Human Theatre and Energetic Alchemy

Somatic Presence in Performance Practice

Richard Martínez

intellect

Bristol, UK / Chicago, USA

First published in the UK in 2026 by
Intellect, The Mill, Parnall Road, Fishponds, Bristol, BS16 3JG, UK

First published in the USA in 2026 by
Intellect, The University of Chicago Press, 1427 E. 60th Street,
Chicago, IL 60637, USA

EU GPSR Authorised Representative
LOGOS EUROPE, 9 rue Nicolas Poussin, 17000, LA ROCHELLE, France
E-mail: Contact@logoseurope.eu

A catalogue record for this book is available from the British Library.

Copy editor: MPS Limited
Cover design: Natalie Thomas and Richard Martínez
Cover image: Inner Currents—AI-generated image created with OpenAI's DALL·E (via ChatGPT). Concept and design by Richard Martínez.
Frontispiece: Ancestral Currents. At the threshold of presence, the inner body awakens. Gesture is seeded in silence, carried by the ancestral currents that shape every performer. AI-generated image created with OpenAI's DALL·E (via ChatGPT).
Production manager: Debora Nicosia
Typesetter: MPS Limited

Hardback ISBN 978-1-83595-276-4
ePDF ISBN 978-1-83595-278-8
ePUB ISBN 978-1-83595-277-1

Printed and bound by Hobbs the Printers Ltd

This is a peer-reviewed publication.

To **Davide La Fauci**,
for standing beside me through my deepest challenges,
for seeing me when I couldn't see myself,
and for believing in the breath I hadn't yet found.
Your support has been my grounding—and my flight.

To **my grandmother and grandfather**, who taught me the value of being human before being anything else.
My grandfather used to ask me:
"Are artists born, or are they made?"
This book is my answer:
Artists are born—every time they remember how to feel.
They are made—every time they dare to feel it fully.

To **my Puerto Rican family**,
whose presence—near or far—lives in every movement,
every silence, every return.
To **my mentors and masters**,
thank you for pushing me to trust instinct over form,
vibration over voice, and truth over perfection.

To **my Italian family**,
who became more than collaborators—
set designers, costume makers, stagehands, and audience—
but companions in art and in life.
Thank you for following me across Italy,
lifting every beam, folding every curtain,
and holding each performance as if it were your own.

To **Italy**, my second home,
for sharing with me the wisdom of its ancestors,
the richness of its traditions,
and the warmth and love of its people.

To **Puerto Rico**,
you are more than a homeland—**you are my root**.
You taught me resilience, creativity, dignity in adversity,
and how to keep moving forward,
even when far from you.

This work is as much yours as it is mine.

Contents

List of Figures xi
Credits List xxvii
Glossary xxix
Acknowledgments xxxvii
Preface xxxix
Aracelis Ruiz Reyes
Preface xliii
Fabio Mangolini
Foreword li
Introduction liii

SECTION 1: FOUNDATIONAL CONCEPTS 1

1. Before the Curtain Rises: Foundations of Human Performance 2
An Introduction to the Living Legacy, Language, and Challenge of Human Performance 3

2. Energy Onstage: A Foundation for Human Theatre 10
Part 1—Unveiling the Energetic Core of Human Theatre: A Journey Through Dynamis, Energeia, and Entelecheia 11
Part 2—Unlocking the Energetic Body: Lowen's Bioenergetic Approach 19
Part 3—The Expressive Body: Lessac's Kinesensic Training 30

3. The Energetic Stage: Echoes of the Past 38
Part 1—Tracing the Roots of Codified Art 39
Part 2—The DEE Cycle in Action: Historical Examples and Eastern Parallels 56
Part 3—Embodying the Future: From Lineage to Innovation 62

SECTION 2: CONTEMPORARY APPLICATIONS AND PERSPECTIVES 65

4. The Energetic Body: Performing from Within 66
Part 1—Tracing the Evolution of Artistic Decodification 67
Part 2—Awakened Ground: The Reemergence of Energetic Memory Across Cultures 87
Part 3—Reframing Tradition: Barba's Anthropology and the Pitfalls of Orientalism 94

5. The Energetic Performer: From Within to Without 106
Part 1—Towards an Organic Entelecheia 107
Part 2—Tension: Our Modern Obstacle and Fundamental Tool 115
Part 3—Expressive Alignment and the Performer's Intent 126
Part 4—Energetic Alchemy of the Performer: Healing Through Presence 131
Part 5—Theatre and Trauma: Bridging Performance and Healing 145

SECTION 3: SYNTHESIS AND APPLICATION OF HUMAN THEATRE 163

6. Human Theatre: Embodying the Performer's Heart 164
Part 1—Reframing Dramaturgy: From Ancient Theory to Energetic Expression 165
Part 2—The Language of Energy: Incubation, Experimentation, and Embodied Identity 170
Part 3—Teatro Umano: Building a Practice 176
Part 4—Dramaturgy in Action: Genres, Children, and the Unexpected 189
Part 5—Shifting Paradigms: Postdramatic Influences and Theatrical Hybridity 193
Part 6—Poetics of Objects, Masks, and Energetic Transference 198
Part 7—Human Theatre and Dramaturgy: A Meta-Perspective 202
Part 8—Conclusion: Human Theatre as a Living Dramatic Language 206

7. Unmasking Vulnerability Onstage: A Practical Guide to Emotional Presence 210
Part 1—Foundations of Embodied Vulnerability 211

Part 2—Human Theatre in Practice: Case Study and Reflection 219
Part 3—It's Your Turn: Training for Human Theatre 231

About the Author 243
Bibliography 245
Index 251

Figures

Note to the Reader

Some of the images in this book were created using artificial intelligence, specifically with **DALL·E**, an image-generation tool developed by OpenAI. These visualizations were crafted not to replace traditional artistic methods, but to **illustrate complex concepts** and to help **make the invisible visible**—giving form to energetic, emotional, and somatic states that often resist linear description. They serve as visual companions to the ideas explored in the text, expanding the ways in which Human Theatre can be perceived and embodied.

1.0	The First Impulse. AI-generated image created with OpenAI's DALL·E (via ChatGPT).	2
1.1	A simplified timeline tracing the evolution of human performance from early ritual and oral tradition to contemporary performance practice. AI-generated image created with OpenAI's DALL·E (via ChatGPT).	4
1.2	A comparative breakdown of Traditional Theatre and Human Theatre. AI-generated image created with OpenAI's DALL·E (via ChatGPT).	5
1.3	Actor versus Performer. AI-generated image created with OpenAI's DALL·E (via ChatGPT).	6
1.4	Zones of Muscle Tension and Energy Flow. AI-generated image created with OpenAI's DALL·E (via ChatGPT).	7
1.5	The DEE Cycle as Energetic Alchemy. AI-generated image created with OpenAI's DALL·E (via ChatGPT).	8
2.0	Sensation in Descent. AI-generated image created with OpenAI's DALL·E (via ChatGPT).	10

2.1 The dancer's body as a vessel of energy. AI-generated image created with OpenAI's DALL·E (via ChatGPT). 12

2.2 The Performer–Energy–Audience Flow. AI-generated image created with OpenAI's DALL·E (via ChatGPT). 13

2.3 Usage of the word "energy" over time, according to Google Books Ngram Viewer. Screenshot. 13

2.4 The DEE Cycle. AI-generated image created with OpenAI's DALL·E (via ChatGPT). 15

2.5 The DEE Cycle in Nature: A plant's life cycle. AI-generated image created with OpenAI's DALL·E (via ChatGPT). 16

2.6 The DEE Cycle in the Energetic Body. AI-generated image created with OpenAI's DALL·E (via ChatGPT). 16

2.7 The DEE Cycle Embodied. (from left to right) (1) Dynamis; (2) Energeia; (3) Entelecheia. AI-generated image created with OpenAI's DALL·E (via ChatGPT). 18

2.8 Breath, Voice, and Presence. AI-generated image created with OpenAI's DALL·E (via ChatGPT). 18

2.9 The DEE Cycle mapped through the human form. AI-generated image created with OpenAI's DALL·E (via ChatGPT). 19

2.10 Five key zones of energetic significance. AI-generated image created with OpenAI's DALL·E (via ChatGPT). 20

2.11 The Performer as an Energetic System. AI-generated image created with OpenAI's DALL·E (via ChatGPT). 22

2.12 Grounding and Trembling in the Performer. AI-generated image created with OpenAI's DALL·E (via ChatGPT). 23

2.13 The River Within. AI-generated image created with OpenAI's DALL·E (via ChatGPT). 24

2.14 Energetic Pathways in Motion. AI-generated image created with OpenAI's DALL·E (via ChatGPT). 25

2.15 Grounding exercise. AI-generated image created with OpenAI's DALL·E (via ChatGPT). 26

2.16 Cat–Cow Stretch. AI-generated image created with OpenAI's DALL·E (via ChatGPT). 27

2.17 Scream therapy. AI-generated image created with OpenAI's DALL·E (via ChatGPT). 28

2.18 Breath of Life. AI-generated image created with OpenAI's DALL·E (via ChatGPT). 29

2.19 Movement and Dance. AI-generated image created with OpenAI's DALL·E (via ChatGPT). 30

2.20 The vibrating performer, visual metaphor for Arthur Lessac's Kinesensic approach. AI-generated image created with OpenAI's DALL·E (via ChatGPT). 31

2.21 Arthur Lessac *(top)* and Deborah Kinghorn *(bottom)*. Image courtesy of Deborah Kinghorn and Lessac Institute; archival details not provided. 32

2.22 Organic Instructions and the DEE Cycle. AI-generated image created with OpenAI's DALL·E (via ChatGPT). 33

2.23 Organic Instruction in Motion. AI-generated image created with OpenAI's DALL·E (via ChatGPT). 34

3.0 The Lineage Within. AI-generated image created with OpenAI's DALL·E (via ChatGPT). 38

3.1 The Codified Stage. AI-generated image created with OpenAI's DALL·E (via ChatGPT). 40

3.2 Javier Hernández *(top)* and Hernández performing *(bottom)*. Image courtesy of Javier R. Hernández; archival details not provided. 41

3.3 The Split Between Form and Impulse. AI-generated image created with OpenAI's DALL·E (via ChatGPT). 42

3.4 "Michelangelo's Hand." Photograph by Richard Martínez, during mime training school, 2009. 43

3.5 The Author in a "Giving Statue" Pose. Photograph by Richard Martínez, during mime training school, 2009. 44

3.6 Analysis of the "Statue of Shyness." Photograph by Richard Martínez, during mime training school, 2009. 45

3.7 Embodied Elegance: A Tribute to Kunqu. AI-generated image created with OpenAI's DALL·E (via ChatGPT). 47

3.8 Kunqu Gesture and Mime Hand Design: *The Dream of Visiting the Garden. (left)* Illustration by the author representing a Kunqu hand gesture from *The Dream of Visiting the Garden*. AI-generated image created with OpenAI's DALL·E (via ChatGPT). *(right)* Similar hand shape from mime training. Photograph by Richard Martínez, during mime training school, 2009. 49

3.9 Gesture as Dialogue: Kunqu and Mime in Parallel. *(left)* Author's illustration comparing the Kunqu gesture from *The Dream of Visiting the Garden*. AI-generated image created with OpenAI's DALL·E (via ChatGPT) with *(right)* the "Margarita" hand design from mime training. Photograph by Richard Martínez, during mime training school, 2009. 49

3.10 Mei Lanfang's Gesture: A Comparative Study. *(left)* Illustration by the author of a hand gesture performed by Mei Lanfang. AI-generated image created with OpenAI's DALL·E (via ChatGPT). *(right)* Similar shape from mime training. Photograph by Richard Martínez, during mime training school, 2009. 50

3.11 Gesture Across Traditions: Kunqu and Indian Classical Theatre. Visual comparison between Kunqu Theatre *(left)* and Indian Classical Theatre *(right)*. AI-generated image created with OpenAI's DALL·E (via ChatGPT). 51

3.12 Hand Gesture in Kutiyattam: Embodying the Heroine. Photograph by Richard Martínez, 2025. 52

3.13 Illustration of a Kutiyattam Performance. AI-generated image created with OpenAI's DALL·E (via ChatGPT). 52

3.14 Yakshagana Performance of the Ramayana. AI-generated image created with OpenAI's DALL·E (via ChatGPT). 53

3.15 Embodiment and System: Deburau and Delsarte in Contrast. AI-generated image created with OpenAI's DALL·E (via ChatGPT). 55

3.16 One Performer, Many Shadows. AI-generated image created with OpenAI's DALL·E (via ChatGPT). 57

3.17 The DEE Cycle as Universal Structure. AI-generated image created with OpenAI's DALL·E (via ChatGPT). 58

3.18 Parallel Energies: Aristotle and Cheuk Fung. AI-generated image created with OpenAI's DALL·E (via ChatGPT). 59

3.19 A Universal Path: The Performer at the Crossroads of Tradition. AI-generated image created with OpenAI's DALL·E (via ChatGPT). 61

3.20 Energy Through Time: The Performer as Bridge. AI-generated image created with OpenAI's DALL·E (via ChatGPT). 63

4.0 Axis of Being. AI-generated image created with OpenAI's DALL·E (via ChatGPT). 66

4.1 Todd Farley, Father of Modern Christian Mime. Image courtesy of Todd Farley; archival details not provided. 68

4.2 *Moses*, a performance by Todd Farley (QR code). AI-generated image created with OpenAI's DALL·E (via ChatGPT). 70

4.3 *Silencio Lúdico*: The Author's Embodied Inquiry (QR code). AI-generated image created with OpenAI's DALL·E (via ChatGPT). 71

4.4 Gilda Navarra: Master of Silence. Photograph by Arturo Melero, *Ballets de San Juan* / Gilda Navarra (1960), from the Arturo Melero Negative Collection, Dance Archive, University of Puerto Rico, Río Piedras Campus. Courtesy of Isamar Abreu Gómez. 72

4.5 Fusion of Theatre and Flamenco. In the photograph: Gilda Navarra. Image from *Detrás del silencio* by Gilda Navarra and Jorge Rigau. Courtesy of Alberto Rigau; archival details not provided. 73

4.6 Gilda Navarra directing a rehearsal of *The Soldier's Tale*, 1971. Image from *Detrás del silencio* by Gilda Navarra and Jorge Rigau. Courtesy of Alberto Rigau; archival details not provided. 74

4.7 Gilda Navarra's Taller de Histriones. Image from the Gilda Navarra Collection, Victoria Espinosa Documentary Archive Room, José Emilio González Humanities Documentation Center, Faculty of Humanities, University of Puerto Rico, Río Piedras Campus. Courtesy of José A. Robledo González. 75
4.8 Gilda Navarra with classmates at Étienne Decroux's studio, New York, 1961. Image from *Detrás del silencio* by Gilda Navarra and Jorge Rigau. Courtesy of Alberto Rigau. 76
4.9 Gilda Navarra *(left)* and Yaraní del Valle *(right)*. Image courtesy of Prof. Rosa Luisa Márquez; archival details not provided. 77
4.10 Gilda Navarra in *Asíntota: The Stillness That Speaks*. Photograph by Arturo Melero, *Ballets de San Juan* / Gilda Navarra (1960), from the Arturo Melero Negative Collection, Dance Archive, University of Puerto Rico, Río Piedras Campus. Courtesy of Isamar Abreu Gómez. 78
4.11 The Fundamental Energy of the Human Soul. A visual of Gilda Navarra's inner charge. Image from *Detrás del silencio* by Gilda Navarra and Jorge Rigau. Courtesy of Alberto Rigau; archival details not provided. 79
4.12 Gilda Navarra, professor at the University of Puerto Rico and pioneer. Image from *Detrás del silencio* by Gilda Navarra and Jorge Rigau. Courtesy of Alberto Rigau; archival details not provided. 79
4.13 Fabio Mangolini: Bearer of the Commedia dell'Arte. Image courtesy of Fabio Mangolini; archival details not provided. 80
4.14 The Mask as Portal: Crafted by the Sartori Legacy. In the photograph: Fabio Mangolini. Image courtesy of Fabio Mangolini; archival details not provided. 82
4.15 Mapping Koshi: Fabio Mangolini's *Diagram of Energetic Grounding* (from Fabio Mangolini's doctoral thesis "Attraversando il ponte" ["Crossing the Bridge"]). Courtesy of Fabio Mangolini. 84

4.16 The Alchemy of Presence: Fabio Mangolini in Motion. AI-generated image created with OpenAI's DALL·E (via ChatGPT). 86

4.17 Lineage in Motion: Mangolini and the Masters. Image courtesy of Fabio Mangolini; archival details not provided. 87

4.18 Koshi Across Cultures: Flamenco and the Energetic Spine. *(left and center)* Navarra and a flamenco dancer. *(right)* Diagram of koshi. *(left)* Image from *Detrás del silencio* by Gilda Navarra and Jorge Rigau. Courtesy of Alberto Rigau; archival details not provided. *(center)* Image courtesy of the author; archival details not provided. *(right)* Diagram from Fabio Mangolini's doctoral thesis "Attraversando il ponte" ("Crossing the Bridge"). Courtesy of Fabio Mangolini. 89

4.19 Bomba and the Embodied Pulse of Koshi. AI-generated image created with OpenAI's DALL·E (via ChatGPT). 89

4.20 Awakening Inner Structure: Alignment as Energetic Source. AI-generated image created with OpenAI's DALL·E (via ChatGPT). 91

4.21 Scott Putman, creator of EBAS and Architect of Spinal Flow. Photograph by Barbara Shore. Image courtesy of Scott Putman; archival details not provided. 92

4.22 Koshi in Action: Scott Putman and the Architecture of Alignment. *(left)* Scott Putman in performance. *(center)* Visual representation of Triangulation. Photograph by Barbara Shore. Image courtesy of Scott Putman; archival details not provided. *(right)* Diagram of Centerline. Images courtesy of the author; archival details not provided. 93

4.23 Arthur Lessac demonstrating the C-Curve. Image courtesy of Deborah Kinghorn and Lessac Institute; archival details not provided. 94

4.24 A Luminous Body in Motion: Grounded Radiance. AI-generated image created with OpenAI's DALL·E (via ChatGPT). 95

4.25 Two Energies, Two Paradigms: Exertion versus Entelecheia. AI-generated image created with OpenAI's DALL·E (via ChatGPT). 97

5.0 Gesture Becoming Form. AI-generated image created with OpenAI's DALL·E (via ChatGPT). 106

5.1 Stanislavski's Organic Cycle: Perezhivanie in Motion. AI-generated image created with OpenAI's DALL·E (via ChatGPT). 109

5.2 Stanislavski's Inner Web: Emotion, Memory, and Action. AI-generated image created with OpenAI's DALL·E (via ChatGPT). 110

5.3 André Casaca, founder of Teatro C'art and creator of Comical-Relational Education. Image courtesy of André Casaca; archival details not provided. 111

5.4 André Casaca's Embodied Approach: Where Vulnerability Becomes Expression. Image courtesy of André Casaca; archival details not provided. 112

5.5 The Casaca Spiral: Presence Through Instinct, Play, and Embodied Poetics. AI-generated image created with OpenAI's DALL·E (via ChatGPT). 113

5.6 The Bioenergetic Body: Lowen's Somatic Bridge to Expressive Freedom. AI-generated image created with OpenAI's DALL·E (via ChatGPT). 114

5.7 The TDTETE Model: Tension as Rhythmic Catalyst in the Energetic Cycle. AI-generated image created with OpenAI's DALL·E (via ChatGPT). 116

5.8 The TDTETE Spiral: Tension as Rhythmic Reset. AI-generated image created with OpenAI's DALL·E (via ChatGPT). 117

5.9 Koshi as Energetic Axis: Diagram by Fabio Mangolini. Diagram from Fabio Mangolini's doctoral thesis "Attraversando il ponte" ("Crossing the Bridge"). Courtesy of Fabio Mangolini. 119

5.10 Koshi serves as the performer's core axis. AI-generated image created with OpenAI's DALL·E (via ChatGPT). 120

5.11 Lowen's Adaptive Cycle of Tension: From Mobilization to Exhaustion. AI-generated image created with OpenAI's DALL·E (via ChatGPT). 121
5.12 Cultural Conditioning and Tension: Habit, Posture, and the Path Back to Flow. AI-generated image created with OpenAI's DALL·E (via ChatGPT). 122
5.13 Unconscious Tension in the Performing Body. AI-generated image created with OpenAI's DALL·E (via ChatGPT). 123
5.14 Tension as Embodied Narrative. AI-generated image created with OpenAI's DALL·E (via ChatGPT). 124
5.15 The Mind–Body Divide: From Fragmentation to Integration. AI-generated image created with OpenAI's DALL·E (via ChatGPT). 125
5.16 Energetic Alignment: From Intention to Expression. AI-generated image created with OpenAI's DALL·E (via ChatGPT). 126
5.17 Communication Channels: Releasing the Constriction Rings. AI-generated image created with OpenAI's DALL·E (via ChatGPT). 128
5.18 Spontaneity as Energetic Freedom. AI-generated image created with OpenAI's DALL·E (via ChatGPT). 129
5.19 Artaud's Vision: Theatre as Plague—A Sacred Confrontation. AI-generated image created with OpenAI's DALL·E (via ChatGPT). 132
5.20 Models of Catharsis: A Legacy in Four Voices (Aristotle; Freud; Artaud; and Somatic Practice). AI-generated image created with OpenAI's DALL·E (via ChatGPT). 134
5.21 Artaud's Energetic Catharsis: Inner Forces Unleashed. AI-generated image created with OpenAI's DALL·E (via ChatGPT). 135
5.22 From Tension to Transformation: Trauma's Journey Through the Performer's Body. AI-generated image created with OpenAI's DALL·E (via ChatGPT). 136

5.23 The Body as Tapestry: Trauma as Energetic Memory. AI-generated image created with OpenAI's DALL·E (via ChatGPT). 140

5.24 Suspension Before Expression: Masks from the Author's Collection. Photograph by Richard Martínez, taken in 2021 during rehearsal and mask creation. 143

5.25 Mask as Mirror: A Student's Therapeutic Exploration. Exercise by student D. at Teatro Umano. Photograph by Richard Martínez, taken in 2021 during rehearsal and mask creation. 144

5.26 Grounded versus Ungrounded: Tension in the Pelvic Floor. Diagram comparing a body holding unconscious tension in the gluteal and perianal region *(left)* with one that is released and grounded *(right)*. AI-generated image created with OpenAI's DALL·E (via ChatGPT). 152

5.27 Human Theatre: A Space of Transformation: The core journey of Human Theatre. AI-generated image created with OpenAI's DALL·E (via ChatGPT). 158

6.0 Heart of Resonance. AI-generated image created with OpenAI's DALL·E (via ChatGPT). 164

6.1 The Human Theatre Proposal: Energy as Dramaturgy. Evolution from traditional dramaturgy toward Human Theatre. AI-generated image created with OpenAI's DALL·E (via ChatGPT). 166

6.2 The Evolution of Dramaturgy: From Aristotle to Human Theatre. AI-generated image created with OpenAI's DALL·E (via ChatGPT). 168

6.3 The DEE Cycle of Human Theatre: From Inner Potential to Embodied Expression. DEE Cycle interwoven with the foundational tools of Human Theatre. AI-generated image created with OpenAI's DALL·E (via ChatGPT). 169

6.4 Performing Without Words: Expressive Language Beyond Text. AI-generated image created with OpenAI's DALL·E (via ChatGPT). 170

6.5 Embodied Displacement in Motion. Mid-scene from the Italian premiere of *Voyage* (still frame from the video recording). Courtesy of the author. 172

6.6 *(top)* The Ocean Between Us. Final scene from *Voyage*. *(bottom)* The Weight of Inheritance. Still frames from the video recording of *Voyage*, Italian premiere. Courtesy of the author. 173

6.7 Fragmented Belonging. Performance of *Voyage* at the International Theatre Festival in Croatia. Still frame from the video recording of *Voyage*, Croatian premiere. Courtesy of the author. 174

6.8 *(left)* QR code accessing selected scenes from *Voyage*. *(right)* Testimony from the Audience, a message received after the show. Image courtesy of the author; archival details not provided. 174

6.9 Teatro Umano Masks: Raw Faces of Energetic Expression. Photograph by Richard Martínez, taken in 2021 during rehearsal and mask creation. 176

6.10 Teatro Umano Logo: A Visual Manifestation of Energetic Presence. Image courtesy of the author; archival details not provided. 177

6.11 The Trio in Tension. A masked trio mid-dialogue in *Desconocido*. Photograph by Maurizio Cugno, Umbria, Italy, *c*. 2020. 179

6.12 Anna and Giuseppe: Two Acts of Presence. *(left)* Anna, the seamstress protagonist, with a humanoid mask. *(right)* Giuseppe delivering the opening letter from the battlefield. Photographs by Maurizio Cugno, Umbria, Italy, c. 2020. 180

6.13 The Arrival of the Stranger. Guglielmo enters Anna's shop in *Desconocido*. Photograph by Maurizio Cugno, Umbria, Italy, c. 2020. 181

6.14 Structural Map of *Desconocido*. AI-generated image created with OpenAI's DALL·E (via ChatGPT). 182

6.15 The Humanoid Character: Stillness Before Emergence. AI-generated image created with OpenAI's DALL·E (via ChatGPT). 183

6.16 *Desconocido*: The Humanoid Body in Energetic Expression. Triptych with three moments from *Desconocido*: *(top)* Guglielmo salutes an unseen presence; *(center)* Don Geraldo's exaggerated theatricality disrupts the moment, while Anna and Rossella respond; *(bottom)* Anna cradles her child and clutches a letter. Photographs by Maurizio Cugno, Umbria, Italy, c. 2020. 184
6.17 Minimalism as Portal: Inviting the Audience's Imagination. Still frame from the video recording of *Desconocido*, Florence, Italy. Courtesy of the author. 185
6.18 Gesture as Geography: Expanding the Stage Through Movement. Still frame from the video recording of *Desconocido*, Florence, Italy. Courtesy of the author. 185
6.19 The Stillness of Grief: Collective Imagination Through Silence. Anna receives Giuseppe's farewell letter in *Desconocido*. Photograph by Maurizio Cugno, Umbria, Italy, c. 2020. 186
6.20 Ritual, Listening, and Care in the Theatre of *Desconocido*. *(left)* Rossella raises a disinfectant bottle like a sacred relic. *(center)* A nurse's stethoscope crosses theatrical distance; Rossella listens not just to breathe, but to the unspoken truth beneath the mask. *(right)* A moment of care—Rossella examines Guglielmo, while Anna witnesses from afar. Photographs by Maurizio Cugno, Umbria, Italy, c. 2020. 186
6.21 Geraldine: Poise as Performance, Mask as Metaphor. From *Desconocido*. Photograph by Maurizio Cugno, Umbria, Italy, c. 2020. 187
6.22 Don Geraldo: Comedy and Crisis in a Single Gesture. From *Desconocido*. Photograph by Maurizio Cugno, Umbria, Italy, c. 2020. 188
6.23 QR code to access scenes from *Desconocido*. 188
6.24 *Desconocido* (Final Scene). Still frame from the video recording of *Desconocido*, Florence, Italy. Courtesy of the author. 189
6.25 *Bar Moments* (Final Scene): Linear principle. Still frame from the video recording of *Bar Moments*, Arezzo, Italy. Courtesy of the author. 190

6.26 Touring *Mundo Nocturno* (Year Two): Symbolic Simplicity in Design. Second-year version of *Mundo Nocturno* in Argentina. Image courtesy of the author; San Luis, Argentina, 2013. 192
6.27 The Puppet and the Red Hat: Traditional Aesthetics for Energetic Engagement. From the earlier year's festival in Argentina. Image courtesy of the author; San Luis, Argentina, 2012. 193
6.28 From Gesture to Presence: The Evolution Toward Physical Theatre. AI-generated image created with OpenAI's DALL·E (via ChatGPT). 194
6.29 The Postdramatic Field: Fragmentation, Embodiment, and Co-Creation. AI-generated image created with OpenAI's DALL·E (via ChatGPT). 196
6.30 Embodied Memory: A Landscape Beyond Language. AI-generated image created with OpenAI's DALL·E (via ChatGPT). 197
6.31 Emotional Minimalism in Motion: Bausch and Teatro Umano in Dialogue. *(left)* Dancer in the spirit of Pina Bausch. *(right)* Teatro Umano performer. AI-generated image created with OpenAI's DALL·E (via ChatGPT). 199
6.32 Overlapping Worlds: The Poetic Intersection of Tanztheater and Teatro Umano. Venn diagram mapping the shared territory between Pina Bausch's Tanztheater and Teatro Umano's embodied dramaturgy. AI-generated image created with OpenAI's DALL·E (via ChatGPT). 200
6.33 Diagram illustrating the poetic intersection of Object Theatre and Mask Work within Teatro Umano's methodology. AI-generated image created with OpenAI's DALL·E (via ChatGPT). 200
6.34 Object as Character, Absurdity as Mirror. Photographs of solo clown act. Still frame from the video recording of *Una passeggiata di merda*, Italian premiere. Courtesy of the author. 200
6.35 QR code for *Una passeggiata di merda*, a short clown performance by the author. 201

6.36 Koshi as Core: Radiating Presence Through Energetic Projection. AI-generated image created with OpenAI's DALL·E (via ChatGPT). 202
6.37 Dramaturgy as Creative Framework: A Living Cycle. AI-generated image created with OpenAI's DALL·E (via ChatGPT). 203
6.38 Universality Through Suggestion: The Power of Minimalism. AI-generated image created with OpenAI's DALL·E (via ChatGPT). 205
6.39 Cyclical Dramaturgy: A Model of Emotional Return and Energetic Flow. AI-generated image created with OpenAI's DALL·E (via ChatGPT). 206
7.0 Carrying the Invisible. AI-generated image created with OpenAI's DALL·E (via ChatGPT). 210
7.1 Vulnerability as Presence. AI-generated image created with OpenAI's DALL·E (via ChatGPT). 212
7.2 The Performer as Vessel. AI-generated image created with OpenAI's DALL·E (via ChatGPT). 213
7.3 Intuition in Motion. AI-generated image created with OpenAI's DALL·E (via ChatGPT). 214
7.4 Energetic Transmission Through Embodied Gesture. AI-generated image created with OpenAI's DALL·E (via ChatGPT). 215
7.5 The Energetic Compass of Human Theatre. AI-generated image created with OpenAI's DALL·E (via ChatGPT). 217
7.6 The Cycle of Emotional Echo. Step-by-step visualization of how mirror neurons are activated in masked performance. AI-generated image created with OpenAI's DALL·E (via ChatGPT). 218
7.7 The Performer as Resonant Filter. AI-generated image created with OpenAI's DALL·E (via ChatGPT). 219
7.8 The DEE Cycle Embodied in Ensemble Work. AI-generated image created with OpenAI's DALL·E (via ChatGPT). 219
7.9 Publicity and synopsis for *Bar Moments*. Photograph by Maurizio Cugno, Umbria, Italy, c. 2020. 220

7.10 Embodied Archetypes. *(left)* Lila channels lived trauma. *(center)* Magdalena embodies repression. *(right)* Truffini asserts power through angular, dominating movement. Still frames from the video recording of *Bar Moments*, Tuscany. Courtesy of the author. 220
7.11 Gianni personifies fascist-era machismo. Still frame from the video recording of *Bar Moments*, Tuscany. Courtesy of the author. 221
7.12 Lila's Final Gesture. Still frame from the video recording of *Bar Moments*, Tuscany. Courtesy of the author. 222
7.13 Sister Magdalena silences joy. Still frame from the video recording of *Bar Moments*, Tuscany. Courtesy of the author. 224
7.14 Maia stands as a living thread between generations. Still frame from the video recording of *Bar Moments*, Tuscany. Courtesy of the author. 224
7.15 Lili's entrance. Still frame from the video recording of *Bar Moments*, Tuscany. Courtesy of the author. 225
7.16 *(left)* Gianni steals alcohol. *(right)* Lila's betrayal realized. Still frames from the video recording of *Bar Moments*, Tuscany. Courtesy of the author. 225
7.17 *(top)* Magdalena initiates a symbolic confrontation. *(bottom)* Lila interrupts the staged conflict and shares the symbolic "cake." Still frames from the video recording of *Bar Moments*, Tuscany. Courtesy of the author. 226
7.18 Lila's moment of reckoning. Still frame from the video recording of *Bar Moments*, Tuscany. Courtesy of the author. 226
7.19 Symbolic liberation: Lila releases the weight of institutional control. Still frames from the video recording of *Bar Moments*, Tuscany. Courtesy of the author. 227
7.20 *Bar Moments*, QR code. 227
7.21 Embodied Resistance: The DEE Cycle in Action. AI-generated image created with OpenAI's DALL·E (via ChatGPT). 228
7.22 Vulnerability, Empathy, and Energy: The Performer's Inner Compass. AI-generated image created with OpenAI's DALL·E (via ChatGPT). 229
7.23 Human Theatre as an Evolving Energetic Language. AI-generated image created with OpenAI's DALL·E (via ChatGPT). 231

Credits

Special thanks to the following custodians and contributors for generously providing the photographs that appear throughout this book. Their visual contributions help give form to memory, embodiment, and the energetic presence at the heart of Human Theatre.

Alberto Rigau
FIGURES 4.5, 4.6, 4.8, 4.11, 4.12, 4.18 *(left)*
From the book *Detrás del silencio* by Gilda Navarra and Jorge Rigau.

André Casaca
FIGURES 5.3, 5.4

Caroline Montes
FIGURES 6.5, 6.6, 6.7
With appreciation for her permission to use these images.

Deborah Kinghorn and the Lessac Training & Research Institute
FIGURES 2.21, 4.23

Fabio Mangolini
FIGURES 4.13, 4.14, 4.15, 4.17, 4.18 (*right*), 5.9

Isamar Abreu Gómez
FIGURES 4.4, 4.10
Photographs by Arturo Melero
Ballets de San Juan / Gilda Navarra (1960)
Arturo Melero Negative Collection, Dance Archive, Arts and Music Collection, Library System, University of Puerto Rico, Río Piedras Campus.

Javier R. Hernández
FIGURE 3.2

José A. Robledo González
FIGURE 4.7
Photos from the Gilda Navarra Collection, Victoria Espinosa Documentary Archive Room, José Emilio González Humanities Documentation Center, Faculty of Humanities, University of Puerto Rico, Río Piedras Campus.

Maurizio Cugno
FIGURES 6.11, 6.12, 6.13, 6.16, 6.19, 6.20, 6.21, 6.22, 7.9
Photographs of *Desconocido* by Maurizio Cugno

Rosa Luisa Márquez
FIGURE 4.9

Scott Putman
FIGURES 4.21, 4.22
Photograph credit: Barbara Shore

Todd Farley
FIGURE 4.1

Glossary

This glossary defines key terms and concepts used throughout the book. It is intended to provide a reference framework for understanding the philosophical, somatic, and theatrical methodologies discussed.

A

Actor A practitioner who traditionally embodies a character through scripted performance, often emphasizing psychological realism, narrative, and representation.

Amplification (Energetic) The practice of using breath, gesture, and attention to increase the expressive power of inner emotion or impulse without exaggeration.

Awareness The conscious attention to sensation, breath, thought, and emotion—internally and externally. In Human Theatre, awareness is the foundation for transformation: it allows the performer to perceive tension, energy, impulse, and resonance in real time. Awareness is not just observation; it is a form of presence.

B

Bioenergetics A somatic therapeutic approach developed by Alexander Lowen, integrating body awareness, breath, and movement to release stored tension and repressed emotions.

Body Dramaturgy A dramaturgical approach in which the body—not the text—is the primary site of meaning-making, storytelling, and expression.

Breath-Sensing A core element involving conscious perception of the breath as a physical and emotional experience. It also serves as an anchor in trauma-informed performance.

C

C-Curve (Lessac) A foundational physical alignment practice in Lessac training that emphasizes koshi awareness, core support, and a dynamic, balanced verticality.

Catharsis From Aristotle's *Poetics*, the purging or emotional release that occurs when audiences experience intense emotions through theatre. In Human Theatre, catharsis is not only for the audience, but also for the performer.

Character Armor A concept developed by Wilhelm Reich referring to chronic muscular tension patterns that form as defense mechanisms against emotional pain.

Coherence (Somatic) A state in which the performer's breath, posture, impulse, and attention are aligned, producing clarity in action and reception. Somatic coherence supports both artistic expressiveness and energetic safety.

Co-Poiesis (Co-Poetic Space) The shared creative space between audience and performer, where meaning is not given but generated in the moment through presence and suggestion.

D

DEE Cycle (Dynamis–Energeia–Entelecheia) A core concept of Human Theatre, adapted from Aristotelian terms:

1. **Dynamis**: Latent potential, intention or emotional charge; the inner charge that precedes movement.
2. **Energeia**: Activation or flow; the expression of that intention through energetic presence and internal coherence.
3. **Entelecheia**: Realization or fulfillment; when the action has fully manifested, completing its cycle with resonance and purpose.

Documentary Theatre A genre of performance constructed from real-life testimonies, documents, interviews, or personal narratives, often used to elevate underrepresented voices or explore sociopolitical topics.

Dramaturgy The theory and structure of dramatic work. In this book, it includes not only narrative construction but also energetic, spatial, and emotional architecture.

Dynamis Latent energy or emotional charge before movement or expression.

E

Embodied Testimony A performance approach where the body carries and communicates lived experience, often replacing or complementing spoken word.

Embodiment More than physical presence, embodiment is the integration of thought, feeling, and sensation into unified, expressive being. It is when the performer is not "showing" something—but *being* it. In Human Theatre, embodiment is a form of energetic truth: a performance that rises from within the body, not imposed upon it.

Empathy (Mirror/Embodied) The performer's capacity to resonate with and transmit emotional states, engaging the audience's mirror neuron system. In Human Theatre, empathy is cultivated not through imitation, but through embodied presence and vibratory truth.

Energeia The moment potential becomes action—energy in motion and expression.

Energetic Alchemy The transformational process in which inner sensations, emotions, and tension are metabolized through the body and expressed as meaningful, resonant performance.

Energetic Authenticity A state in which performers' internal emotional and physical state are fully aligned with their external expression, allowing audiences to feel a real connection.

Energetic Body in Action A performer's body actively expressing presence, intention, and internal flow. This is not mechanical movement, but dynamic expression charged with meaning. The energetic body in action is where breath, impulse, and sensation converge—where movement becomes message and presence becomes power.

Energetic Containment The ability to hold emotional intensity without suppression or leakage. Containment creates safety and control within.

Energetic Flow The continuous movement of energy within the performer, from grounding and breath through movement and voice.

Energetic Listening The practice of receiving and responding to a partner's presence not only through dialogue but through breath, rhythm, and subtle movement. This non-verbal attunement deepens relational presence.

Energetic Transference The phenomenon in which the emotional or physical state of the performer is transmitted (often nonverbally) to the audience through gesture, presence, and rhythm.

Energetics Energetics refers to the lived experience of vibratory tone and physical presence as a felt, resonant flow—prioritizing internal coherence over visible effort. This framework contrasts with performance models that define energy in terms of muscular exertion or dramatic tension.

Entelecheia The realization or fulfillment of potential—where energy becomes fully integrated and embodied.

Extra-Daily Techniques Stylized, intentional behaviors in performance that deviate from ordinary (daily) movement. Introduced by Barba to define heightened stage behavior across cultures.

Everyday Techniques Barba's term for ordinary, habitual behavior shaped by one's social and cultural context. Used to contrast with theatrical stylization, though often misunderstood in his work.

F

Frame (in Composition) A moment or visual image that contains multiple meanings and invites audience reflection. A framing device in non-linear dramaturgies.

G

Gesture-Memory The way movement and physical patterns recall emotional or autobiographical experiences stored in the body.

Grounding A somatic practice of connecting the body to the earth and feeling one's weight through the feet and legs. It is essential for energetic stability and emotional safety.

H

Human Theatre An embodied performance methodology developed by the author, grounded in the DEE Cycle, somatic awareness, energetic presence, and minimal reliance on verbal language. It centers the performer's humanity as the core expressive tool.

Humanoid Character A masked, non-verbal figure that transcends identity categories such as nationality, race, or gender—used to project and receive universal human emotions through energy and breath.

I

Immediacy (in Performance) The quality of being fully in the present moment during a performance, often experienced as a heightened sense of presence, responsiveness, and truth.

Impulse The origin point of an action or gesture in the body—pre-verbal, pre-rational. In Human Theatre, impulse is the raw energetic charge that arises before thought or control. It is a marker of authenticity and a gateway to presence.

Inner Child (Metaphor) Used in Human Theatre as a visualization and healing metaphor for the most sensitive, creative, and vulnerable part of the self. This metaphor becomes performative through breath, tone, and energetic release.

Interoception The internal perception of bodily states (heartbeat, breath, hunger), crucial in both trauma healing and actor training for building emotional self-awareness.

K

Kinesensic A term coined by Arthur Lessac to describe the felt sense of physical and vocal vibration. Kinesensic training emphasizes awareness of internal sensation to guide movement and speech.

Koshi (**腰**) A Japanese term referring to the pelvic center of gravity. In Human Theatre, koshi is essential for energetic projection, grounding, and core alignment. Closely linked to the Lessac C-Curve.

L

Lessac Kinesensics A voice and body training method developed by Arthur Lessac, emphasizing breath, tone, and the body's innate energy to support expressive communication. Influential in the development of Human Theatre.

Lokadharmi In Indian dramaturgy, a realistic mode of theatrical presentation grounded in everyday behavior and naturalistic expression. Defined in the *Natyashastra*.

M

Mask Work The use of masks in training and performance to eliminate facial expression and emphasize gesture, breath, and embodied presence. In Human Theatre, it neutralizes identity to prioritize energy.

Mimestry A pantomime-based expressive technique created by Todd Farley, combining movement, gesture, and spirituality to narrate complex stories without dialogue.

Mirror Neurons Neural circuits that allow individuals to empathize with the emotions or actions of others by mentally simulating them. Key to understanding emotional contagion in performance.

Model TDTETE (**Dynamis → Energeia → Entelecheia**) A foundational energetic model in Human Theatre that maps the transformation of intention into embodied action, using both Aristotelian and somatic frameworks. Each stage corresponds not only to a phase of expression but also to a specific type of **tension** the performer experiences and utilizes.

1. **Dynamis**: The tension of **potential**. Latent energy or emotional charge that has not yet moved. This is the moment of intention, of the "not-yet," where the impulse begins to gather.
2. **Energeia**: The tension of **activation**. Energy is in motion but not yet released. It flows through the breath, koshi, and body's alignment. This is the performer's energetic presence: a controlled, alive stillness or movement that is not mechanical but charged.
3. **Entelecheia**: The tension of **completion**. The action reaches its final form, fully realized and resonant. The energy is no longer building or held—it has been released into meaningful gesture, expression, or stillness.

This model recognizes that performance is not just a sequence of actions but a cycle of tensions—held, transformed, and released. In Human Theatre, TDTETE becomes a map of **how energy lives inside the performer**, turning internal movement into external impact.

Movement and Dance Intuitive movement practices that access emotional or energetic states.

N

Natyadharmi A stylized, symbolic performance mode described in the *Natyashastra*. It uses gesture, codified action, and abstraction, contrasting with Lokadharmi realism.

Natyashastra A classical Indian treatise on performance arts by Bharata Muni. It outlines theories of acting, dance, music, aesthetics (rasa), and dramaturgy foundational to Indian theatre.

Non-Textual Dramaturgy A compositional strategy where meaning emerges from visual, spatial, kinetic, and sonic elements rather than spoken dialogue.

O

Object Theatre A theatrical approach in which objects—sometimes abstract or metaphorical—are used to express human emotions or ideas. Related to puppetry and physical theatre.

P

Performing Arts An umbrella term that includes theatre, dance, music, mime, clowning, and other live art forms where the human body is the primary medium of expression. In contrast to traditional theatre, the performing arts emphasize physicality, presence, and often non-verbal communication.

Performer In Human Theatre, a being who channels energetic presence rather than portraying a character. The performer's task is not to represent, but to present.

Playfulness (as Process) A vital principle in Human Theatre, where creative exploration is rooted in curiosity, not perfection. Playfulness enables risk-taking, disarms egoic control, and encourages presence through spontaneity.

Physical Theatre A genre of performance in which movement, gesture, and the body are central narrative tools, often blending elements of dance, mime, and traditional acting.

Presence (Energetic) A quality of full awareness, attention, and embodiment onstage. Presence in Human Theatre is not just about focus—it is a felt experience of aliveness.

Presence (Relational) Beyond the individual, relational presence refers to the awareness of and connection with others onstage and in the audience. It is co-created, attuned, and dynamic.

R

Resonance In voice training and energetic work, resonance refers to the vibration and projection of tone throughout the body. Resonance is both literal (sound) and symbolic (emotional).

Restoration (in Performance) A process through which the performer returns to a grounded, regulated state following emotional or physical intensity. In trauma-informed Human Theatre, restoration practices are integrated into both rehearsal and live work.

Repatterning The conscious reorganization of physical, emotional, and neurological patterns within the performer. Repatterning involves identifying habitual responses—such as tension, breath holding, or defensive posture—and gradually replacing them with patterns that support energetic flow, presence, and freedom. In Human Theatre, repatterning is a form of energetic alchemy: it transforms lived experience into expressive capacity through breath, intention, and embodied awareness.

S

Somatic Awareness Conscious attention to bodily sensation, breath, and alignment. A fundamental pillar in trauma-informed performance and Human Theatre methodology.

Structure (Internal/External)

- **Internal structure**: The emotional and energetic sequence within a scene or performance
- **External structure**: The visible plot or narrative sequence for the audience

Somatic Intelligence The body's innate ability to sense, regulate, and express energy and emotion. Somatic intelligence involves listening to internal cues—breath, posture, sensation—and responding with awareness. In Human Theatre, it is a guiding force that replaces control with connection, allowing the performer to move from instinct rather than imitation.

Somatics A field of practice and study that focuses on the body as experienced from within. Somatics emphasizes awareness, sensation, and the internal perception of movement and energy, often used in healing, education, and performance training.

Stillness (Energetic) Stillness is not the absence of movement, but a state of suspended energy. In Human Theatre, stillness holds charge, breath, and intention, often creating more impact than motion.

T

Tamé (溜め) A Japanese concept in traditional theatre and martial arts referring to **the gathering and storing of energy** before its release. In performance, tamé is the pause that holds tension, the breath before the gesture. It is not stillness, but **potential energy in suspension**, enhancing the impact of what follows. In Human Theatre, tamé embodies the moment where Dynamis waits to become Energeia.

Tonal Dramaturgy A structure based not on narrative but on shifts in emotional tone, energy, and rhythm. It emphasizes experiential flow over plot development, key in Human Theatre compositions.

Threshold Moment A transitional phase within performance or training where the performer crosses from habitual behavior into heightened presence or vulnerability. Thresholds are often subtle, sensed internally rather than marked externally.

Tone-Sensing A practice where vocal tone is experienced as vibration and energy, helping actors align voice and emotion.

Trauma-Informed Performance A method of rehearsal and creation that prioritizes psychological safety, regulation of the nervous system, and consent in working with vulnerable material.

Trembling Response A sign of energetic release, often occurring during grounding or breathwork. In Bioenergetics and Human Theatre, trembling is welcomed as a return to flow.

U

Universality Through Suggestion A guiding principle of Human Theatre: that ambiguity and minimalism invite the audience to project its own meaning, making the performance universally resonant.

V

Verticality A performer's sense of aligned, supported posture that connects koshi (pelvis) to crown (head), allowing grounded presence and full breath.

Voice as Vibration An understanding of voice not merely as sound or projection, but as a somatic and emotional vibration that resonates through the body and space.

Vulnerability (as Power) In Human Theatre, vulnerability is not weakness but an open state of being that allows authenticity, empathy, and transformation onstage.

Y

Yūgen (幽玄) A Japanese aesthetic principle meaning **"subtle grace"** or **"profound mystery."** Yūgen refers to the beauty that lies beneath the surface—suggested rather than shown, felt rather than explained. In performance, it's the **quiet emotional resonance** that lingers in silence, in gesture, in space. Human Theatre embraces yūgen by inviting audiences to co-create meaning through ambiguity and energetic presence.

Acknowledgments

This book was not written alone. It was breathed, trembled, and whispered into being through the bodies, voices, and hearts of many.

To Davide, your support has been the silence beneath my voice, the stillness beneath my trembling, the ground beneath every leap.

To my grandmother and grandfather, thank you for teaching me that to be human is to care, to listen, to be present. My grandfather's question—"Are artists born, or made?"—never left me. This book answers with every breath, every page, every trembling gesture: Artists are born through sensation, and made through surrender.

To my Puerto Rican family, your strength lives in my voice, your stories move in my breath. You gifted me music, resilience, and a cultural heartbeat I carry on every stage.

To Puerto Rico, you are not just my homeland—you are the root of this work. You taught me how to endure and how to speak, how to turn survival into rhythm, and silence into presence. Even from afar, your spirit guides me.

To my mentors and teachers, thank you for inviting me to risk presence over performance, to meet the unknown, and to breathe through it.

To my Italian family, thank you for becoming set designers, costume makers, audience, and lifters of every curtain. You didn't just help me build stages—you helped me build belonging.

To Italy, thank you for becoming a second home—for the wisdom of your traditions, the love of your people, and the space to grow something sacred from something painful.

To every performer, student, and witness who stepped into this work with openness and courage— your vulnerability made this book possible.

This is for you.

And because of you.

Preface

Aracelis Ruiz Reyes

Process. One of my favorite words.

The emergence of life—being born, growing, evolving, and leaving a mark on the path you choose—unfolds through a process. When you finally arrive at your intended destination, more than the celebration of achievement itself, it will be the memories of that journey—the process—that truly bear fruit in your life. Whether it brought you pain, joy, or both, the process is the great agent of transformation.

The book you are about to enter is the fruit of one such process—a journey of life walked by someone passionately devoted to the performing arts and so much more. Passion alone was not enough. The author gathered, with meticulous care, scientific grounding, and strategic clarity, every "brick" necessary to give structure and solidity to his vision: Human Theatre.

Nothing in this book is placed without purpose. With deep responsibility and a masterful sequence, the author draws from the works, movements, and disciplines born of pioneers and visionaries from every corner of the world and every epoch. Watching how he compares, cross-references, and applies their insights becomes an act of reverence—honoring those who once theorized about the origins of human expression: the inner world, the self. From ancient ritual and Aristotle's triad of Dynamis–Energeia–Entelecheia, to the Commedia dell'Arte, from Lowen's Bioenergetics and Arthur Lessac's Kinesensics, to the legacies of Barba, Navarra, and Farley, the scope of this theoretical and practical framework is vast and vibrant.

This establishes the author's authority and legitimacy in developing Human Theatre, built on his lifelong exploration of the body as an instrument of truth.

We could call this vision globalist, in the truest sense. It is the ideal foundation for Human Theatre. Each reader is invited to witness how humanity—across cultures and eras—has approached the body as a vehicle to communicate, express, reveal, and purify. Whether as a way of life or within performance, the body becomes a sacred conduit.

Conceptually, each element discussed in these pages is presented with clarity and fidelity. And yet, the author also reclaims and reinterprets concepts that have been long misunderstood—offering a fresh lens through which to view ideas like tension and vulnerability.

In terms of structure, the dynamic interplay between the text and its accompanying illustrations is striking. These visuals do more than complement the reading; they transport us into a workshop, where each idea can be tested, expanded, and embodied. It's here that the educator in the author shines.

To me, one of the most meaningful contributions in this work is the vision of Human Theatre as a tool for healing, rehabilitation, rediscovery, and decoding the body. In doing so, its reach is not limited to professional performing arts. It becomes a resource for therapists, educators, healthcare practitioners, and others. This quality extends the impact of the work—making it not only relevant but essential in today's society and its challenges.

Let us return to where we began—*process*. In Human Theatre, the process takes precedence over the outcome.

The process heals. The process creates. The process expresses.

It does not merely produce a product—it embodies it. And in that embodiment, theatre becomes *human*.

On a more personal note, I cannot close without sharing how Richard and I first met.

It was August of 2003. I had been assigned to a rural school nestled in the beautiful countryside of our beloved Yabucoa. I hadn't chosen to go there. Few know that during that season, I was surrounded by sadness and depression. I didn't want to be there.

And then, into my small classroom walked a ninth-grade class—lively, diverse, full of energy. Teenagers, in all their glory. It didn't take long to notice one student: poised, respectful, mature, brilliant, knowledgeable beyond his years. I kept asking myself, *Who is this young man?*

That's how our student-teacher relationship began—one that would soon evolve into friendship, and later, family. Richard and his classmates had no idea that they were God's instruments in lifting me out of bed every morning and giving me a reason to show up.

Soon after, we began creating together: outdoor rehearsals, short plays, and a comedy festival titled "A Carcajada Limpia"—dedicated to the great Puerto Rican comedian José Miguel Agrelot, who had passed in early 2004. The students researched his life through newspapers, created exhibits, and presented stellar work. I was so proud that I documented it all with photos—some of which were even published. Seeing their faces light up, holding the newspaper, seeing their work—an unforgettable day.

Among all the projects, one stood out for its content, structure, and excellence: the work of Richard Martínez. I still keep that assignment, preserved with love.

That class graduated. What we thought would be goodbye, was only a turning point. That very August, the Specialized School of Fine Arts opened in neighboring Humacao—a dream come true. A professional theatre, state-of-the-art facilities, and a full academic and artistic program.

I will never forget the call:

RICHARD: "Señora", I have news—they just accepted me into the School of Fine Arts!

ME: Richard! I'm so happy! But wait ... I also have news! *(pause, imaginary drumroll ...)* They just selected me to be part of the faculty at the School of Fine Arts!

We were going to continue together.

The rest is history. I'd need another book—or three—to recount what we achieved and lived in those years. And even after, we never lost touch. As friends. As family. And always, to this day, he still calls me "Señora."

As someone who has studied the Stanislavski method, one of my favorite concepts is the *unbroken line*: the actor's ability to stay fully connected to their objective from beginning to end, uninterrupted by distractions.

Richard is not a character—he is a person. But from the moment I met him, I've witnessed in him a continuous line: of talent, of excellence, of an unrelenting desire to learn, to create, to overcome. Even in a field where excellence can provoke envy, where many seek to dim the light rather than fuel it, Richard burns too brightly—like trying to put out a wildfire with a glass of water.

I always knew that line would take him far. But its magnitude still amazes me. *Pride* is too small a word.

It was my honor to be his first theatre teacher.

But greater still is the honor of inviting you to read this book—a work that, without a doubt, will hold a lasting place in the theoretical foundation of contemporary and future performing arts.

More than a method—it is a lived experience. More than a theory—it is a therapy. More than a book—you hold in your hands a masterwork, a tribute.

Aracelis Ruiz Reyes, M.Ed.

Preface

Fabio Mangolini

There are books that, once read and studied, offer new perspectives and open up often unexplored paths. These are important books that become milestones for the future because they resonate, connecting familiar places through unexpected threads, like those that connect stars in constellations. They are also important books because they attempt to clarify terms and concepts that are sometimes used excessively and often improperly. Even more so, they clarify them by merging theory and practice. How many times, in our theatre practice, have we used or heard the terms "energy" and "dynamism" used, often associating them with different categories in each person's practice and thinking? And each time, these terms are defined by their complexity and interpretability. Clarifying does not mean giving peremptory and definitive definitions, but trying to offer a frame of reference, a sort of map like those medieval maps that highlighted known places by connecting them with imaginary lines. This is what the book you are holding in your hands right now does, offering you a sort of map to help you find a way. This alone makes it not only a useful book, but also a necessary one, the result of research and knowledge that has become increasingly experiential. I imagine the author of this book a bit like the character Palomar, the fruit of Italo Calvino's imagination, when on a trip to Japan he is confronted with the mystery of the Ryoanji Zen garden in Kyōtō:

> He prefers to take the more difficult path, trying to grasp what the Zen garden can give him by looking at it in the only situation in which it can be seen today, sticking his neck out among other necks.
>
> What does he see? He sees the human species in the age of large numbers, spreading out in a levelled crowd but still made up of distinct individuals, like this sea of grains of sand that submerges the surface of the world [...]. He sees the world nevertheless continuing to show the heavy burdens of its nature, indifferent to the fate of humanity, its hard substance irreducible to human assimilation [...]. It sees the forms in which human sand aggregates tending to arrange themselves according to lines of movement, patterns that combine regularity and fluidity like the straight or circular tracks of a rake [...]. And between humanity-sand and world-rock, one senses a possible harmony, as

> between two non-homogeneous harmonies: that of the non-human in a balance of forces that seems to respond to no design; that of human structures that aspire to a rationality of geometric or musical composition, never definitive ...[1]

Of course, the beauty of theatre does not lie merely in the appreciation of its parts, but in the totality of its experience, which is realized in its becoming, in its *making*. Its realization onstage, despite its *ephemeral nature*, establishes a relationship between *performance and audience* that goes beyond simple *admiration* to become an *experience*, that is, an activity. The goal of theatre is, therefore, the *aesthetic experience* that moves along the dual axis of artistic production, on the part of the performer, and *experiential activity*, on the part of the audience. The actor becomes an instrument of the audience's activity, provoking their emotions and producing them through his or her own action onstage. In the same way, the *allied arts*, i.e. all the arts that make up the theatrical act, contribute to building the audience's experience by influencing its perceptive qualities.

It is on the actor's ability to constantly reach the audience's perspective during their action, at the very moment of the performance, that the audience's appreciation and the ability of the spectators to transcend the fragmentary quality of the *allied arts* and bring them together into a productive whole rests. The actor is not only a producer of meaning, but also a creator of emotions that are conveyed in a unicum that develops on an axis ranging from semantic perception to a cognitive state, ending in a contemplative dimension. The actor must capture *the essence of the emotion* to be conveyed, despite the ephemeral nature of the performance. To achieve this goal, the actor must operate on two levels, internal and external, revealing the latter to the audience so that the audience, in turn, can reach a state of interiority and contemplation.

Pure theory? No, praxis that becomes theory and then praxis again in an eternal cycle. To remain in that corner of the world where Italo Calvino's Palomar moved, let us stay in Japan and call upon someone who was a performer, theorist, teacher and philosopher of theatre: Zeami.

In one of his shortest and most dense treatises, *Kyūi*,[2] written in 1424, Zeami analyses the art of acting, distinguishing it into nine levels, nine steps ranging from the state of *soen*, raw nature, to that of *myōka fū*, the "flower of tranquil balance," that is, the state in which the actor, having surpassed full awareness of his art, finally grasps its mystery by sharing it with the audience. In this final stage of his art, which Zeami translates into the metaphorical image "at Silla the sun shines at midnight," we see the extreme limit of the art of the Nō actor, that is, the goal towards which the actor strives throughout his life and on which the maximum success of the aesthetic experience that takes place onstage depends. In this stage, where the brilliance of the sun and the deep darkness of the night converge, the actor reaches the fullness of Nothingness, which encompasses every kind of emotion, testifying with his presence onstage to the abyss that transforms him into dazzling light. In this final stage of consciousness, the actor, through performance, encounters the consciousness of the spectator at a level "where logical discrimination is suspended and a direct perception of the mystery or emptiness from which forms spring forth can be realised,"[3] thus creating an event of gnoseological significance, the aesthetic experience.

According to Zeami, the effectiveness of a performance lies in the relationship between the actor and the audience. The performer's constant goal must therefore be to keep the audience's interest constantly unaltered. In a passage from another treatise, *Kakyō*, from 1424, Zeami says that the actor must be able to create a performance in which the audience, "both those who know the art and those who are new to it, can shout in unison, 'How interesting!'"[4] The *kan* ("emotion") aroused in the spectator must not derive merely from the momentary attraction of their attention but from the actor's ability and skill in arousing in the audience a series of interconnected emotions, ranging from anticipation to surprise to delight. Zeami considers these emotional responses to be symptomatic of the audience's involvement with the actor onstage and constitute what Zeami calls *mezurashi* or *omoshiroi*: those moments in a performance that appear artistically and aesthetically unexpected. These emotions are a first "emotional degree" to which the actor must aspire and are defined, in another treatise, the *Kyakurayka*, as "participatory emotional responses."[5] In one of his later treatises, *Shugyoku tokka*, written in 1428, Zeami offers a detailed view of this "emotional degree," highlighting the self-reflective quality of the actor's activity when *omoshiro* is achieved.

Therefore, when Zeami refers to *omoshiroi*, he does not simply mean the audience's appreciation of the actor's skilful use of art, but goes much further: he refers to an aesthetic effect that is produced *simultaneously* between the actor and the audience in an *immediate and preconscious correspondence*. Through his art ("singing and dancing"), the act produces an immediate impact on the audience's inner ear, which is activated in the immediacy of the sphere of *Non-mind*. Both the actor and the audience correspond, therefore, within the immediate aesthetic experience of Nō. The experience of the performance, which is realized through the actor's skills and the *allied arts*, creates a state of *non-mind*, and therefore *emptiness*, in the spectator, and takes the form of a gnoseological experience. Distinguishing between preconscious response, conscious response and articulated response, Zeami traces the suggestions of *Kyūi*, addressed to the art of the actor, back to the dynamics of the communicative relationship between the stage and the audience. The liveliness of Nō consists in the constant attempt to achieve this state of emotional immediacy between actor and audience: in the actor through his art and in the audience through the disposition to which the actor's art invites, when, through that same state, one reaches a state of consciousness (subjectively), *omoshiro* is achieved.

This advanced state of "preconscious" emotionality is not defined by Zeami with the term *kan* ("emotion") but with *mushin-no-kan*, meaning "emotions that go beyond the conscious mind," or, more literally, "emotions without mind," where 'mind' refers to the whole that encompasses both the sphere of thought and that of personal and egocentric emotions.[6] This subtle emotion created through the art of the actor strikes the viewer so intensely (like light coming out of a cave) that they lose themselves in the experience. However, this is not a hypnotic state, but a genuinely aesthetic experience. For Zeami, this lofty goal of the actor becomes the goal of the art of Nō and translates into inducing the viewer to transcend their egotistical being in order to discover a more direct perception of reality within things. In essence, it is the creation of a cathartic effect that frees the viewer, even if only for a moment, from the world of their personal and emotional concerns.[7]

Whenever Zeami uses the term *kan* ("emotion") in direct reference to the actor, he does so in contexts that do not refer directly to his personal emotion. Rather, he uses this term to denote the *sensitive intuition* that the actor controls and develops onstage: the perception that the actor develops in what Zeami calls "the opportune moment that corresponds to the emotion of the audience."[8] This *sensitive intuition* developed by the actor helps him to develop a strong and immediate relationship with the audience, which he can then guide through the aesthetic experience of Nō by revealing the nature of the character he is portraying onstage. The actor's emotion therefore involves his own skills, not so much from a purely technical point of view, but in his ability to deeply identify the dynamics of the character he is portraying. Thus, by denying the actor's personal emotion, what the audience perceives is an effect created by the actor without perceiving how this effect was produced.[9] At the same time, however, at the highest level of skill, the actor experiences a state of *mushin* ("no-mind" or "emptiness") that allows him to connect with the audience. Only when the actor frees himself from his personal feelings, i.e. by creating *mushin*, will he be able to deeply grasp his art.

The actor is not required to possess the simple technical skill capable, at most, of producing *kan* ("emotions") in the audience, but to transcend it, through training and experience, to reach the personal experience of *mushin*, the act of contemplation, leading the audience through *mushin-no-kan*, that is, the emotion of contemplation, the representation of *mu*, the highest aesthetic value of *gei-dō*. What we have so far defined as performance, in Nō transcends itself to become a shared experience between actor and audience, in Zeami's time as in contemporary Nō. The tension that is created in the theatre space, between the stage and the audience, becomes the aspiration of human beings to grasp, even if only for a fleeting and immediate moment, the experience of *mu*. In this aspiration, in this common tension, lies the activity of actor and audience, which is mutual in that it is reciprocated. In this tension, therefore, lies beauty, not as an exposition of verisimilitude, but as a common search for profound truth that transcends human limitations.

In the introduction to the English translation of Zeami's major treatises, Masakazu Yamazaki, a man of the theatre as well as a theorist, offers a clear view of the problem by comparing Zeami's positions with those of Diderot and Archer, who are certainly closer to us.

> What Zeami stresses in his teachings to actors, is none other than "becoming" and the possession of "one mind." He calls the actor who has acquired that ability one who can show Internalization (*yūshufū*). Internalization requires that an actor become the complete master of his own movements, and according to Zeami it denotes a state in which the flow of movement has become so well assimilated that the actor loses even the consciousness of controlling it.
>
> In this regard, one can say that this great artist's theory of acting went beyond the argument prevalent in the West since the eighteenth century concerning the opposition between masks and faces. Diderot's stand was that acting which moves the audience rises out of the actor's conscious manipulation of his body. Archer's idea was that, on the contrary, such acting came spontaneously from the actor's own feeling. These two views clearly correspond to the contrast between Zeami's "imitation" and "becoming." However, Zeami did not see the mask and the face as requiring a choice among alternatives; rather he wanted the actor to unify the two while retaining a positive consciousness of their opposition. In connection with the expression of a strong emotion, in particular, Zeami strictly demanded this ambiguous attitude. He carefully warned the actor against indulging in his own emotions as well as using his technique to manipulate them. [...] What Zeami taught specifically to the actors in order to make them tackle this contradictory task of acting was, first, to understand a role in terms of an attitude, and, second, to see action as a rhythmical structure. Either of these can become a direct aim for an actor's efforts, and they may be described as the focus for his consciousness, giving him a target for his attention and saving him from confusion and disruption.[10]

When an actor becomes a master, he is not only skilled in his craft, but also becomes aware of the creative expression that he can convey through it: he can express himself directly without being inhibited by personal concerns. Only then can he devote himself to the contemplative state to be achieved during the performance. Theatrical art, as conceived by Zeami and still understood today by Nō professionals and taken by the actor to its extreme consequences of mastery, is therefore the basis of Nō, not its ultimate goal.

In Nō, the actor's body extends to the boundaries of the space experienced and seen by the spectator, going beyond them. The actor's body becomes emblematic of the question of meaning as a producer of activity that transforms the time and space of the action, suspending them. Similarly, on the part of the spectator, the aesthetic process stops, also suspended, in the manipulation of time and space induced by the actor. At that juncture, which is defined by the term ma, in the indefiniteness of space-time suspension, in the density of emptiness, lies the whole transformation and encounter.

NOTES

1. Italo Calvino, *Palomar* (Mondadori, 1990), 93.
2. J. Thomas Rimer and Masakazu Yamazaki, *On the Art of the N. Drama: The major Treatises of Zeami* (Princeton University Press, 1984), 120–25. Toshihiko Izutsu and Toyo Izutsu, *The Theory of Beauty in the Classical Aesthetics of Japan* (Martinus Nijhoff, 1981), 97–104.
3. Gioia Ottaviani, *Introduzione allo studio del teatro giapponese* (La Casa Usher, 1994), 131.
4. Mark J. Nearman, "*Kaky*: Zeami's Fundamental Principles of Acting," *Monumenta Nipponica* XXXVII, 3, (1982–83): 51.
5. Mark J. Nearman, "*Kyakurayka*: Zeami's Final Legacy for the Master Actor," *Monumenta Nipponica* XXXV, 2, (1980): 178.
6. Mark J. Nearman, "Feeling in Relation to Acting: An Outline of Zeami's Views," *Asian Theatre Journal* 1, 1, (1984): 42.
7. As Nearman points out, "paradoxically, this spiritually therapeutic goal bears a resemblance to Bertolt Brecht's *Verfremdungseffekt* wherein the performance is viewed and experienced as fully as possible by the spectator for his evaluation. That is, the spectator enters into a heightened state of consciousness rather than remaining caught up in an emotionally blinding feeling of sympathy for a fictitious hero whose innate, absolute goodness and rightness are never called into question. Similar to Brecht, Zeami seems to call for a transcendence of societal values that will allow the viewer to see the essential nature of a character beyond a level of sentimental heroism" (Nearman 1984: 43).
8. Nearman, "*Kaky*" (1982–83): 461–62.
9. Nearman, "*Kaky*" (1982–83): 489–91.
10. Rimer and Yamazaki, *On the Art of the N. Drama*, xli–xii.

REFERENCES

Izutsu, Toshihiko, and Toyo Izutsu. *The Theory of Beauty in the Classical Aesthetics of Japan*. Martinus Nijhoff, 1981.

Nearman, Mark J. "*Kyakurayka*: Zeami's Final Legacy for the Master Actor." *Monumenta Nipponica* XXXV, 2, (1980): 153–87.

Nearman, Mark J. "*Kaky*: Zeami's Fundamental Principles of Acting." *Monumenta Nipponica* XXXVII, 3, (1982): 333–74.

Nearman, Mark J. "*Kaky*: Zeami's Fundamental Principles of Acting." *Monumenta Nipponica* XXXVII, 4, (1983): 459–96.

Nearman, Mark J. "Feeling in Relation to Acting: An Outline of Zeami's Views." *Asian Theatre Journal* 1, 1, (1984): 40–51.

Ottaviani, Gioia. *Introduzione allo studio del teatro giapponese*. La Casa Usher, 1994.

Rimer, J. Thomas, and Masakazu Yamazaki. *On the Art of the N. Drama: The major Treatises of Zeami*. Princeton University Press, 1984.

Foreword

This book is not the result of theory alone—it was born of necessity. It arose at the intersection of art and healing, where performance became more than expression; it became a lifeline. A path back to presence, to breath, to embodiment. Human Theatre emerged from a series of questions that haunted me: Why did my body betray me onstage? Why did my breath vanish under pressure? Why did emotions overwhelm rather than empower? And why did the sacred connection with the audience feel so terrifying?

These questions came not only from my artistic practice—but from my life.

When the pandemic stripped away distractions and illusions, it also took from me my last refuge: the stage. What was left was silence—and in that silence, I was forced to meet myself. Raw. Untethered. Unfiltered. And in that stillness, I began to realize that the tools I had gathered—Lessac's Kinesensics, somatic practices, the mask, and the DEE Cycle—were not just techniques for performance. They were tools for survival. They were bridges back to myself.

This book is for anyone who uses their body as a vessel for expression, connection, or healing. It is for actors, movers, therapists, educators—for those exploring the intersection of trauma and creativity, nervous system regulation and stage presence, silence and voice.

It is a book about energetic alchemy: the transformation of tension into movement, of silence into voice, of pain into power. And it is, above all, a book about hope—about reclaiming our expressive potential through embodiment and energy.

I offer this work not as a finished method, but as a living proposal. A process. A practice that continues to evolve with every performer who dares to explore it.

To those who have felt estranged from their own expressive power, To those who never quite fit the mold, To those whose voices have been silenced by shame, trauma, or tradition— This book is for you.

May it give you permission to breathe again. To listen. To tremble. To transform. May it return you to your voice—and to the body that holds it.

Welcome to Human Theatre.

Introduction

Modern theatre often finds itself entangled in technical mastery, yet disconnected from the visceral human truth it once embodied. Performances, while polished, can feel emotionally distant—more representation than revelation. In this book, we explore an alternative: **Human Theatre**—a practice rooted not in artifice, but in energetic presence, embodiment, and transformation.

Human Theatre invites performers, educators, movers, and healers to return to the source: the body. It is an evolving methodology that reclaims the stage as a space of real, lived alchemy, where breath, sensation, and energy shape performance beyond character or plot.

This is not a manual of technique, nor a reinterpretation of canonical styles. It is a proposal for a different kind of presence—one that begins with vulnerability, somatic awareness, and the courage to let energy move through you. At the heart of this work is the **DEE Cycle**—Dynamis (potential), Energeia (action), and Entelecheia (realization)—an ancient framework repurposed here to guide performers toward authentic expression and embodied storytelling.

Rather than following a linear structure, the book unfolds organically:

1. It begins with a philosophical and somatic inquiry into **energy**: what it is, how it flows through the body, and why it matters onstage.
2. It then dives into **practical explorations** through **bioenergetics**, **Lessac Kinesensics**, breathwork, and embodied voice.
3. It offers **movement-based and vocal exercises**, not as techniques to master, but as invitations to feel and transform.
4. Along the way, it dialogues with **theatrical traditions**, interrogates codification, and honors the lineage of embodied wisdom.

This work is for anyone seeking to integrate their inner world with their expressive power. Whether you're a theatre artist, therapist, dancer, or teacher, Human Theatre offers a path back to presence—a way to stand onstage and say, with your whole being: *I am here.*

Let this book be a companion in your journey—a mirror, a map, and a breath.

SECTION 1

FOUNDATIONAL CONCEPTS

Chapter 1

Before the Curtain Rises: Foundations of Human Performance

1

Before the Curtain Rises: Foundations of Human Performance

An Introduction to the Living Legacy, Language, and Challenge of Human Performance

Before delving into the philosophical and somatic foundation of energy onstage, this opening section provides a brief overview—both conceptual and practical—of the key themes that shape Human Theatre. Think of it as a prelude: a moment to ground ourselves in the history, vocabulary, and challenges that await the performer on this transformative journey.

The Historical Roots of Human Expression in Performance

The impulse to perform is ancient. Long before theatre buildings, scripts, and directors, human beings danced, chanted, and embodied stories around fires and in temples—moments captured in the evolving lineage shown in **Figure 1.1**. Performance was not entertainment—it was **ritual**, **healing**, and **transformation**.

In cultures across the world—from the masked dances of West Africa to Japanese Nō theatre, from Greek tragedy to Indigenous ceremonies—the performer's role was to *channel*, *invoke*, and *commune*. These practices were often inseparable from spirituality, nature, and communal memory. Movement and sound were not just aesthetic choices; they were energetic forces, capable of invoking the sacred and transmitting unspoken truths.

FIGURE 1.0: The First Impulse. From grounded stillness, the first impulse rises. Breath, weight, and intention converge as the performer steps into motion. AI-generated image created with OpenAI's DALL·E (via ChatGPT).

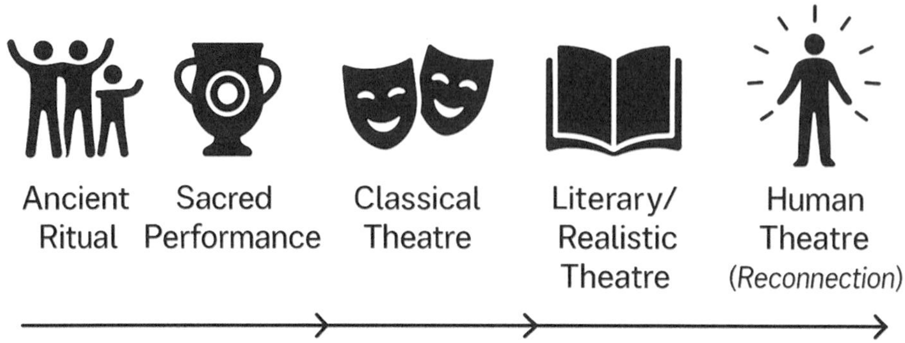

FIGURE 1.1: A simplified timeline tracing the evolution of human performance—from early ritual and oral tradition to classical theatre, modernism, and the emergence of contemporary performance practice. This visual highlights the deep historical roots that continue to inform the performer's craft. AI-generated image created with OpenAI's DALL·E (via ChatGPT).

Human Theatre seeks to reclaim this lineage.

While many modern performance styles evolved through religious liturgy or courtly entertainment, they gradually shifted toward narrative, text, and psychological character building—moving further from the body and from immediacy. This shift culminated in the dominance of Western naturalism, where performance became an imitation of real life, often prioritizing intellectual analysis over **embodied experience.**

But deep in the theatre's DNA is something more primal. The performer was once a vessel, a bridge between inner and outer worlds, between the personal and the collective. Human Theatre returns to this lineage—not as a nostalgic revival, but as a radical reconnection to what it means to **be alive and present in front of others.**

Performing Arts: Definition and Distinctions from Traditional Theatre

The term *performing arts* encompasses a wide variety of disciplines—including dance, music, circus, clowning, and physical theatre—where the human body becomes the central instrument of expression. Unlike traditional theatre, which often centers on text and scripted performance, performing arts prioritize presence, movement, and immediacy. They allow performers to communicate not only through words but through *gesture, space, silence, and breath.*

In this context, **Human Theatre** is rooted in the performing arts but distinguishes itself through its emphasis on energetic transmission and the DEE Cycle. It invites performers to abandon the illusion of character and narrative in favor of *direct, embodied communication.* This type of theatre doesn't aim to recreate life—it *generates lived experience* through the performer's present and authentic being.

Where traditional theatre might construct a fictional world for the audience to observe, Human Theatre breaks that fourth wall not through direct address, but through energetic authenticity. The performer doesn't hide behind a character; they become a *channel* for lived human experience. This shift from representation to presence marks a fundamental transformation in the understanding of what it means to perform.

In this sense, Human Theatre returns to something primal. It echoes ancient ritual and communal storytelling, where performance was a shared energetic act, deeply tied to life, healing, and transformation. It reclaims the stage not just as a place for entertainment—*but as a sacred space for real human connection.* Unlike traditional theatrical frameworks that prioritize character, plot, and directorial control, Human Theatre is rooted in the lived body and the energetic encounter between performer and audience.

A side-by-side comparison of these approaches is illustrated in **Figure 1.2**, where the contrast between representation and presence becomes visually apparent. This comparison encapsulates the shift from theatrical illusion to energetic authenticity.

Key Distinctions Between Actor and Performer

While often used interchangeably, the roles of *actor* and *performer* carry significant differences—especially in the context of Human Theatre.

Actors are traditionally linked to character embodiment, scripted dialogue, and the recreation of behavior shaped by dramatic circumstances. Their role is often centered on illusion: creating the impression of a life that

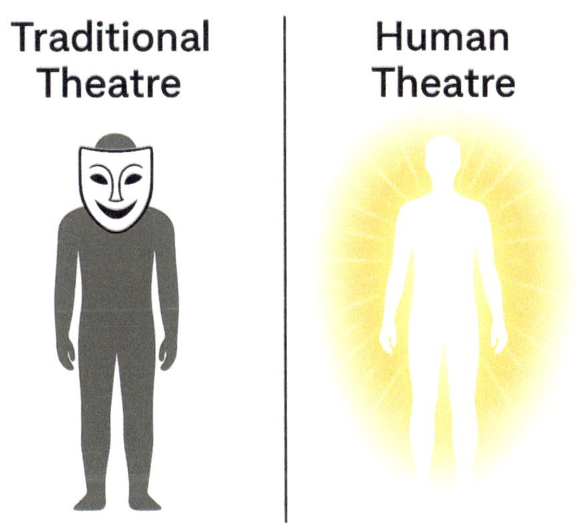

FIGURE 1.2: A comparative breakdown of Traditional Theatre and Human Theatre. While Traditional Theatre emphasizes scripted narrative, fixed staging, and character portrayal, Human Theatre prioritizes presence, transformation, and the performer as a living conduit of energy and experience. AI-generated image created with OpenAI's DALL·E (via ChatGPT).

exists independently of their own. This model has dominated Western theatre, emphasizing *interpretation* of text and psychological realism.

A **performer**, in contrast, is a vessel of presence and energetic transmission. They are not concerned primarily with creating characters but with activating truth through action. Performers work with their own bodies, breath, voice, and intention—not to become someone else, but to *reveal something essential* within themselves. This makes the performer an *instrument of the moment*—always listening, always responding, always alive.

In Human Theatre, the performer is a generator of *Energeia*. They are not representing; they are *presenting*. This distinction is key: to represent is to construct an external image, but to present is to offer one's self—fully, vulnerably, and energetically.

As illustrated in **Figure 1.3**, the distinction between actor and performer is not simply one of technique, but of presence. The actor, grounded in representation, constructs a character from the outside in. The Human Theatre performer, by contrast, channels vulnerability and Energeia from within—presenting rather than portraying. This image crystallizes the essence of Human Theatre: a move from illusion to transmission, from mimicry to embodied truth.

Moreover, while actors may rely on craft and technique to convey emotion, performers draw from embodied memory and subconscious resonance. Their gestures are not stylized for effect; they are *energetically charged*. The DEE Cycle—*Dynamis*, *Energeia*, *Entelecheia*—is in constant motion within the performer, making their presence dynamic, rooted, and real.

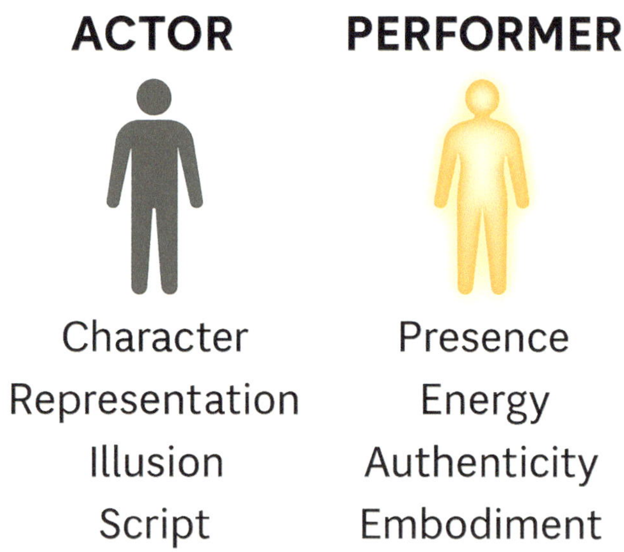

FIGURE 1.3: Actor versus Performer. On the left, the actor represents a character; on the right, the performer becomes a vessel for presence and transformation. This contrast reflects a shift from theatrical illusion to energetic authenticity—where the body is not just portraying, but transmitting. AI-generated image created with OpenAI's DALL·E (via ChatGPT).

This is not to devalue the work of actors or the traditions they come from. Rather, it's to reclaim a space in the theatre where *aliveness*, *response*, and *self-awareness* are as important as technique. In doing so, Human Theatre invites the performer and the actor to become more than a medium for storytelling—they become a mirror for the human condition.

Challenge for the Performer: Managing Muscle Tension

A common obstacle for the modern performer is not a lack of skill or imagination—but tension. Muscle tension acts like static in a communication system, distorting the clarity of emotional and physical transmission. It disconnects breath from voice, movement from impulse, intention from action.

In Human Theatre, **energy must flow freely** through the body to activate the DEE Cycle. When muscles are rigid, the performer's Energeia is blocked, the transformation toward Entelecheia is stifled, and the connection with the audience weakens.

Tension often arises from external pressure: the need to "perform well," to control the body, to meet expectations. But it also comes from deeper internalized patterns—trauma, shame, self-judgment. These are not just psychological concepts; they are embedded in the tissue of the body.

As shown in **Figure 1.4**, the visual map of common tension zones—including the

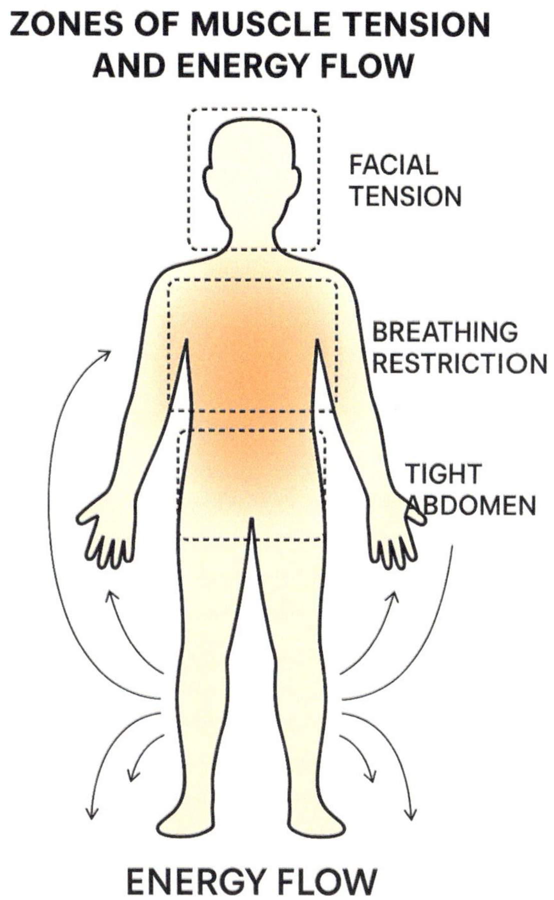

FIGURE 1.4: Zones of Muscle Tension and Energy Flow. This diagram highlights common areas in the body where performers tend to store tension, interrupting the free movement of breath, voice, and Energeia. Releasing these zones allows the DEE Cycle to flow more fully through the performer. AI-generated image created with OpenAI's DALL·E (via ChatGPT).

jaw, shoulders, diaphragm, and pelvis—offers a somatic reference point for understanding how blocked musculature can disrupt energetic flow and compromise expressive freedom.

To manage this, performers must first become aware. Where is the tension? What is its shape? What thought or memory causes it to surface? Then comes **release**—through breath, sound, posture, and awareness. This is not about "relaxation" as passivity, but about *readiness*—a state where the performer is open, alert, and energetically available.

This is why Human Theatre places such emphasis on breath, presence, and embodiment. A relaxed jaw, an open chest, a grounded pelvis—these are not merely anatomical concerns; they are gateways to freedom. They allow for authenticity to emerge and communication to become resonant, not mechanical.

The Energetic Alchemy of the Performer

In Human Theatre, the body is more than a vessel—it is a crucible. Within it, *energy*, *memory*, *intention*, and *breath* combine and transform. This is the energetic alchemy of the performer.

This energetic transformation is visually captured in **Figure 1.5**, which places the performer within the triangular flow of **Dynamis, Energeia, and Entelecheia**. More than a diagram, it symbolizes the alchemical core of Human Theatre: where energy becomes action, action becomes presence, and presence becomes meaning.

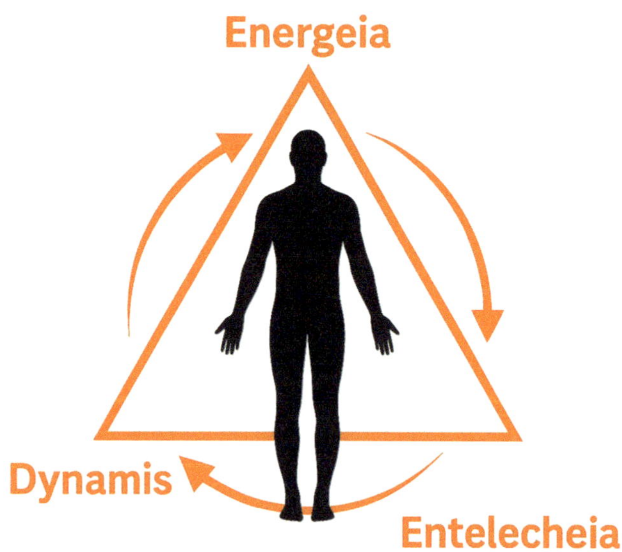

FIGURE 1.5: The DEE Cycle as Energetic Alchemy. Within the triangle of transformation—Dynamis, Energeia, Entelecheia—the performer stands as a living crucible. Energy becomes action, action becomes presence, and presence becomes meaning. Human Theatre is forged in this cycle. AI-generated image created with OpenAI's DALL·E (via ChatGPT).

When performers step onstage, they bring with them a lifetime of sensations, histories, and emotions. If these remain unconscious or repressed, their body may move, but their presence remains dim. The goal of Human Theatre is to awaken that internal current—to transform *Dynamis* ("potential energy") into *Energeia* ("manifested action") and then into *Entelecheia* ("a moment of realized impact").

This cycle doesn't merely help with performance—it generates performance. Each breath taken with awareness fuels Energeia. Each moment of stillness becomes a charged pause, where the audience leans forward, unconsciously breathing with the performer. The mirror neurons fire. Empathy is kindled. A silent form of communication begins.

The alchemy occurs not in complexity, but in *authenticity*. It's not about doing more—it's about doing *truthfully*. When performers breathe with intention, move with awareness, and listen with their whole body, the audience receives more than a show—they receive a *transmission*.

In this way, Human Theatre becomes not a performance of life, but a form of *living*. It is a space where the performer is not a role but a resonator, transforming energy into meaning, and presence into collective experience.

Having traced the ancestral pulse of performance, redefined the contours of what it means to be a performer, and acknowledged the challenges of tension, energy, and embodiment, we now turn to the lifeblood of Human Theatre: energy itself. What is this invisible current that animates the stage, electrifies a gesture, or makes silence sing? In the next chapter, we dive into the philosophical and somatic roots of energy in performance, and how the DEE Cycle—Dynamis, Energeia, Entelecheia—becomes the alchemical core of transformative theatre.

Reflection: The Performer as Portal

We began by tracing the roots of human expression, from ancient rituals to contemporary stages. We questioned the boundaries between actor and performer, theatre and presence, illusion and truth. And we discovered that Human Theatre does not begin with a role or a script—it begins with a body. A breath. A charge of potential waiting to become. The distinctions explored in this chapter are not just conceptual. They are **energetic choices**. To perform is not merely to do—it is to **transmit**. To allow something to pass through you that is larger than character or story. Something vibratory. Something human. You are not the illusion. You are the threshold. The performer is not a mask—but a portal.

As we continue into deeper practices of energy, breath, and sensation, carry this with you:

The work of Human Theatre is not to imitate life—it is to become fully **alive** within it.

Chapter 2

Energy Onstage: A Foundation for Human Theatre

2

Energy Onstage: A Foundation for Human Theatre

Part 1—Unveiling the Energetic Core of Human Theatre: A Journey Through Dynamis, Energeia, and Entelecheia

The Spark Within: Unpacking Energy in Performance

Imagine dancers leaping across the stage, their body a taut spring of energy—each muscle firing with controlled precision. As shown in **Figure 2.1**, this moment captures pure energetic presence: breath, impulse, and intention unified in motion. The image is not just a demonstration of technique, but a visceral embodiment of what we mean by "energy" long before it becomes theory. Their eyes blaze with intensity, drawing you into a story told not through words, but through vibration, breath, and emotion.

This kind of connection—the dancers' bodies, their internal charge, and the way that energy reaches you—is the heart of this chapter. And it's not just about dance. It is the invisible current beneath all performance—and life itself.

In this section, we delve into the elusive yet powerful nature of energy. It's a word we use constantly, yet in performance it transcends physical exertion. Energy is what creates the invisible thread between performer and audience, the deeply emotional current that bridges experience and expression (see **Figure 2.2**).

So—what does energy mean to you? Maybe sunlight, movement, or the tension in your shoulders after a long day. We turn to language for clarity. The *Oxford English Dictionary* offers a few familiar definitions: "The strength and vitality required

FIGURE 2.0: Sensation in Descent. Energy travels downward through the body, rooting the performer in gravity. Awareness is sculpted from the inside outward. AI-generated image created with OpenAI's DALL·E (via ChatGPT).

for physical or mental activity," "power derived from the utilization of resources," and "the capacity of matter to perform work."

These definitions offer structure, but they fall short of capturing what energy means inside a performance—the kind that pulses between bodies, breath, and space.

Culturally, the word itself has gathered momentum. As shown in **Figure 2.3**, the use of "energy" in literature has climbed steadily since the 1750s. This mirrors its expansion across disciplines—physics, metaphysics, wellness, and art. We've begun to lean on this word to name something vital, but often intangible. Its elasticity makes it powerful—but also difficult to define.

Now, think back: Have you ever been moved by a performance? Was it the dialogue—or something else? Something in the air, between performer and audience? That "something" is what we're chasing here.

FIGURE 2.1: The dancer's body as a vessel of energy—each gesture becomes a transmission, bridging emotion and audience. An embodied example of Dynamis flowing into Energeia. AI-generated image created with OpenAI's DALL·E (via ChatGPT).

To understand energy in performance, we must look beyond modern definitions and reach back to ancient philosophy—specifically the Greek concept of **Energeia**, the root of our modern word "energy." This takes us to Aristotle's[1] model of transformation: **Dynamis–Energeia–Entelecheia.** Known throughout this book as the **DEE Cycle**, it offers a living framework for understanding how energy transforms from potential into expression—and finally, into meaning.

This book approaches the DEE Cycle not just as theory, but as practice: a choreography of impulse, alignment, and resonance. Here, ancient philosophy meets modern science. Energy becomes not a metaphor, but a sensation. Not an idea, but experience.

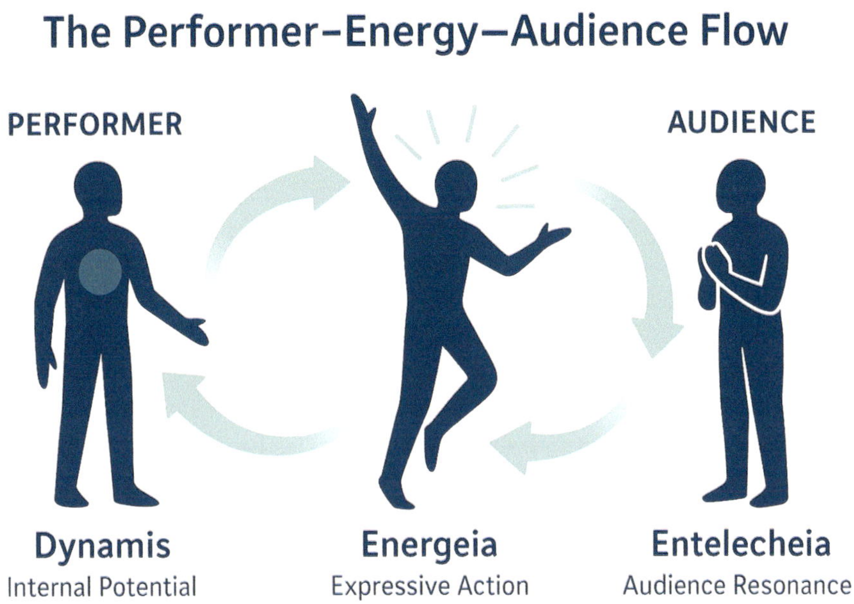

FIGURE 2.2: The Performer–Energy–Audience Flow. A visual representation of how internal potential (Dynamis) transforms into expressive action (Energeia), resulting in audience resonance (Entelecheia). Energy flows back and forth between performer and audience, creating a shared emotional circuit. AI-generated image created with OpenAI's DALL·E (via ChatGPT).

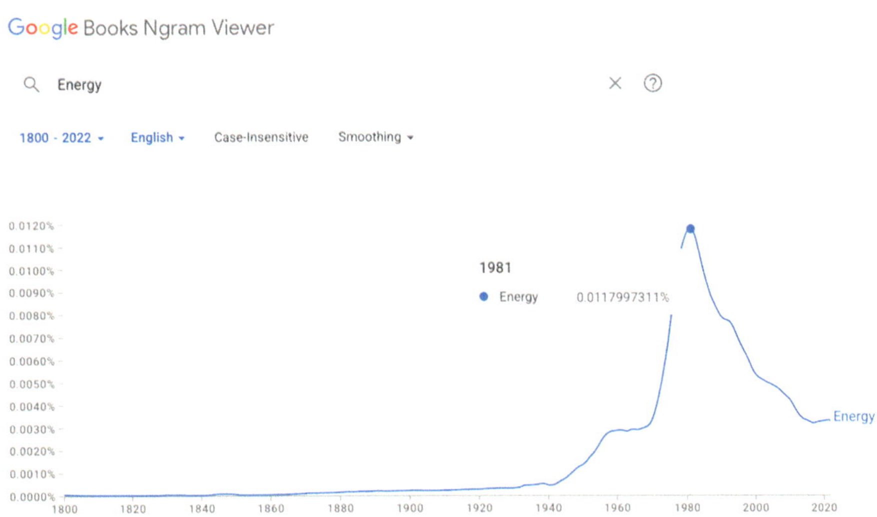

FIGURE 2.3: Usage of the word "energy" over time, according to Google Books Ngram Viewer. The rise in frequency reflects its growing cultural, scientific, and artistic relevance. Google Books Ngram Viewer, screenshot.

Tracing Energy's Roots: Aristotle and the DEE Cycle

Modern definitions of "energy," while useful, rarely address its purpose or depth within human expression—especially in the realm of performance. They often frame energy as a quantifiable force or resource, but this perspective doesn't capture the emotional and expressive reality of what we experience onstage.

To truly understand energy as a performative phenomenon, we must return to its philosophical roots. That journey leads us to ancient Greece—specifically to **Aristotle**, and his triadic formulation of change: **Dynamis, Energeia, and Entelecheia.**

These interwoven concepts form the basis of what this book calls the **DEE Cycle**—a living rhythm of transformation that operates not only in theatre but in the body, in breath, and in life itself.

Let us unfold these three stages as they apply to performance:

- **Dynamis** (*δύναμις*): The charge. It is potential not yet expressed—a breath held, a thought forming, the silence before the scene begins.
- **Energeia** (*ἐνέργεια*): The fire. Energy in motion. A breath released, a step taken, the voice emerging. This is the body in action, alive and aware.
- **Entelecheia** (*ἐντελέχεια*): The echo. Fulfillment—not as completion, but as resonance. It is the moment when intention has become expression, and expression lands as presence.

These are not sequential steps. The DEE Cycle is a **perpetual rhythm**, a current moving through the performer's body in rehearsal, improvisation, and performance. It pulses in moments of intensity, stillness, and transformation.

This conceptual flow is illustrated in **Figure 2.4**—a triangle of lived energy: **Dynamis**, the internal charge; **Energeia**, the expressive unfolding; and **Entelecheia**, the reverberation of meaning through presence. The performer stands within this cycle—not as a passive subject, but as an alchemist of embodied change.

For clarity, **Table 2.1** summarizes the three terms from Aristotle's framework, linking ancient meaning with their theatrical embodiment.

TABLE 2.1: Dynamis, Energeia, and Entelecheia in the progression from potential to expressive action.

Greek Term	**Philosophical Meaning**	**Example in Performance**
Dynamis (*δύναμις*)	Latent potential; capacity that is not yet action.	A performer in stillness, charged before the first line is spoken.
Energeia (*ἐνέργεια*)	Energy in motion; actualization of potential.	The unfolding of gesture, the rise of voice, the breath initiating movement.
Entelecheia (*ἐντελέχεια*)	Fulfillment; completion through expression.	The moment a gesture or scene lands with emotional resonance—where meaning is felt, not just shown.

The interpretation of these Aristotelian terms has sparked rich philosophical debate[2] over the centuries. Their meanings—especially the distinction between what something **could become** and what it **already is**—have been explored and contested by generations of scholars.

Thinkers such as **Ricardo Yepes**, known for his detailed work on Aristotle's metaphysics, have helped clarify the historical ambiguities surrounding these concepts. This philosophical depth is essential for understanding how the DEE Cycle operates not only in theory, but in performance practice—where potential becomes action, and action becomes presence.

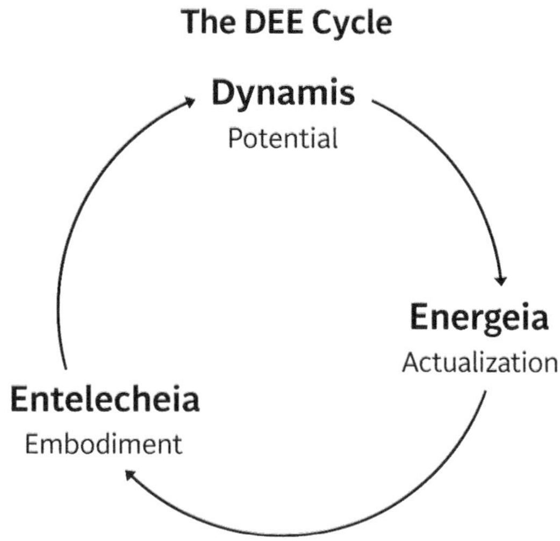

FIGURE 2.4: The DEE Cycle. A conceptual triangle representing the continuous transformation of energy within the performer: from latent intention (Dynamis), to energetic activation (Energeia), to complete expression or realization (Entelecheia). This diagram marks the foundational structure of energetic embodiment in Human Theatre. AI-generated image created with OpenAI's DALL·E (via ChatGPT).

A Natural Analogy: The Plant as Energetic Cycle. To visualize the DEE Cycle, imagine the life of a plant:

- **Dynamis**: The seed contains the blueprint and hidden energy to become a full-grown plant. The potential is present, but nothing is visible yet.
- **Energeia**: The seed germinates, roots push downward, stems reach upward. This is the active process of becoming.
- **Entelecheia**: The plant blooms. Its purpose is fulfilled as it flowers and spreads seeds of its own.

Just as energy transforms within the performer, so too does it cycle through nature. One of the simplest and most intuitive analogies for the DEE Cycle is the life of a plant—a movement from **seed**, to **growth**, to **bloom**.

This natural rhythm mirrors the performer's process: from the inner charge of intention (Dynamis), to the expressive unfolding of movement or sound (Energeia), to the flowering of presence onstage (Entelecheia).

Figure 2.5 illustrates this organic progression. In the soil, the seed holds its latent potential. With the right conditions, it sprouts upward—energy moving into form. And in full bloom, the plant is not simply complete, but fully present: radiating color, form, and vitality.

This cycle isn't linear—it repeats. A single performance contains many moments of Dynamis, Energeia, and Entelecheia, unfolding like petals and returning to the root.

Why the DEE Cycle Matters in Performance. Understanding energy through the DEE Cycle shifts us from a mechanistic view of acting to one rooted in **transformation**. It gives us language for something often left unspoken: how internal impulses move through the body, how performance becomes more than pretending, and how **truth emerges through presence**.

You don't just act a role—you **activate** it. You don't merely speak lines—you **channel energy**.

The DEE Cycle helps us frame this subtle, deeply human process of energetic transmission. It clarifies what happens when the performer stops "doing" and begins **becoming**—when performance is no longer a mask, but a conduit.

As illustrated in **Figure 2.6**, this cycle lives within the body. It starts in the belly, rises with the breath, expresses through gesture or voice, and lands in the space between performer and audience.

Now that we've mapped the DEE Cycle from its philosophical roots to its energetic logic, the next step is to **embody it**. How does this cycle live in your nervous system, your breath, your posture, your memory? That's where we're headed next.

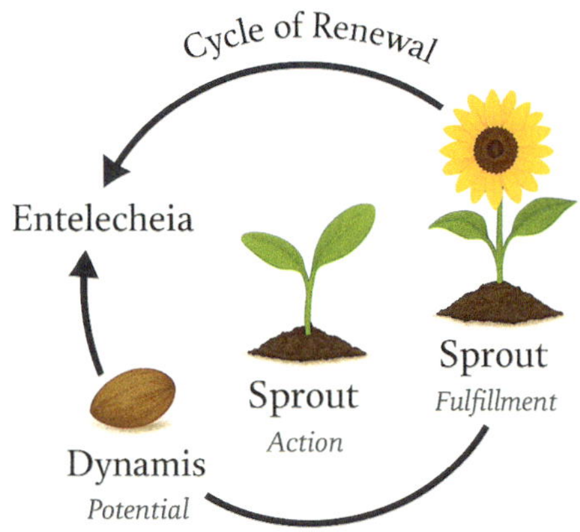

FIGURE 2.5: The DEE Cycle in Nature: A plant's life cycle illustrates the transformation of potential (seed) into action (sprout) and fulfillment (flower). AI-generated image created with OpenAI's DALL·E (via ChatGPT).

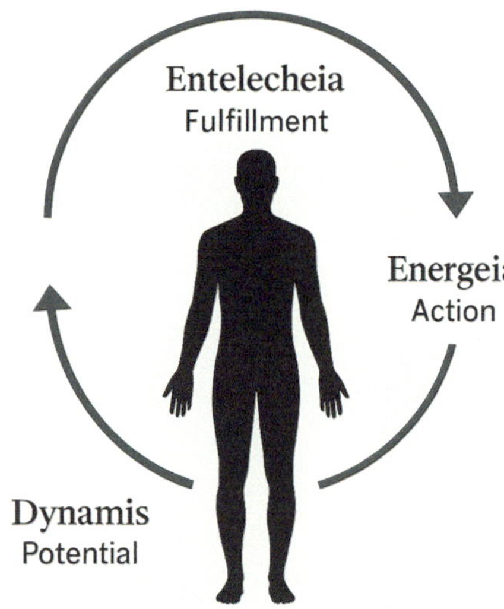

FIGURE 2.6: The DEE Cycle in the Energetic Body. A visual metaphor of how potential (Dynamis) becomes action (Energeia) and fulfillment (Entelecheia) within the living performer. The cycle illustrates energy as it flows through the body and back again—creating presence through transformation. AI-generated image created with OpenAI's DALL·E (via ChatGPT).

From Abstract to Embodied: The Energetic Body

Understanding energy as a philosophical or theoretical concept is only the beginning. For the performer, energy is not just an idea—it's a **felt reality**, something we experience in the breath, the muscles, the gut, and the space between us and others. This is where theory must be translated into practice—where the **DEE Cycle becomes flesh.**

Every emotion, thought, and memory we carry manifests in our bodies. Tension patterns, breathing rhythms, vocal habits, and posture all hold traces of our lived experience. This is why embodied practice is not a luxury—it's a necessity. The body is not just the container of our instrument; **it is the instrument**.

To work with this instrument, the performer must cultivate **somatic intelligence**: the ability to perceive, interpret, and transform inner sensation into expressive action. This capacity—reading the body from within and transmitting its truth outward—is what defines the *energetic body in action*.

Bridging Somatics and Philosophy. To fully grasp the concept of the energetic body, we must draw from somatic traditions that view the body not merely as biomechanics but as a site of memory, healing, and transformation. Think of the work of **Alexander Lowen**,[3] **Wilhelm Reich**,[4] and more recent somatic methodologies. These perspectives affirm that unexpressed emotions, trauma, or repressed impulses do not vanish—they lodge themselves in the body as chronic tension, fatigue, or numbness.

In performance, this means that actors are never a blank slate.[5] They bring their entire embodied history into the rehearsal room or onto the stage. Human Theatre does not ask performers to suppress this history—it invites them to recognize it, engage with it, and transform it.

Here, the DEE Cycle applies profoundly:

- **Dynamis**: A stored emotion or tension—a latent energetic charge.
- **Energeia**: The conscious engagement with that charge—through breath, voice, or movement.
- **Entelecheia**: The moment of release, connection, or transformation—energetically and artistically.

As seen in **Figure 2.7**, this progression can be visualized in the performer's body: from the stillness charged with potential, to the surge of expressive motion, and finally to the presence that lands with emotional and somatic fulfillment. These aren't fixed stages—they are living states, continually in motion.

FIGURE 2.7: The DEE Cycle Embodied. *(from left to right)* (1) **Dynamis**—A performer in stillness, charged with internal potential. (2) **Energeia**—Energy in motion, expressed through breath, voice, or movement. (3) **Entelecheia**—A moment of lived fulfillment, presence, and artistic completion. Together, the sequence illustrates the transformation of energy from within to without—body, action, and realization in performance. AI-generated image created with OpenAI's DALL·E (via ChatGPT).

Breath, Voice, and Presence. Key access points to the **energetic body** are breath and voice. Breath is not just a physiological necessity—it's a bridge between the **autonomic and voluntary nervous systems,** a thread connecting instinct to intention. The way we breathe influences how we move, how we feel, and how we speak.

Voice, similarly, is not merely sound. It is **vibration in motion**—shaped breath that carries emotion, memory, and presence. In performance, the voice becomes the audible echo of the performer's energetic state. It doesn't just fill space; it resonates through it.

As illustrated in **Figure 2.8**, breath and voice form the **core channels** of presence in Human Theatre. This image captures how breath initiates energetic flow, and how voice amplifies that flow into communicative presence.

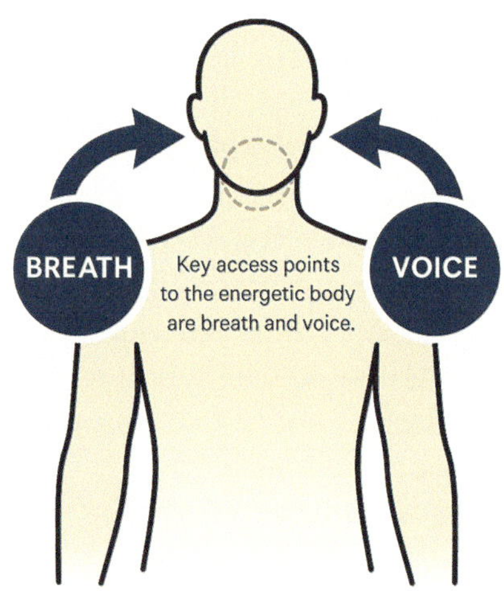

FIGURE 2.8: Breath, Voice, and Presence. This diagram highlights breath and voice as foundational energetic channels in Human Theatre. Breath is the initiator of movement, emotion, and awareness—bridging the instinctive and the intentional. Voice, shaped by breath and embodied tension, becomes more than sound: it is emotional vibration made audible. Together, breath and voice anchor the performer's presence, transforming inner sensation into communicative resonance. This image underscores how these elements are not tools for performance—they are the performance. AI-generated image created with OpenAI's DALL·E (via ChatGPT).

Cultivating breath awareness and vocal freedom allows performers to unlock blocked energy, release chronic tension, and reclaim their full expressive range. These are not abstract ideals—they are **trainable capacities**, grounded in both **ancient performance wisdom** and **contemporary neuroscience.**

Repatterning the Performer. Training the energetic body requires more than repetition or refined technique. It involves **repatterning**—a slow, conscious rewiring of physical habits, emotional reflexes, and neurological pathways.

The performer becomes a kind of alchemist: not just repeating actions, but **transforming personal material into artistic presence.**

In this way, the **DEE Cycle** is not a formula. It is a path of embodiment. It teaches us to listen deeply, move intentionally, and express fully—not only as performers, but as human beings.

Part 2—Unlocking the Energetic Body: Lowen's Bioenergetic Approach

From Concept to Practice: Embodying the DEE Cycle

The DEE Cycle—**Dynamis, Energeia, Entelecheia**—is not merely a theoretical model; it is a living process that unfolds through the body. The shift from concept to practice begins the moment the performer turns inward—not to command the body, but to listen to it.

At this stage, the body ceases to be an instrument of external control and becomes a field of sensation, memory, and impulse. The performer's task is no longer performance but attunement—to the subtle rhythms of breath, vibration, and tension. This is where philosophy becomes physiology—where energy becomes experience.

To embody the DEE Cycle is to engage in transformation. It begins with **Dynamis**—the latent charge, the emotional memory, the breath before expression. It unfolds into **Energeia**—movement, vibra-

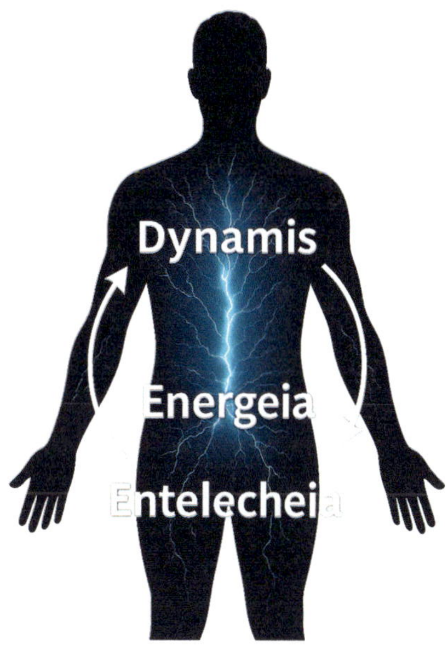

FIGURE 2.9: The DEE Cycle mapped through the human form. Dynamis (potential), Energeia (expression), and Entelecheia (impact) flow like an electrical current through breath, sensation, and presence. This cycle is not symbolic—it is visceral, neurological, and somatic. AI-generated image created with OpenAI's DALL·E (via ChatGPT).

tion, sound. And if the performer remains open and unblocked, the cycle completes in **Entelecheia**—a moment of realization, fulfillment, presence.

Figure 2.9 illustrates this cycle as it flows through the human form—not as abstract theory but as a somatic, neurological, and energetic reality. The triangle of transformation becomes a map for truth in motion.

This is not metaphorical. It is muscular. Electrical. Felt.

Alexander Lowen's Bioenergetics: From Reich to Bioenergetics

The body remembers what the mind forgets.

This truth is foundational to Human Theatre, and no one has explored it more deeply than Alexander Lowen. Building upon the radical work of Wilhelm Reich, Lowen illuminated the relationship between emotional history and bodily form—not as metaphor, but as physiological and expressive truth.

Reich, a student of Freud, was one of the first to link psychological repression to physical muscular tension. His theory of **character armor** described how unresolved emotions manifest in chronic muscular contractions, distorting breath, posture, and the flow of vital energy. The body, in his view, did not merely reflect the psyche—it actively held it.

Figure 2.10 illustrates five key energetic zones identified in Bioenergetics, offering a visual reference for understanding how emotional experience is mapped onto physical form.

Lowen expanded this theory into a full-bodied, accessible

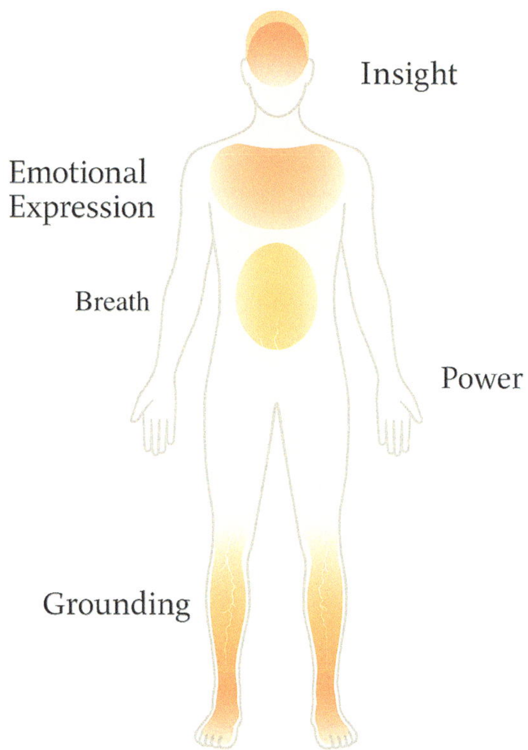

FIGURE 2.10: This diagram maps five key zones of energetic significance: grounding in the legs, power in the pelvis, breath in the diaphragm, emotional expression in the chest, and insight in the head. These zones are not only physiological—they are emotional gateways. Opening them unlocks presence, vitality, and embodied truth. AI-generated image created with OpenAI's DALL·E (via ChatGPT).

methodology: **Bioenergetics**. He saw the body not only as expressive, but as *intelligent*. It knows how to shake, weep, reach, collapse, and rise in ways that spoken language cannot capture. He proposed that true healing—emotional, psychological, and creative—required not just insight, but movement.

Bioenergetic exercises involve breath, voice, and physical positioning designed to unearth and release stored tension. Trembling legs in a grounding posture, an open throat during a primal yell, or sobs shaking the diaphragm—these are not malfunctions. They are *signs of reactivation*, of the DEE Cycle flowing again through the performer's system.

For the performer, these tremors and surges are not disturbances. They are **the fire of presence**. They signal that energy is moving:

- From **Dynamis** (charged potential);
- Through **Energeia** (embodied expression);
- Into **Entelecheia** (realized presence).

Bioenergetics teaches that performers' resonance is inseparable from their inner release. The more they attune to and liberate their body's stored histories, the more transparent, human, and *alive* their performance becomes.

The Concept of Energy in Bioenergetics: A Deeper Look

In Bioenergetics, energy is not a vague metaphor or mystical abstraction—it is lived, felt, and measurable. It moves through the body as breath, sensation, emotion, and muscular charge. Alexander Lowen didn't theorize energy as a symbolic force; he treated it as a biological and emotional truth.

For Lowen, energy is life itself. It animates our movements, fuels our expressions, and defines our ability to feel deeply and fully. When energy flows freely, we are vital, expressive, and present. When blocked—by trauma, repression, or chronic tension—the body contracts, breath shortens, and emotional presence dims.

This flow isn't linear—it pulses. It charges, discharges, regulates, and restores in a rhythm that echoes natural cycles. Just as the nervous system shifts between activation and rest, the performer's energy flows through expansion and return.

Bioenergetics teaches that this capacity for energetic flow is shaped by life experience. A child taught not to cry might tighten the throat. Performers shamed into silence may flatten their breath. These adaptations become embodied, forming invisible but powerful patterns of tension and protection.

The work of the performer, then, is to restore this full energetic pathway—from **Dynamis** (stored charge), to **Energeia** (expressive action), to **Entelecheia** (completion and presence). Not through force, but by reawakening flow. **Figure 2.11** illustrates this process as a living, moving cycle. Energy doesn't just support performance—it *is* performance.

This is the alchemy at the heart of Human Theatre. Through grounding, breath, movement, and voice, the performer becomes a vessel for energetic transformation—not only for the role, but for themselves.

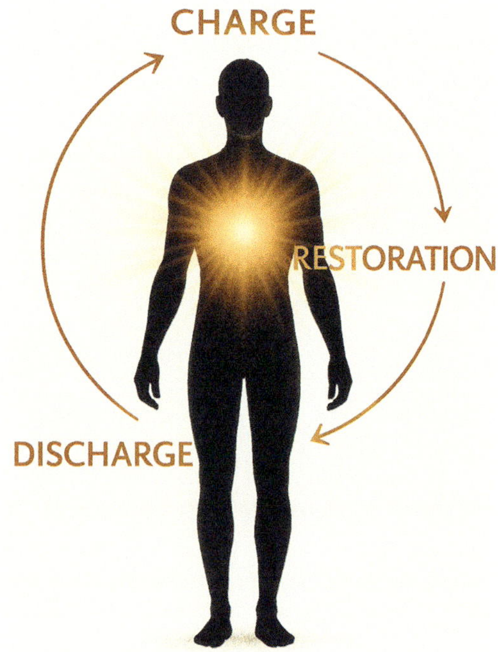

FIGURE 2.11: The Performer as an Energetic System. Energy moves in biological rhythms—charging, expressing, and restoring—while tracing the DEE Cycle of **Dynamis, Energeia, and Entelecheia**. This is not symbolic; it is **muscular, electrical, and emotional**. The performer's body becomes a living system of transformation, where performance is not imitation but alchemy—a real, felt process of becoming. AI-generated image created with OpenAI's DALL·E (via ChatGPT).

Grounding and Trembling: The Foundations of Bioenergetic Work

In the language of Bioenergetics, grounding is not a metaphor—it is a physical practice. It is a return to the body, to the earth, and to the present. To ground is to feel your own weight, to allow your energy to descend through the legs and into the floor. It is the opposite of dissociation. It is presence made tangible.

Grounding reawakens the lower body—an area often neglected in daily life and in many performance traditions. Tight hips, locked knees, and collapsed arches are not merely postural habits; they are symptoms of a deeper disconnection from the performer's primary energetic foundation.

And then something extraordinary happens: the body begins to tremble.

Trembling is not a loss of control—it is a return to aliveness. It signals that energy, once held in muscular armor, is now free to move. Legs may shake, breath may deepen, and emotions may surface. This involuntary trembling, a core aspect of Bioenergetics, is the body's way of discharging stored tension and reanimating presence.

Figure 2.12 illustrates this process: The performer grounded through the legs and pelvis, releasing internal charge as visible tremors. These are not distractions—they are invitations. To tremble onstage is not to falter but to awaken. It means the DEE Cycle is fully engaged: energy flowing from Dynamis (potential), through Energeia (activation), toward Entelecheia (embodied realization).

Grounding and trembling are the **somatic roots** of energetic expression. Without them, performance remains stylized or intellectual. With them, it becomes **vibrant, real, and unforgettable.**

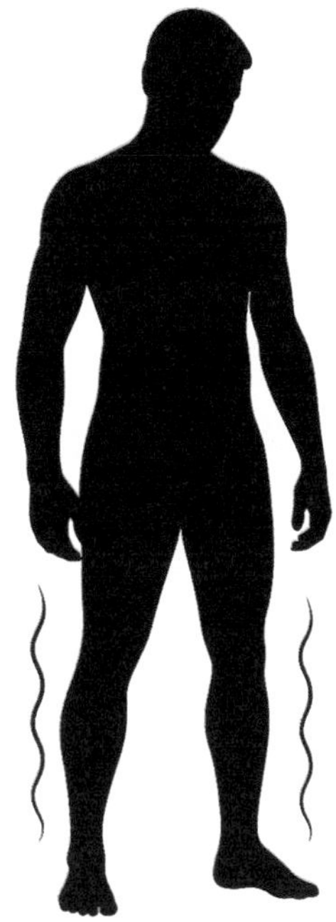

FIGURE 2.12: Grounding and Trembling in the Performer. When the performer reconnects to the earth through the legs and pelvis, stored tension begins to release as tremors. These trembles are signs of energetic unblocking—vital steps in activating the DEE Cycle from within. AI-generated image created with OpenAI's DALL·E (via ChatGPT).

The Flow of Energy in Bioenergetics: A River Within

Energy does not move in straight lines. It flows, ripples, surges, and retreats. In Bioenergetics—and in Human Theatre—this movement is like a river running through the body, carving new paths through old terrain.

This flow is not metaphorical. It is **biological and emotional.** Energy rises from the ground (legs, feet, koshi), is propelled by breath, moves through the diaphragm, resonates in the chest, and is expressed outward through gesture, voice, or gaze. When this current is open, the performer feels alive, present, and expressive. When it's blocked, movement feels heavy, breath shallow, and emotion muted.

Figure 2.13 visualizes this concept, portraying energy as a rising current within the performer's body—an inner river that supports presence and expression.

The river can be turbulent—especially as it meets muscular armor formed from years of tension or silence. But with sustained practice, the body learns to trust the current. Breath deepens. Expression softens. Presence returns.

This flow doesn't only affects the body. It also transforms how time and space are experienced. Performers in energetic flow moves differently—more fluidly, more economically. Their presence expands beyond the outline of their body. Their silence is not empty—it hums. Their stillness holds charge.

In this state, the **DEE Cycle** is not a concept—it is a current:

- **Dynamis** bubbles in the gut or chest.
- **Energeia** surges through movement or voice.
- **Entelecheia** arrives in a moment of energetic resonance shared with the audience.

Like water, energy doesn't need to be forced. It only needs to be **unblocked, trusted, and followed**.

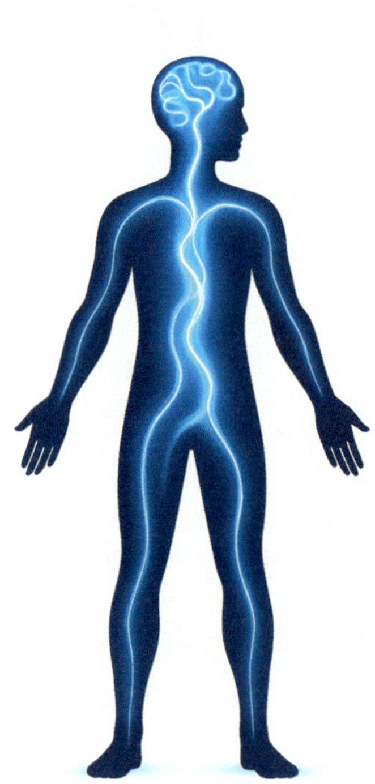

FIGURE 2.13: The River Within. A stylized representation of energy flowing through the performer's body—from the feet, through the legs, pelvis, chest, arms, and head, radiating outward. This inner current is not symbolic—it is **somatic reality**. It forms the energetic backbone of presence and expression in Human Theatre, where movement is not imposed but arises from flow. AI-generated image created with OpenAI's DALL·E (via ChatGPT).

Practicing the Flow: From Concept to Body

Energy is not a theory—it is a **felt experience**. Now that we've explored its rhythms, its blockages, and its potential within the body, it's time to step into practice.

The exercises that follow invite you to **feel energy for yourself**—not as a performer, not as an observer, but as a human being in motion.

These are not techniques to master. They are **experiments in presence**. Each one engages your breath, your body, and your attention in ways that can awaken, release, and integrate energy.

Approach them with gentleness. With curiosity. There is nothing to force—only something to notice. Let the flow begin.

FIGURE 2.14: Energetic Pathways in Motion. A visual representation of embodied flow through the body—each posture reflects a distinct moment in the cycle of release, expansion, contraction, and grounding. These figures invite the performer to move beyond fixed form and into felt sensation, where energy becomes expression and presence becomes embodied practice. AI-generated image created with OpenAI's DALL·E (via ChatGPT).

Figure 2.14 offers a visual introduction to this practice-based approach, depicting the body in five stages of energetic motion—each a gateway to awareness, release, and presence.

Disclaimer: Practicing with Care and Awareness

The exercises presented in this section are intended as practical examples to illustrate concepts discussed in the context of Bioenergetics and the flow of energy within the body. It is important to note that engaging with pent-up emotions can be a deeply personal and sometimes challenging experience. Not everyone may feel prepared or comfortable to address their emotions in this way.

I encourage individuals to approach these exercises with mindfulness and self-compassion. If you find that exploring these practices brings up discomfort or overwhelming feelings, consider seeking the guidance of a qualified professional, such as a therapist or counselor, to provide support and assistance in your journey toward emotional health and well-being.

Remember that everyone's path is unique, and it is essential to prioritize your own comfort and safety.

Exercise 1: Grounding
Purpose: Enhance connection to the earth and increase body awareness.
Instructions:

1. Stand with your feet hip-width apart, grounding firmly into the floor.
2. Close your eyes and take a deep breath, feeling your weight descend through your feet.
3. Visualize roots extending from the soles of your feet deep into the earth.
4. With each exhale, imagine tension flowing downward, while the earth's energy supports you.
5. Repeat for five to ten minutes, scanning for areas of tension and consciously releasing them.

Figure 2.15 illustrates the energetic visualization of this practice, reinforcing the downward grounding flow and rooted stance.

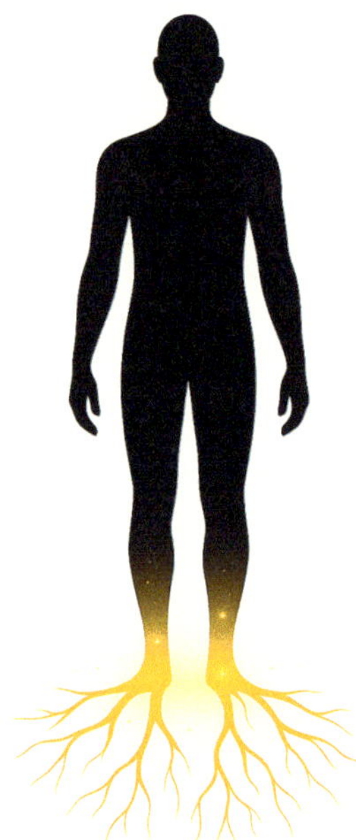

FIGURE 2.15: Grounding exercise. A human silhouette stands rooted to the earth, with energetic flares radiating downward—symbolizing the flow of energy into the ground. This practice reconnects the performer to **bodily presence, stability**, and the quiet support of the earth beneath them. Grounding is not stillness—it is the foundation of aliveness. AI-generated image created with OpenAI's DALL·E (via ChatGPT).

Exercise 2: Cat–Cow Stretch
Purpose: Open the spine and release tension in the back, chest, and abdomen.
Instructions:

1. Begin on all fours, with your hands under your shoulders and knees under your hips.
2. Inhale deeply as you arch your back, lifting your head and tailbone toward the sky (Cow Pose).

3. Exhale slowly as you round your spine, tucking your chin to your chest and drawing your belly inward (Cat Pose).
4. Continue flowing gently between these two positions for about five minutes, allowing the breath to guide your movement.
5. With each round, notice where your body resists or softens. Allow emotional tension to rise and release without judgment.

Figure 2.16 demonstrates the rhythmic flow between extension and flexion that characterizes this breath-led spinal movement.

FIGURE 2.16: Cat–Cow Stretch. A stylized silhouette flows between spinal extension and flexion. This breath-led movement invites the release of tension along the spine, chest, and belly—softening muscular armor and restoring energetic flow. It is both a reset and a return: to sensation, to breath, to presence. AI-generated image created with OpenAI's DALL·E (via ChatGPT).

Exercise 3: Scream Therapy

Purpose: Release stored emotional tension and stimulate energetic discharge through vocal expression.

Instructions:

1. Find a private, comfortable space where you feel emotionally and physically safe.
2. Stand with your feet planted or sit upright with both feet on the floor.

3. Begin by breathing deeply and slowly, allowing your awareness to settle into your body.
4. As you exhale, allow a **primal scream** to emerge—uncensored, unfiltered. Let the sound rise from your belly and move through your throat.
5. Don't worry about how it sounds. Follow your instincts. Scream once or many times, for 30 seconds to two minutes.
6. When finished, sit quietly and observe the sensations in your body. Notice any emotional shifts or sensations of release.

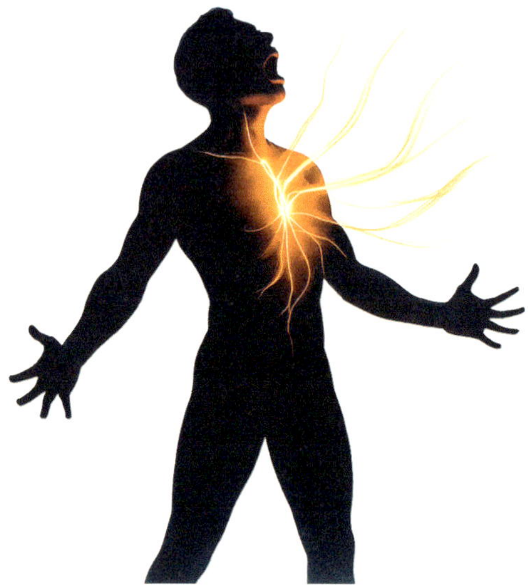

FIGURE 2.17: Scream therapy. A performer's silhouette caught mid-scream, arms extended, energy radiating from the core and throat. This practice invites suppressed emotions to surface and move through sound—transforming inner tension into release, voice into liberation. AI-generated image created with OpenAI's DALL·E (via ChatGPT).

Figure 2.17 visually captures this moment of primal expression and energetic discharge.

Exercise 4: Breath of Life

Purpose: Increase oxygen flow, expand energetic awareness, and support emotional regulation through conscious breathing.

Instructions:

1. Sit or lie down in a comfortable position. Gently close your eyes.
2. Inhale deeply through your nose, letting your belly rise, then your ribs, then your chest.
3. Pause briefly at the top of the breath, noticing the fullness of your body.
4. Exhale slowly through your mouth, allowing any tension to melt away with the breath.
5. As you continue, **visualize each inhale filling your body with vibrant energy,** and each exhale releasing stress, resistance, or emotional weight.

6. Repeat this cycle for five to ten minutes, staying attuned to sensation, temperature, or subtle vibrations in your body.
7. Let the breath become your rhythm, your guide, and your cleansing wave.

Figure 2.18 conveys the internal spaciousness and subtle vitality awakened through this breath-based practice.

FIGURE 2.18: Breath of Life. A reclining silhouette bathed in currents of breath. This image captures the cyclical intelligence of inhale and exhale—a rhythm that regulates, grounds, and reawakens energetic flow. Breath is not only survival—it is presence in motion. AI-generated image created with OpenAI's DALL·E (via ChatGPT).

Exercise 5: Movement and Dance

Purpose: Stimulate full-body energy flow and foster authentic self-expression through intuitive movement.

Instructions:

1. Find a space where you can move freely without judgment or restriction.
2. Choose music that resonates with your current emotional state or intention.
3. Begin standing still. Let the music enter your body—through your breath, your spine, your skin.
4. Allow your body to move however it wants. Don't try to choreograph—**just respond**. Maybe it begins with a hand, a sway, a stomp, or a shake.
5. Follow the impulse, let your breath guide you, and allow movement to emerge from sensation, not from thought.
6. Continue for ten to twenty minutes, exploring dynamics—stillness and speed, softness and strength, contraction, and release.
7. Let the movement express something unspoken. Let it *become the language of your energy.*

Figure 2.19 captures the raw, expressive freedom of this movement-based exploration.

Reflection: Listening to the Current

FIGURE 2.19: Movement and Dance. A dynamic silhouette in motion, surrounded by swirling energetic trails. This image evokes the freedom of embodied expression—where movement becomes the medium through which emotion, breath, and energy flow as one. AI-generated image created with OpenAI's DALL·E (via ChatGPT).

You have now stepped into the living body of this work—not as an observer, but as a participant.

These practices are not just exercises. They are invitations to feel your own energetic truth. To listen to what lives beneath the surface. To allow it space to move, tremble, release, and rise.

Whether you felt a subtle shift or a flood of sensation, know that you are engaging with a river that has always been there. It does not need to be tamed or dramatized. It needs to be welcomed.

With each breath, each grounding, each cry or movement, you are deepening your capacity for presence.

This is where Human Theatre begins—not in the performance, but in the willingness to feel.

As we move forward, carry this awareness with you. The stage is not separate from the self. The energy you cultivate in stillness becomes the current that animates your voice, your gesture, your presence.

You are not here to imitate life—you are here to become it.

Part 3—The Expressive Body: Lessac's Kinesensic Training

From Therapeutic to Artistic: Lessac and Kinesensic Principles

If Lowen's work reawakens the body's natural energy flow, Arthur[6] Lessac's approach teaches us how to **shape and amplify that energy into expressive artistry**. Where Bioenergetics often works from the inside out—releasing tension, surfacing emotion—Lessac's *Kinesensic Training* begins with the **felt sense of vocal and physical vibrancy,** leading to freedom, precision, and resonance.

Lessac believed that the body is innately musical—that breath, movement, and sound are not separate elements of performance but interconnected **vibratory phenomena.** His training emphasizes *"kinesensic" awareness*—a term he coined to describe **sensation as the primary guide** for physical and vocal expression.

Rather than teaching a "correct" way to speak or move, Lessac encouraged performers to follow **how it feels** when the body is vibrating optimally. A lifted tone, a buoyant step, a resonant hum—these are not the results of technical control, but of **energetic awareness.** Performers learn to tune their body as an instrument, discovering that efficiency, beauty, and clarity emerge naturally when sensation is trusted.

Figure 2.20 illustrates this concept, showing the performer's body resonating with vibratory energy—sound and sensation flowing from breath to limb, from voice to presence.

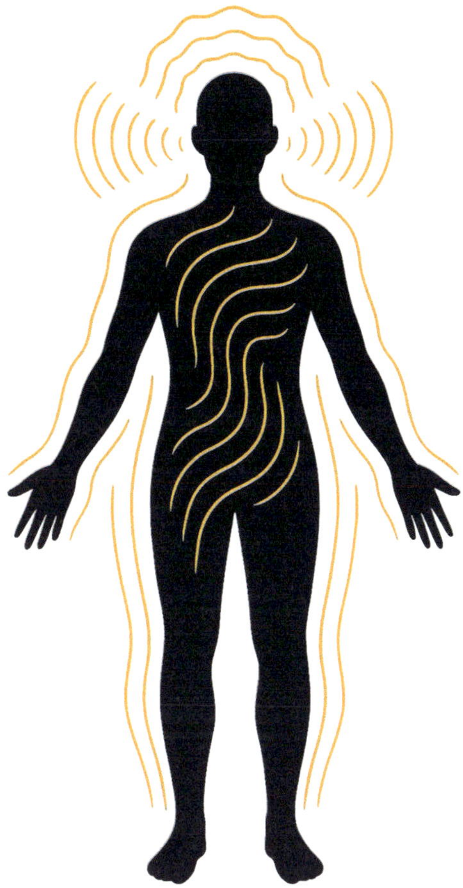

FIGURE 2.20: The vibrating performer. A visual metaphor for Arthur Lessac's Kinesensic approach, where resonance is experienced as a full-body phenomenon. Vibration travels through bones, breath, and voice, inviting the performer to embody sensation and sound in a unified, expressive presence. This is not a metaphorical vibration—it is felt, lived, and vibrationally attuned to the performer's inner life. AI-generated image created with OpenAI's DALL·E (via ChatGPT).

In this sense, Lessac's method is not merely pedagogical—it is **transformational.** It bridges the **therapeutic and the artistic,** allowing performers to feel emotionally grounded while achieving expressive range and creative nuance.

Kinesensics doesn't override emotion—it refines the **vehicle through which emotion travels.** When a performer feels vibration in the bones, lift in the breath, and tone in the voice, they are no longer pushing. They are resonating.

Arthur Lessac and "Kinesensic" Training: A Holistic Approach

Arthur Lessac's work offers a powerful complement to the bioenergetic principles of Lowen. Where Bioenergetics emphasizes release and grounding, Lessac's **Kinesensic Training** focuses on **vibratory awareness and expressive potential.** Together, they form two halves of the same circle: **energy in flow and energy in form.**

Lessac's method is grounded in the belief that the human/performer is a naturally expressive being—not something to be corrected or controlled, but **rediscovered.** His approach centers on the *"feeling process"*—the internal sensations of movement, voice, and breath—as the most authentic guide to performance. He called this felt sense "Kinesensics," from the Greek *kinesis* (movement) and *aesthesis* (sensation).

This training cultivates not just technical skill, but **sensory intelligence.** Performers learn to feel lift in the breath, tonal clarity in the voice, and harmonic movement in the body. These are not imposed patterns—they are internal discoveries. The result is an expression that feels both **natural and heightened,** alive and precise.

My own work has been profoundly shaped by Lessac's lineage, especially through the teaching and mentorship of **Deborah Kinghorn,** who carries Arthur's philosophy with deep integrity and embodied wisdom (see **Figure 2.21**). Her work reminds us that voice and movement are not tools for performance—they are expressions of the **energetic human spirit.**

FIGURE 2.21: *(top)* Arthur Lessac, whose method is grounded in resonance flowing through voice, breath, and movement as a unified current. *(bottom)* Deborah Kinghorn, Master Teacher and contemporary practitioner, continues this lineage by tuning the body through vibration and felt awareness.

Kinesensic training invites the performer to become **both resonator and listener**, attuned to the subtle sensations that precede thought or emotion. The performance, then, becomes an extension of that awareness—not a demonstration, but a vibration.

This is the kind of artistry that does not demand attention—it draws it. Not by force, but by frequency.

Organic Instructions as Activators of the DEE Cycle: A Pathway to Embodied Expression

Traditional performance training often emphasizes external correction: *Adjust your pitch, control your breath, straighten your spine.* But Human Theatre, informed by the DEE Cycle and the vibratory intelligence of the body, invites something different—something deeper.

It invites us to **listen first**. As shown in **Figure 2.22**, organic instructions move the performer through four distinct phases: from natural engagement to physical sensation, emotional evocation, and finally expressive action.

In this context, *organic instructions* are not commands or fixed techniques. They are **internal cues**—sensory, vibratory, and intuitive—that awaken the DEE

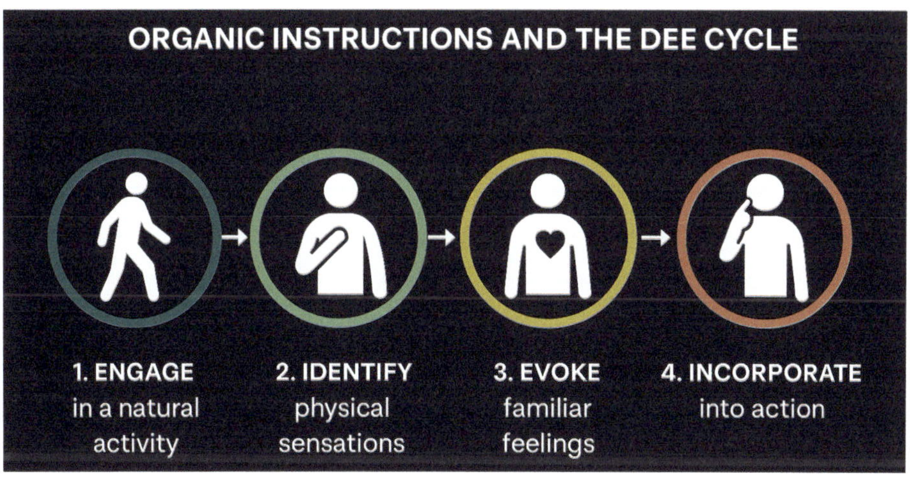

FIGURE 2.22: Organic Instructions and the DEE Cycle. This diagram illustrates the four key stages of Lessac-inspired organic instruction: (1) Engaging in a natural activity, (2) identifying physical sensation, (3) evoking emotional resonance, and (4) transforming it into expressive action. Each step reanimates the DEE Cycle—guiding the performer from Dynamis (internal potential), through Energeia(activated sensation), toward Entelecheia (embodied realization). This process awakens expression from within, rather than layering it from the outside. AI-generated image created with OpenAI's DALL·E (via ChatGPT).

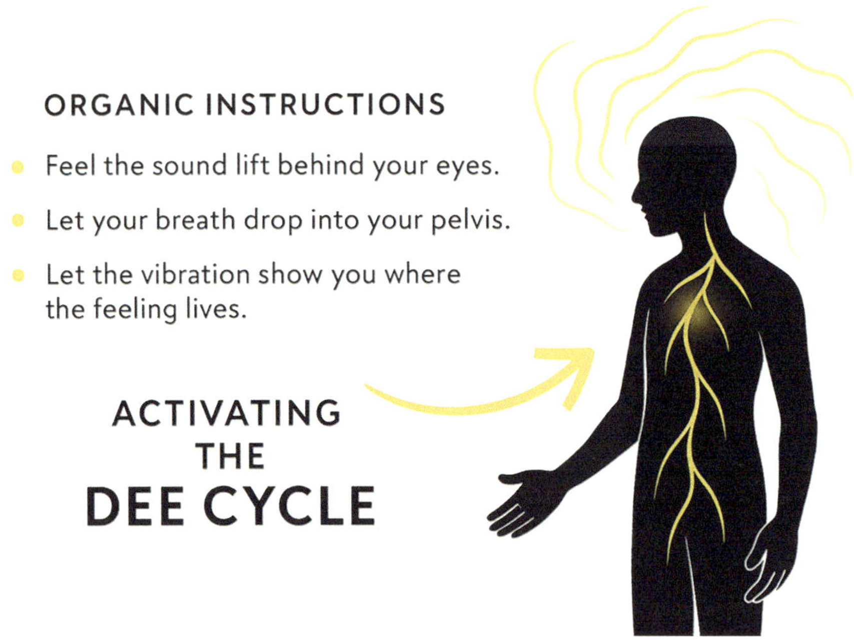

FIGURE 2.23: Organic Instruction in Motion. This image symbolizes how sensation-based cues awaken vibrational awareness throughout the performer's body. Rather than imposing external form, organic instruction activates inner resonance—inviting the DEE Cycle to unfold naturally: from latent charge (Dynamis), to expressive flow (Energeia), to embodied presence (Entelecheia). The body doesn't perform—it listens, responds, and reveals. AI-generated image created with OpenAI's DALL·E (via ChatGPT).

cycle from within. This concept, developed and championed by **Arthur Lessac**, invites performers to **discover rather than imitate**, and to allow **sensation to guide expression.** Rather than telling the performer what to do, organic instructions invite them to **notice, feel, and respond.** As illustrated in **Figure 2.23**, this internal activation supports the performer's energetic flow, grounding expression in felt sensation rather than forced technique.

The Steps of an Organic Instruction

1. **Sense:** Begin with **somatic awareness.** The performer is invited to feel—where is the energy gathering? Where is it blocked? What wants to move?
2. **Language That Activates:** The instruction is delivered using **imagery or sensation-based language**, not analytical terms. These cues are meant to bypass intellect and stimulate **vibratory or kinesthetic awareness**—instead of "project

your voice," we say: *Feel the sound lift behind your eyes*—instead of "open your chest," we ask: *What happens when your breath drops into your pelvis?*

3. **Energetic Activation**: The instruction stimulates **Dynamis** (potential energy), inviting **Energeia** (expressive movement) to emerge. The body **responds**, rather than obeys.
4. **Witnessing and Trusting the Response**: The performer **notices** what happens—not just physically, but emotionally and energetically. This is the moment of **Entelecheia**—the realization, the becoming, the embodied truth.

A Real Example: The Actor Who Stopped "Trying"

In one workshop, an actor struggling with emotional connection in a monologue kept being told to "go deeper" and "connect more." But no amount of intellectual effort or external correction was working.

Instead, I asked: "Let the sound vibrate behind your cheekbones. Don't try to feel. Let the vibration show you where the feeling lives."

Something shifted. He paused. His breath softened. The next line came—not louder, not more emotional—but **alive**. It carried resonance. Something had been **activated**, not forced.

This is the essence of the DEE Cycle in practice: **Dynamis** awakened, **Energeia** expressed, and **Entelecheia** realized. These instructions don't impose—they **activate**. They spark **Dynamis**, awaken **Energeia**, and allow **Entelecheia** to emerge not through effort, but through resonance.

This approach mirrors how the body learns naturally—through **sensation and repetition**, not critique and control. It respects the performer's inner wisdom and supports self-discovery over performance mimicry.

When we use organic instructions, we speak to the **body's language**. The language of vibration. Of breath. Of energetic response. And when we do this, performance becomes not something we direct, but something we **receive**—a lived alchemy in motion.

This is where Lessac's Kinesensics and the DEE Cycle converge. In the performer's body. In the performer's breath. In the moment when instruction becomes transformation.

Becoming the Current: The Performer's Energetic Journey

You have now traveled through the many layers of the performer's body—not only its muscles and breath, but its memory, vibration, and potential. What began as an exploration of energy has become an **invitation to transformation**. From the trembling release of Bioenergetics to the resonant lift of Kinesensic awareness, the body has revealed itself not as an object to shape, but as a **source of intelligence**—a living current of energy, sensation, and meaning.

At the center of it all is the **DEE Cycle.** Not as a concept, but as a process. A loop. A pulse. A breath. In every exercise, in every instruction, we've returned to this rhythm: **Dynamis—the charge; Energeia—the expression; Entelecheia—the arrival.** You've seen how performers can access it through grounding, vibration, voice, and movement. But beyond the exercises and diagrams, the deeper question remains: *Can you trust your body to lead? Can you let energy move before your mind makes sense of it? Can you listen—not to the voice in your head, but to the one rising from your bones?*

This is the heart of Human Theatre. Not performance for performance's sake, but **performance as presence.** Not expression as decoration, but **expression as transmission.**

You are not here to represent. **You are here to resonate.**

NOTES

1. Aristotle's *Poetics*, one of the earliest surviving works of dramatic theory and literary criticism in the Western tradition. Focused primarily on tragedy, it outlines essential elements such as plot (mythos), character (ethos), and catharsis, offering a foundational framework for understanding dramatic structure and the emotional effects of theatre. His influence remains central to classical and contemporary performance theory.
2. The debate centers on the nuanced meanings of "Dynamis," "Energeia," and "Entelecheia" in aristotelian philosophy. "Dynamis" refers to potentiality, while "Energeia" is actuality, indicating the fulfillment of potential. "Entelecheia" is closely associated with "Energeia" and denotes the realization of potential. Scholars debate their precise interpretations and interrelationships, particularly in explaining change, movement, and existence. This discussion is crucial in interpreting Aristotle's explanation of creation and purpose, impacting metaphysics, ethics, and natural philosophy.
3. Alexander Lowen, an American psychiatrist and psychotherapist, developed Bioenergetic Analysis, a psychotherapy integrating physical, emotional, and psychological self-dimensions. Trained in psychoanalysis, Lowen emphasized bodily awareness and expression in healing emotional and psychological issues. He believed repressed emotions manifest as physical tension, and releasing this through movement and breath facilitates psychological healing. Lowen's influential books, *The Language of the Body* and *Bioenergetics*, highlight the body-mind connection, impacting humanistic psychology and body-oriented therapies.
4. Wilhelm Reich was an Austrian psychoanalyst and a student of Sigmund Freud, best known for his pioneering work in the connection between emotional repression and physical tension. He developed the concept of "character armor," describing how chronic muscular

patterns reflect and defend against unresolved emotional experiences. Reich's work laid the foundation for body-oriented psychotherapy and profoundly influenced practices like bioenergetics, somatic healing, and contemporary actor training.

5. The phrase "actors are never a blank slate" challenges the notion of the performer as a neutral or empty vessel. In reality, every actor carries a lived history—embodied knowledge, social context, and personal memory—that informs and shapes their presence onstage. This stands in contrast to the philosophical concept of tabula rasa, suggesting that performers begin not from nothing, but from a complex interplay of prior experiences, identities, and cultural imprints. In performance, acknowledging this "non-blank" state deepens authenticity and embodiment.
6. Arthur Lessac, an American speech and movement theorist, actor, director, and teacher, developed the "Kinesensic" methodology, a comprehensive approach to voice and body work. This methodology integrates physical movement and vocal expression to enhance communication and self-awareness. Lessac believed the body and voice are interconnected, and freeing tension in the body improves vocal health and expressive abilities. He trained actors, performers, and educators, advocating for a holistic approach to performance that considers emotional and physical aspects. Lessac authored influential books on voice and movement, and his methods continue to be taught worldwide.

Chapter 3

The Energetic Stage: Echoes of the Past

3

The Energetic Stage: Echoes of the Past

Part 1—Tracing the Roots of Codified Art

Immersion in the Codification of Art

The stage is never neutral. Long before lines are memorized or lights are hung, the space of performance holds **imprints**—ritual echoes, aesthetic codes, unspoken rules passed down through generations. The performer doesn't merely step onto a platform—they step into a history. And that history is **energetically charged.** (See **Figure 3.1**: The codified stage as a space marked by memory and form.)

In this section, we examine how performance spaces and styles have been shaped by **codification**: the formalization of movement, voice, gesture, and structure into repeatable systems. These systems—whether born of ritual, religion, or empire—defined what "art" should look and feel like. Over time, they became not just tools of transmission, but tools of **containment**.

Codification can act as both **container and cage**. It preserves knowledge, but it also dictates boundaries—what is acceptable, what is beautiful, what is correct. And this has deep implications not just for art, but for the **energetic freedom** of the performer.

When the body is trained to obey a system, something else may begin to disappear: **spontaneity, presence, authenticity**. What began as sacred repetition can harden into performative repetition—ritual without vibration.

But to understand how we arrived here, we must enter the roots of codification. We must ask: Who decided what "art" is?—Who was allowed to perform?—What energy was preserved—and what was silenced?

FIGURE 3.0: The Lineage Within. Every gesture carries a history. Behind the performer, the echoes of multiple traditions rise, shaping the living body of theatre. AI-generated image created with OpenAI's DALL·E (via ChatGPT).

This is not merely an academic inquiry. It is an **energetic excavation.**

As we move through this chapter, we will trace not only the history of theatrical form, but the **energetic fingerprints** left behind—onstages, bodies, and traditions. We will look deeply at the tension between structure and freedom, repetition and presence, and tradition and truth.

To reclaim the **energetic stage,** we must first understand the **architecture of its memory.**

FIGURE 3.1: The Codified Stage. A performer stands at the intersection of structure and spirit, surrounded by invisible frameworks of ritual, tradition, and artistic lineage. Even in stillness, the space vibrates with inherited codes—gestures passed down, postures shaped by culture, silence charged with history. Performers do not just move within a frame—they carry its echoes in their body. AI-generated image created with OpenAI's DALL·E (via ChatGPT).

A Personal Encounter with Mime

I didn't choose mime. It arrived like a whisper—quiet, unfamiliar, and oddly magnetic. I was young, and my body was restless. I didn't yet have a language for the sensations that lived beneath my skin. But when I saw a mime move, *everything inside me leaned forward.* There was no speech, no character in the traditional sense. Just energy. Precision. Stillness that trembled with meaning.

Mime was the first form that **spoke to my inner world without asking me to explain it.** It demanded control, yes—but not to suppress. It asked for presence. For listening. For stillness that breathes and gesture that resonates. I remember the moment I first pressed my palms against invisible air and felt *resistance.* It wasn't pretend. It was a real engagement—**an energetic contract with space.**

Training in mime exposed me to the beauty and the burden of codified form. The precision of gesture. The shaping of time and breath into pure rhythm. The sacred geometry of the body in motion. But over time, I also began to feel the edges of that form. Where was *my* energy in all of this? Could I still feel *Dynamis* beneath such structured repetition? Was there room for impulse?

This tension surfaced years later in a performance I witnessed by **Javier Hernández** (see **Figure 3.2**), a talented performer from my community and my dear friend. His movements were deliberate, grounded, emotionally raw. And yet—I couldn't connect. I watched, respectful, but distanced. His work felt foreign to me, even though he was of my culture. Or maybe *because* he was of my culture—and expressing it in ways I had not yet learned to welcome in myself.

I realized, with some discomfort, that I had brought preconceptions into that space. Unspoken expectations about what mime should be. About what good energy looks like. About who gets to take up space and how.

Javier's performance became a **mirror**, one I hadn't asked for. It showed me the places in myself where I still clung to aesthetic purity, to unconscious judgment shaped by Eurocentric ideals. It forced me to ask: *What energies have I unconsciously learned to reject? What traditions have I internalized as superior?*

In that moment, mime became more than technique. It became **an inquiry**—into form, freedom, lineage, and listening. This inner tension—the split between form and impulse—finds visual echo in **Figure 3.3**, where two embodied states coexist: one contained, one reaching. Between them lies the fertile space where Human Theatre emerges.

Mime taught me how to **shape space**, how to **feel silence**, and how to **make the invisible felt**. But it also taught me how easily codification can **mask vitality** when form is prized over flow. And how quickly we internalize those forms—not just in our bodies, but in our judgments.

FIGURE 3.2: *(top)* Javier Hernández, professional mime and dear friend. *(bottom)* Hernández performing, embodying emotional intensity through expressive movement in a dimly lit theatre.

From this tension, the seeds of Human Theatre began to sprout—not as a rejection of form, but as a reclamation of the **energy beneath it**.

A visual depiction of the inner split between form and impulse.

FIGURE 3.3: The Split Between Form and Impulse. A visual metaphor for the tension between codified structure and embodied desire. One figure stands composed, stylized, contained. The other reaches, cracks, and surges, breaking form to reclaim impulse. Between them lies the rift—and the possibility—where Human Theatre is born. AI-generated image created with OpenAI's DALL·E (via ChatGPT).

Unlocking the Code: Discovering Hand Design

When I entered the School of Classical and Contemporary Pantomime, I encountered an approach to training that was both physical and philosophical. My curriculum included illusions, technical mime, mime history, style, improvisation, and a rigorous laboratory of movement and gesture. One of the most foundational courses, Technical Mime I, introduced a concept that would forever change the way I understood the body in space: **Hand Design.**

Hand Design was not simply about how hands *looked*. It was about how they functioned—each with a specific **purpose**, **energy**, and **rhythm**. Each hand design symbolized a concept or emotion and was to be executed with precision and presence. We documented these designs in a personal manual, complete with **photographs and descriptions**, to serve as a reference for future teaching or deeper study.

Among the designs I studied were:

- **Writer's Hand**—Symbolizing creativity.
- **Fan Hand**—Evoking grace.
- **Hand of God**—Representing power.
- **Painter's Hand**—Depicting the act of creation.
- **Michelangelo's Hand**— A form studied for its sculptural tension and balance (see **Figure 3.4**).

Each of these gestures was not isolated. They were practiced and understood within a **system of rhythm**—four basic rhythmic types that gave emotional and energetic shape to every movement:

- **Slow without resistance**—Evoking calm, like a leaf falling gently.
- **Slow with resistance**—Suggesting struggle, like a tree against the wind.
- **Fast without resistance**—Joyful, spontaneous, like a running child.
- **Fast with resistance**—Expressing conflict, power, and opposition.

The training emphasized **not discovery**, but **clarity**. These gestures weren't meant to arise from improvisation or subjective sensation; they were **designed**—intentional expressions of idea, emotion, or state. Codified, yet powerful. Fixed, yet capable of resonant transmission when fully embodied.

FIGURE 3.4: "Michelangelo's Hand."—"Its movement is slow and resistant. It is used for giving, presenting, and pointing" (author's translation). From the author's technical mime course, this hand design was one of several studied for its expressive form, rhythmic intention, and symbolic charge. Practiced not only with physical precision, but with energetic awareness, each hand became a site of transmission—where design met emotion, and gesture carried meaning beyond the visible.

The Statues Speak: Crafting the Body into Meaning

As my mime training deepened, we moved from the study of isolated gestures to the integration of the entire body. This practice, known as the creation of **statues**, challenged us to communicate ideas, emotions, or states with a single physical composition—rigorous, specific, and intentional.

These weren't improvisations. They were precise constructions, based on a **codified system** of bodily expression. The process began with defining the **idea** behind the statue—what the training called a *simple*, *complex in harmony*, or *complex in duel* idea. This idea could be emotional, symbolic, or narrative. Once defined, we then analyzed and constructed the statue using thirteen specific body elements.

TABLE 3.1: The thirteen body elements used in the construction of a statue.

1—Head	2—Neck	3—Waist	4—Chest
5—Pelvis	6—Hands	7—Arms	8—Feet
9—Legs	10—Breathing	11—Balance	12—Weight
13—Face or intention			

Each component was assigned a deliberate position. Was the head projected forward? Rotated? Tilted? Were the arms active in support, or neutral? Was the expression of the face calm, surprised, joyful? Nothing was left to chance. Even the breath mattered. The posture of the statue had to emerge with either an **inhalation** or an **exhalation**, aligning internal sensation with external structure.

We practiced neutral position—called **Double Zero**—to begin. From there, every choice had to be made consciously, based on the idea to be transmitted. When any part of the body was not engaged in communication, it returned to zero. This disciplined framework echoes the **codified theatrical systems of Asian performance traditions**, where actors must master an expressive code before they can interpret roles.

FIGURE 3.5: The Author in a "Giving Statue" Pose. A trained mime posture rooted in codified physical language. This pose embodies the act of giving—through symmetry, breath control, and energetic clarity. It is not simply a position, but a transmission: stillness charged with intention, form shaped by feeling.

This process was not just theoretical. We practiced these statues physically, repeatedly, and with intense detail. One such example from my training is the "**Giving Statue**," which emphasized openness, directionality, and breath-infused presence.

Mime statues are not passive images—they are compressed expressions. Every angle, breath, and micro-adjustment speaks. These statues are not frozen; they are suspended. They vibrate with held intention.

In the **"Giving Statue"** pose (**Figure 3.5**), the performer's body becomes an offering. The arms extend not as decoration, but as energetic extension. Breath is regulated, posture symmetrical, and tension distributed in service of presence. The body doesn't just mimic the idea of giving—it becomes a vessel through which the gesture is transmitted.

Here, codified design becomes something more than aesthetic: it becomes **language**. A visual syntax through which meaning travels—not as narrative, but as vibration.

Each statue embodied the **DEE Cycle** in action:

- The **idea** was the potential—**Dynamis.**
- The activation of the posture was the expression—**Energeia.**
- The **embodied presence** of the final form created the impact—**Entelecheia.**

Another example we analyzed in detail was the "**Statue of Shyness**"—a posture constructed from a defined emotional idea and shaped through the careful articulation of the thirteen elements of mime composition. (See **Figure 3.6**: a moment of emotional clarity, where posture becomes presence.)

Estatua de timidez 20/20

1)Cabeza
    1)Inclinación lateral
2)Cuello
    1)Permanece igual que el doble cero
3)Cintura
    1)Permanece igual que el doble cero
4)Pecho
    1)Permanece igual que el doble cero
5)Pelvis
    1)Se gira levemente al doblar la pierna
6)Manos
    1)Mano de ira
7)Brazos
    1)frente a la pelvis, uno mas arriba que el otro. Hay una inclinación de los hombros
8)Pies
    1)En primera posición giras el tobillo hacia afuera
9)Piernas
    1)Una derecha la otra doblada
10)Rostro o intensidad
    1)Timidez, subiendo las cejas
11)Equilibrio
    1)En el pie que permanece completo en el piso
12)Peso
    1)En el pie que permanece completo en el piso
13)Respiración
    1)Exhalación

FIGURE 3.6: Analysis of the "Statue of Shyness." Created during the author's mime training, this composition reveals how posture becomes emotion. Each detail—tilt of the head, angle of the limbs, breath pattern, balance, and subtle facial tension—converges to express shyness not as a concept, but as a presence. Stillness becomes charged. Gesture becomes feeling made visible. 1—Head: Lateral inclination, 2—Neck: Remains the same as double zero, 3—Waist: Remains the same as double zero, 4—Chest: Remains the same as double zero, 5—Pelvis: Lift it this time by bending the leg, 6—Hands: Hand of anger, 7—Arms: In front of the pelvis. One higher than the other. Shoulders are inclined, 8—Feet: In first position, turn the ankle outward, 9—Legs: One straight, the other bent, 10—Face or intention: Shyness, raising the eyebrows, 11—Balance: On the foot, 12—Weight: The weight is on the ground, and 13—Breathing: Exhalation.

Through these practices, I discovered that mime moves far beyond imitation or silent storytelling. It is a **system of total expression**, where each element—gesture, form, rhythm, and breath—becomes a word in a language spoken without sound. The body doesn't just show—it speaks, it vibrates, it reveals.

In a world increasingly dominated by digital communication and an overabundance of information, mime stands as a powerful reminder of the beauty and strength of **non-verbal communication**. It invites us to feel rather than hear—to move beyond words and immerse ourselves in a universe of pure, visceral expression. Each gesture, each position of the hands, each breath becomes a **dance of precision and meaning**, where silence becomes the blank canvas on which an infinite story is painted.

Mime, in this way, becomes a bridge: Between the tangible and the intangible. Between the visible and the invisible. Between what is said—and what is held in silence.

In the eloquent stillness of a well-executed gesture, we find a connection that **transcends language** and speaks directly to the human soul.

And yet, for a time, these reflections remained quietly stored within me—observations without framework. My experience with Javier's performance, the emotional charge of mime, and the power of codified form all lived somewhere in the background of my understanding, waiting for something to connect them.

That moment came unexpectedly.

It was in a Theatre History class that I first encountered **Asian theatrical traditions**. As I watched archival footage of **Kunqu Theatre**, something stirred. The fluidity of movement, the precision of breath, the profound intentionality of gesture—it all felt **strangely familiar**. I was no longer just watching a performance. I was seeing a mirror.

The similarities were undeniable: The stylized control of the performer's body; the rhythmic clarity of each action; the centrality of **hand gestures** as communicative devices.

These elements echoed exactly what I had studied in mime training. And suddenly, the pieces came together. **Mime** and **Kunqu** were not distant cousins—they were part of a shared lineage of **codified energetic expression**, both rooted in a system where **form channels meaning**, and **gesture carries soul.**

I had just begun to explore the DEE Cycle in my own work, and now I could see it mirrored in Kunqu: The **idea or feeling** (Dynamis); the **action shaped through codified movement** (Energeia); the **presence and impact of the moment fully realized** (Entelecheia)

This revelation opened a new door.

What is Kunqu Theatre, and why does it offer such a compelling example of codified movement in action?

Reflections Between Traditions: Mime and the Wisdom of Kunqu

It began with a video—grainy, distant, and yet deeply alive. I was in a Theatre History class when I first encountered **Kunqu Theatre**, one of the oldest and most refined forms of Chinese opera. The movements were slow, deliberate, and full of silence. But that silence wasn't empty. It was **charged**—with presence, with tradition, with breath.

I found myself leaning in, not to understand, but to **feel**.

The performers moved like calligraphy brought to life. Their hands traced invisible arcs, their feet glided in rhythmic diagonals, their gestures carried the weight of centuries. I wasn't just seeing technique—I was witnessing **codified energy**, a system where movement becomes meaning, and the smallest shift in the wrist could alter the entire emotional architecture of the scene. (See **Figure 3.7**: A stylized representation of a Kunqu scene, where every movement becomes a poetic transmission.)

FIGURE 3.7: Embodied Elegance: A Tribute to Kunqu. This stylized depiction of two performers evokes the elegance and emotional nuance of Kunqu Theatre. Each gesture is precise, yet fluid—charged with centuries of tradition. Each glance becomes a conversation, part of a language where movement and emotion are inseparable. This is not performance as display, but performance as reverence—where stillness breathes and silence speaks. AI-generated image created with OpenAI's DALL·E (via ChatGPT).

Something inside me stirred.

It reminded me of my mime training, but not in a comparative way. Kunqu was not mime. It was its own universe—richer, older, and far more complex in lineage. But the **principle** I recognized was this: **form as vessel**, not as decoration. The gesture was not ornamental. It was **essential**.

In this video, the performer is not simply representing an emotion—they are **channeling it** through a precise, encoded vocabulary. Each movement has a defined meaning, but also a felt rhythm, shaped by the performer's breath and internal timing.

There it was again: the **DEE Cycle**, living quietly beneath the art.

- **Dynamis:** The inner emotional impulse.
- **Energeia:** The codified movement used to express it.
- **Entelecheia:** The moment when the gesture lands, fully present in space.

This was not mimicry—it was **transmission.**

And it was through Kunqu that I first truly understood what my mime teachers had meant when they spoke of **intention within form.** My body remembered the hours spent crafting statues and shaping hand designs, but now those studies were **illuminated** by something older—something that placed those forms within a lineage of global performance traditions.

Kunqu, I realized, wasn't just an aesthetic. It was a **spiritual discipline.** A system where energy flows through culture, body, sound, and silence.

Chinese Theatre: Kunqu Theatre and Mei Lanfang

My introduction to Kunqu Theatre happened during a Theatre History class. I was watching a video—an archival performance of *The Dream of Visiting the Garden*, worn by time, yet quietly glowing with life. I did not know then that I was witnessing one of the most refined forms of traditional Chinese opera. What caught my attention wasn't just the elegance of the music or the richness of the costumes. It was the **body**—how it moved with intention, with formality, yet also with undeniable softness.

Kunqu Theatre, known as one of the oldest extant forms of Chinese opera, is not only a cultural treasure but a living embodiment of **codified performance tradition.** Emerging during the Yuan Dynasty (The Editors of *Encyclopedia Britannica* 2010), Kunqu blends poetry, movement, music, and gesture into a seamless flow of symbolic action—where the boundary between ritual and performance often disappears.

The **hands**, in particular, struck me. Their delicacy. Their clarity. Their rhythm.

It stirred something I didn't expect. I saw in those gestures a resonance with my own training. There, in a form I was unfamiliar with, were echoes of mime—**codified movement**, exact yet expressive. There was control, yes, but not to restrict—it was control in service of emotional precision. Each movement, like a calligraphy stroke, told a story not in literal terms but in feeling.

This discovery was so impactful that I returned to my own documentation—a photograph of myself captured mid-gesture during my mime training—and compared it side by side with a screenshot from the Kunqu performance. (See **Figures 3.8** and **3.9**. A visual comparison between a Kunqu gesture and a mime gesture. Though born from different traditions, both share a commitment to intention, balance, and transmission through form.)

It wasn't about similarity in aesthetics—it was about **shared purpose**. In both traditions, the **gesture carries meaning**, and both demand from the performer not just physical discipline, but internal stillness and clarity of intention.

This realization brought me to **Mei Lanfang**—a legendary figure in Chinese opera and a master of performance who embodied this codified language with extraordinary grace and depth. Though I first encountered him through video fragments, his influence reached far beyond the stage. Known for his portrayal of female roles (dan), Mei Lanfang became a cultural icon in both China and abroad, helping to preserve and internationalize Chinese performance traditions.

Through careful training, stylization, and control, his performances embodied a type of communication that transcended language. His mastery of gesture, movement, and energy aligned perfectly with what I was beginning to understand through the **DEE Cycle**:

- An inner charge (**Dynamis**).
- Manifested in structured action (**Energeia**).
- Culminating in impact and presence (**Entelecheia**).

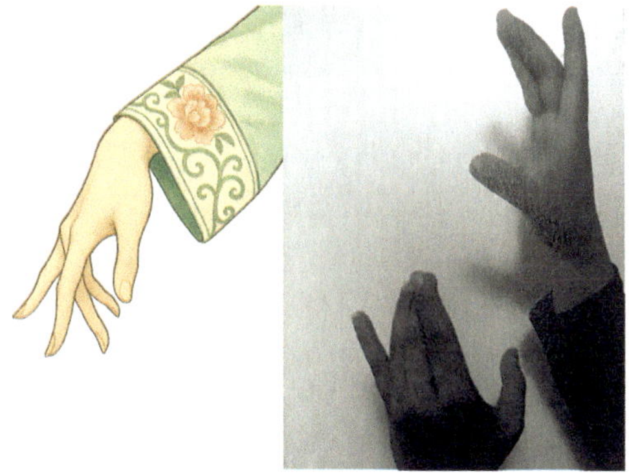

FIGURE 3.8: Kunqu Gesture and Mime Hand Design: *The Dream of Visiting the Garden. (left)* An illustration by the author representing a Kunqu hand gesture from *The Dream of Visiting the Garden.* AI-generated image created with OpenAI's DALL·E (via ChatGPT), juxtaposed with a similar hand shape from mime training *(right)*. This comparison highlights how distinct traditions, though culturally rooted, often converge through shared principles of rhythm, breath, and energetic precision.

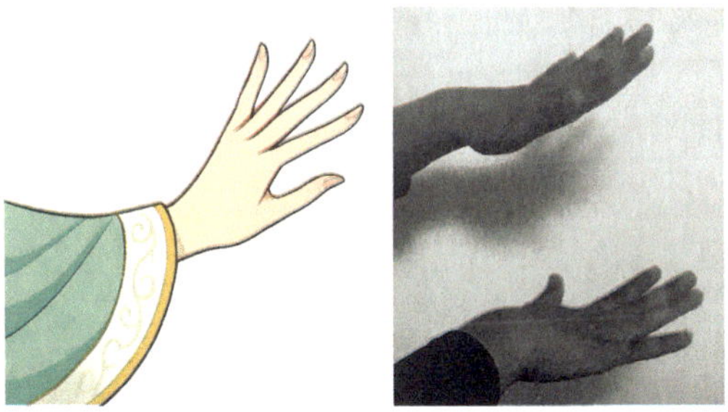

FIGURE 3.9: Gesture as Dialogue: Kunqu and Mime in Parallel. *(left)* Author's illustration comparing the Kunqu gesture from *The Dream of Visiting the Garden*. AI-generated image created with OpenAI's DALL·E (via ChatGPT) with the "Margarita" hand design from mime training *(right)*. Though born of different worlds, both gestures speak through subtlety, suspension, and design—suggesting that gesture can be both culturally specific and universally resonant.

He became a figure of study for me—not just as a performer, but as someone who lived inside a codified tradition while **bringing it to life anew** each time he performed.

In watching Mei Lanfang, and in comparing those gestures with my own mime training (see **Figure 3.10**), I realized that **cultural distance did not mean disconnection**. Instead, it invited **recognition**. My work, grounded in a different tradition, had touched something that was also alive in Kunqu—a shared current of energy, embodied in form, transmitted through time.

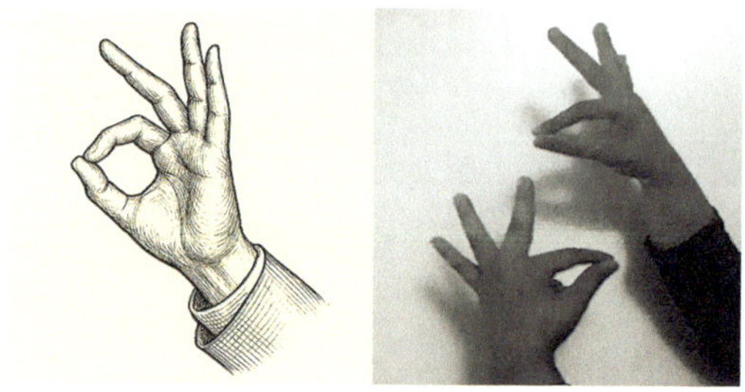

FIGURE 3.10: Mei Lanfang's Gesture: A Comparative Study. *(left)* An illustration by the author of a hand gesture performed by Mei Lanfang. AI-generated image created with OpenAI's DALL·E (via ChatGPT) set alongside a similar shape from mime training *(right)*. This visual invites reflection on how distinct traditions—Kunqu and mime—craft meaning through refined design, emotional charge, and energetic stillness. Across cultures, the hand becomes more than anatomy; it becomes language.

Through the lens of the **DEE Cycle—Dynamis** (the internal charge), **Energeia** (the expressive form), and **Entelecheia** (the fulfilled moment of resonance)—both gestures serve the same function: they become the **visible expression of something invisible.**

In Kunqu, in Mei Lanfang's performance, and in mime, the hand is not just a hand. It becomes a channel for transmission. It is design, breath, memory, and intention—**held in space**, ready to reach another human being.

Toward the Sacred: From Chinese Opera to Indian Classical Theatre

Following my exploration of **Kunqu Theatre** and the legacy of **Mei Lanfang**, I began to sense a recurring truth across world performance traditions: that **gesture, breath, and codification** are not isolated practices—they are woven into the fabric of embodied storytelling across cultures.

This realization led me further south, into the world of **Indian classical theatre**—where the body becomes not just a tool of expression, but a vessel of cosmic significance (see **Figure 3.11**).

In particular, I turned to **Kutiyattam**[1] and **Yakshagana**: Two distinct forms born from different regions and philosophies, yet united by an unshakable reverence for **codified movement, symbolic hand gestures**, and **ritualized presence.**

Where Kunqu had introduced me to the lyrical refinement of gestural storytelling, **Kutiyattam** offered a more meditative, sacred register—gestures performed with precision and gravity, drawing from Sanskrit dramaturgy and temple ritual.

Yakshagana, on the other hand, burst forth with color, rhythm, and mythic intensity—demanding both physical discipline and improvisational boldness.

In both, I found that **Hand Design**—so central to my mime training—resurfaced once again, in new forms, new rhythms, and new cultural vocabularies.

FIGURE 3.11: Gesture Across Traditions: Kunqu and Indian Classical Theatre. A visual comparison between Kunqu Theatre *(left)* and Indian Classical Theatre *(right)*, illustrating how distinct cultural forms converge through refined gesture, symbolic costume, and embodied expression. In both, the performer is not merely presenting movement –they are transmitting meaning through a codified, sacred system, where form becomes feeling and ritual becomes art. AI-generated image created with OpenAI's DALL·E (via ChatGPT).

Indian Theatre: Kutiyattam and Yakshagana

These connections sparked a new interest in exploring codified movement across different cultures, leading me to the rich traditions of Indian theatre. The commonalities I find between Kunqu Theatre, my training, and the famous videos of Mei Lanfang opened up a new world for me. I remembered that during my bachelor's degree I studied the work of Gilda Navarra.[2] In her book *Cartilla de un oficio: Abecedario de un actor-mimo* ("Manual of a Profession: Alphabet of an Actor-mime"), considered a treasure for the history of Puerto Rican theatre, she highlights India as the cradle of the art of mime.

While I won't delve into a full history of Indian theatre, I want to highlight the rigorous training that performers undergo, as it reveals the deep commitment to codified movement that is central to this art form. This training is designed to cultivate the potential (**Dynamis**) for precise and expressive movement, which is then harnessed (**Energeia**) to create a powerful and transformative performance (**Entelecheia**). Sanskrit theatre does not have much written documentation. In fact, it is a style of theatre protected by UNESCO[3] and passed on primarily through oral tradition.

In the context of my research, I have used two performances and a training video to illustrate the similarities between Indian theatre forms and the hand design principles from my mime training.

In the first video, entitled **"Describing a Heroine in Kutiyattam"** (IndiaVideo.org), one can observe the result of an intense and disciplined training to achieve remarkable control over even the smallest movements of the body. In the video, the performer curves his hand into a delicate, rounded shape to describe "the full breasts" of a heroine. This gesture conveys fullness and softness with incredible precision. What struck me was that this hand design is the same as the one I had studied in mime training and had seen in the work of Mei Lanfang. This profound visual connection between traditions is represented in **Figure 3.12: Kutiyattam Gesture of Feminine Symbolism.**

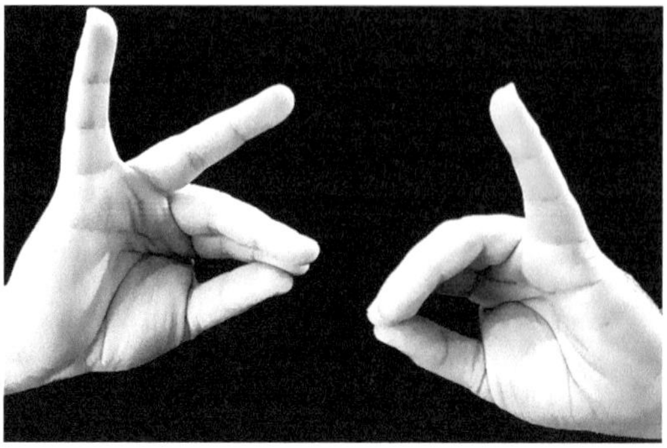

FIGURE 3.12: Hand Gesture in Kutiyattam: Embodying the Heroine. An illustration of a codified hand gesture used in Kutiyattam to describe the "full breasts" of a heroine—expressed not with realism, but through symbolic refinement and stylized poetics.

In another example, **Figure 3.13: Embodied Theatre in Kutiyattam,** the use of the same hand appears again in the video depicting ***Kailasodharanam***, a Kathakali play. Although the subtitles offer a slightly different interpretation of the gesture, the hand design remains consistent, adapted to the style of Kathakali. This affirms the deep integration of codified movement across Indian performance traditions.

FIGURE 3.13: Illustration of a Kutiyattam Performance. This image captures the deeply ritualized structure of a Kutiyattam scene—where movement, gaze, and rhythm are synchronized through codified tradition. The performer becomes a vessel of sacred presence, rooted in centuries of embodied transmission. AI-generated image created with OpenAI's DALL·E (via ChatGPT).

Looking further into contemporary Indian theatre, I examined a Yakshagana performance captured in the video titled **"Yakshagana—Ramayana—1—Shoorpanakha"** (YouTube 2014). Yakshagana, a dance-drama from southern India, incorporates vibrant costumes, makeup, and music. Though less stylized than Kutiyattam or Kathakali, Yakshagana retains expressive hand gestures and dynamic movements. Here, the gestures were freer, with more theatrical spontaneity, possibly reflecting the need to broaden appeal for modern and global audiences. An illustration of the hand used in this scene is shown in **Figure 3.14: Yakshagana and the Epic in Motion.**

These three illustrations represent key observations in this section:

- **Figure 3.12**: Illustration of Kutiyattam Hand Gesture to describe "the full breasts" of a heroine.
- **Figure 3.13**: Illustration of Kutiyattam.
- **Figure 3.14**: A hand gesture from a Yakshagana performance of the Ramayana.

FIGURE 3.14: Yakshagana Performance of the Ramayana. An illustrated hand gesture from a scene of Yakshagana retelling of the Ramayana, where dance, dialogue, and song merge into an expressive totality. The performer's bold gestures, dramatic makeup, and rhythmic presence are not for spectacle—they are tools of transformation, where myth becomes experience and theatre becomes energetic offering. AI-generated image created with OpenAI's DALL·E (via ChatGPT).

The recurrence of these hand designs across diverse Indian theatrical traditions highlights a fundamental principle: codified movement is not a constraint but a liberating structure that allows performers to transcend language, culture, and time. The hands become tools of meaning, shaped by tradition, yet capable of expressing something universal. This is where the DEE Cycle continues to resonate deeply. Each gesture, when rooted in intention and expressed through codified practice, has the power to touch something profound in the viewer.

An Art Codifier in the West

As we journey from the classical and codified traditions of Asia, it is necessary to ask—how did codified movement begin to take shape in the Western world? Which figures first sought to systematize expression through gesture and movement in European performance traditions?

While Eastern theatrical systems such as Kutiyattam and Kunqu have maintained clear historical records of codified gestures, the Western tradition initially developed through more fragmented yet passionate efforts. Two names stand out in this lineage: **Jean-Gaspard Deburau** and **François Delsarte**.

Jean-Gaspard Deburau: Intuition and Expression

Jean-Gaspard Deburau was a French actor and mime who revolutionized pantomime at the Théâtre des Funambules in Paris. Best known for his portrayal of Pierrot, Deburau brought emotional nuance and psychological depth to the traditionally comic role. Although there is no formal manual of his method, scholars such as **Gilda Navarra** identify Deburau as the first Western performer to explore and embody stylized postures that reflected internal emotional states.

Even without a written technique, Deburau intuitively engaged with the same energetic principles we have explored throughout this book—the **DEE Cycle**:

- **Dynamis:** The emotional impulse behind the gesture.
- **Energeia:** The movement used to express it.
- **Entelecheia:** The presence and arrival of meaning in the action.

In this way, Deburau becomes the *ancestor* of Western codification—his work a living embodiment of these principles before they were formally articulated.

François Delsarte: Systematizing the Invisible

If Deburau was the intuitive master, **François Delsarte** was the system builder. A French actor and teacher, Delsarte sought to understand the mechanics of emotional expression and its connection to the body. He developed a full method, later known as the *Delsarte System of Dramatic Expression*, which was published posthumously by his students.

Delsarte's work aimed to codify the relationship between inner experience and outer form. His method categorized physical movements and gestures into detailed systems that corresponded with particular emotional or intellectual states. As noted by Elena Randi (2017), his studies included:

- The connection between gestures and emotions.
- The influence of physical habits on communication.
- The ethical and moral implications of body expression.

Importantly, Delsarte's system resonates today not just in theatre but in virtual performance design. Researchers such as Marsella et al. (2006) have adapted Delsarte's principles to guide the non-verbal behavior of AI and virtual agents, showing the ongoing relevance of codified movement in technology as well as in art.

Reflection: East and West in Dialogue

Looking at Deburau and Delsarte side by side, we find the Western tradition beginning to ask the same questions as Asian theatre: **How does energy move through the body? How does a gesture become meaningful?** (See Figure 3.15.)

Deburau represents the intuitive path—discovering truth through lived performance. Delsarte offers the analytical path—seeking to name and classify that truth.

FIGURE 3.15: Embodiment and System: Deburau and Delsarte in Contrast. A visual juxtaposition of Jean-Gaspard Deburau *(left)*, embodying the emotional nuance of Pierrot through intuitive mime, and François Delsarte *(right)*, whose codified system mapped expressive gestures to specific emotional states. One moved from impulse, the other from diagram—but both sought to give form to feeling. Their divergence mirrors a central question in Human Theatre: Can expression be taught—or only awakened? AI-generated image created with OpenAI's DALL·E (via ChatGPT).

Both approaches echo what we've seen in Kutiyattam, Yakshagana, and Kunqu: that the body, when shaped with awareness, becomes a vessel for transformation.

In this way, the West's journey into codification does not oppose the East's—it begins to rhyme with it. These are not separate stories, but **converging inquiries**, all rooted in the body's capacity to transmit energy, shape meaning, and awaken the audience.

Final Reflections Before Integration

In retracing the Western path toward codification, from the emotive artistry of Deburau to the analytical rigor of Delsarte, we see that the desire to create meaning through form is not confined to any one culture. Delsarte's theories, though born in nineteenth-century France, resonate with the same structural clarity that governs Kunqu, Yakshagana, or mime. What each of these systems shares is a profound understanding of **gesture as language**, and **movement as meaning**.

Delsarte's concept of physical expression acting as a mirror to the internal world aligns perfectly with the **DEE Cycle** we've explored throughout this chapter. His system did not aim to reduce the performer to a set of fixed symbols, but rather to unlock a symphonic relationship between **intention**, **execution**, and **presence**—the very foundation of **Dynamis**, **Energeia**, and **Entelecheia**.

As we now shift our gaze from individual systems to **a comparative analysis of global traditions**, it becomes increasingly clear that these parallels are not mere coincidences—they are echoes of a shared human instinct to **codify expression**, to **ritualize emotion**, and to **transform the body into a sacred instrument of communication** (**see Figure 3.16**).

Part 2—The DEE Cycle in Action: Historical Examples and Eastern Parallels

DEE as a Universal Structure, Seen Across Traditions

By now, the DEE Cycle has been explored as a theoretical framework, a lens through which to view transformation—both in performance and in life. But theory only becomes meaningful when it is **embodied**. And what I've discovered through my training and research is that the DEE Cycle is not a Western invention, nor an isolated idea—it is a **universal pattern**, alive in the world's most refined performance traditions (**see Figure 3.17**).

From **mime to Kunqu**, from **Yakshagana to Lessac's Kinesensics**, I've observed the same energetic pathway over and over again:

FIGURE 3.16: One Performer, Many Shadows. A single performer stands in stillness, casting multiple shadows—each echoing a different theatrical tradition: Kunqu, Yakshagana, mime, Kutiyattam. Charged with radiant energy, the body becomes a vessel of lineage and transformation. The DEE Cycle unfolds here not as theory, but as presence in motion: one breath, many voices; one body, infinite forms. AI-generated image created with OpenAI's DALL·E (via ChatGPT).

- A **charge** begins to build (Dynamis).
- It **moves** through the body with form, breath, and gesture (Energeia).
- And then it **lands**, becoming a moment of presence and impact (Entelecheia).

Each system offers a different language to express it, but the structure remains strikingly familiar.

In **Kutiyattam**, a simple hand gesture expands over time, giving the audience space to feel its energy. In **Yakshagana**, the same energetic buildup surges through rhythmic movement and stylized combat. In **Lessac's work**, vocal vibration and movement become direct conduits of energy. Even **Deburau**, performing silently on a Parisian stage, knew this instinctively—he just didn't have the language for it or never thought about writing it.

The DEE Cycle is not about cultural ownership. It is about **recognizing a deeper logic** that connects embodied traditions. It gives us a tool to understand performance as a **ritual of transmission:** of emotion, of presence, of truth.

In this sense, the DEE Cycle is **not a theory applied to performance**—it is **performance itself.** It is the internal movement of the performer that becomes visible, felt, and shared.

FIGURE 3.17: The DEE Cycle as Universal Structure. A visual representation of the DEE Cycle—Dynamis (potential), Energeia (expression), and Entelecheia (realization)—as a shared energetic pattern seen across performance traditions. Performer silhouettes from mime, Kutiyattam, Kunqu, and Yakshagana form a circular flow, illustrating that while forms may differ, the journey of energy—from impulse to presence—is universal. Across culture, language, and lineage, the body tells the same story: transformation. AI-generated image created with OpenAI's DALL·E (via ChatGPT).

Master Cheuk Fung's Perspective

To deepen our understanding of how the DEE Cycle (Dynamis–Energeia–Entelecheia) functions within performance traditions, it is illuminating to look outside of theatre and examine how energy is understood and applied in other codified systems—particularly in martial arts. One of the most enlightening parallels comes from the perspective of Master Cheuk Fung, a highly respected teacher of traditional Chinese Kung Fu, who speaks with clarity about the relationship between **Yi** (意, intention), **Chi** (氣, energy),[4] and **Li** (力, mechanical force) **(see Figure 3.18)**.

In an interview with his students, Master Cheuk Fung explained how internal energy works in the body:

- **Yi (Intention):** Directs energy and action.
- **Chi (Energy):** Coordinated and concentrated electrochemical energy that manifests in response to Yi.
- **Li (Mechanical Force):** The physical force produced by the transformation of Chi.

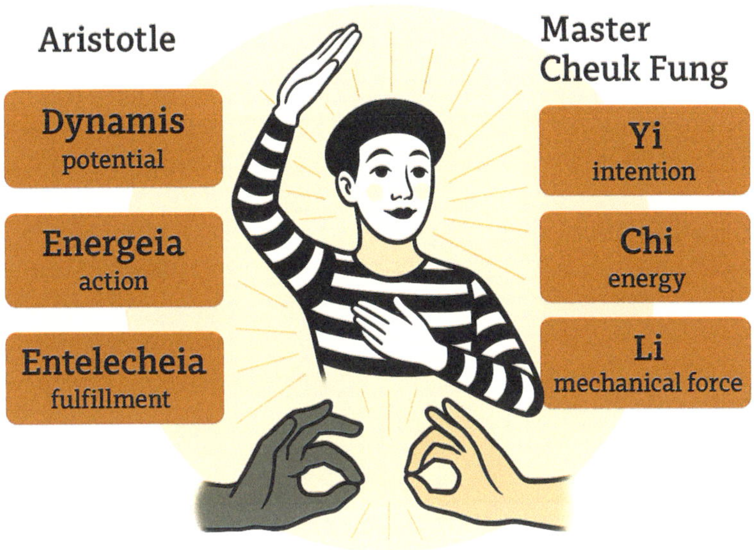

FIGURE 3.18: Parallel Energies: Aristotle and Cheuk Fung. A visual comparison between Aristotle's DEE Cycle—Dynamis (potential), Energeia (activation), and Entelecheia(realization)—and the Yi–Chi–Li sequence from traditional martial arts, as articulated by Master Cheuk Fung: Yi(intention), Chi (energy), and Li (force). Though born of different cultures, both models trace the same path—from invisible origin to embodied action. Energy does not begin in the muscle—it begins in the mind, travels through breath, and arrives in the body. AI-generated image created with OpenAI's DALL·E (via ChatGPT).

Master Cheuk Fung emphasizes that debating the physical existence of Chi is missing the point. What matters is understanding how human energy moves from internal potential (Yi) to visible physical output (Li) through a process rooted in intention and discipline. He explains this transition as a pathway: the body focuses intention, generating nervous system energy (Chi), which then becomes mechanical output (Li) through muscle activation.

This concept mirrors Aristotle's formulation of the DEE Cycle:

- **Dynamis (Potential):** Yi—the performer's inner intention, the spark of potential.
- **Energeia (Action):** Chi—the movement and bioelectric activation of energy through technique.
- **Entelecheia (Fulfillment):** Li—the final physical result of action, visible and complete.

This parallel demonstrates how energy transformation principles can be observed in both martial arts and theatre. While Cheuk Fung learned through years of physical training and intuitive awareness, Aristotle described the same process from a philosophical perspective. Together, they reinforce the idea that the DEE Cycle isn't merely theoretical—it is a lived, embodied experience.

Master Cheuk Fung's teachings help us better understand performance as an energetic process. His system provides an elegant map for how a gesture is born: not from muscle alone, but from thought, through flow, to form.

This connection between DEE and **Yi–Chi–Li** cycles provides a beautiful bridge between East and West, highlighting the **universality of energy-based expression** across traditions. It also offers a valuable reminder that what appears onstage—be it a stylized gesture, a powerful vocal delivery, or a martial strike—always begins somewhere unseen: with intention.

Analyzing Historical Examples

With the DEE Cycle clearly defined and echoed in traditions both Eastern and Western, we now revisit some of the systems introduced earlier to observe how **Dynamis**, **Energeia**, and **Entelecheia** operate within them. This analysis reveals the **energetic logic** behind performance styles that may appear vastly different on the surface but are grounded in the same human impulse: to transmit energy through the body (**see Figure 3.19**).

Mime and the Power of Inner Stillness. In mime, especially the tradition shaped by Jean-Gaspard Deburau, **Dynamis** arises not from external stimulation, but from internal emotional charge. The mime does not speak; they **generate energy** from silence. In each gesture, there is a quiet explosion—**Energeia**—that traverses space with clarity. The audience's recognition, its emotional response, is **Entelecheia**: the final, silent resonance that lands without a word spoken.

Lessac's Kinesensic Training. Lessac's work, expanded upon by master teacher **Deborah Kinghorn**, introduces Energeia not only through gesture but also through **vocal vibration** and **kinesthetic awareness**. A performer who breathes with intention, speaks from resonance, and moves with embodied listening is constantly cycling through DEE:

- **Dynamis**: The internal need to communicate.
- **Energeia**: The shaping of the breath, the vocal tone, the bodily energy.
- **Entelecheia**: The live reception—when the audience feels not the performance, but the presence.

Kutiyattam's Sacred Deliberation. In **Kutiyattam**, we observe the most distilled form of DEE in action. A single gesture may unfold over **minutes**. Here, Dynamis is often tied to mythological or emotional content, prepared through deep ritual and intention. The movement itself—slow, deliberate, held with breath—is **Energeia** incarnate. When the gaze settles, or the hand completes its shape, the pause is **Entelecheia**—the energy arrives fully in the space, untouched by rush or ego.

FIGURE 3.19: A Universal Path: The Performer at the Crossroads of Tradition. A visual rendering of the DEE Cycle as an energetic constant across cultures. The silhouette of a performer stands at the center, where multiple cultural lineages converge—each path representing a unique theatrical tradition. From inner impulse to embodied expression, the journey is shared. The performer becomes both origin and vessel—where many traditions, one energy, flows. AI-generated image created with OpenAI's DALL·E (via ChatGPT).

Yakshagana's Theatrical Codification. The vibrancy and rhythm of **Yakshagana** might suggest spontaneity, but its precision reveals codification. Here, **Dynamis** is often tied to narrative or character archetype. Through dance, rhythm, and heightened gesture, **Energeia** emerges in flamboyant but clearly articulated form. The performer's strike, turn, or cry reaches its peak in **Entelecheia**—when the audience sees not just character, but conviction.

Kunqu and the Gesture as Calligraphy. In Kunqu, the gesture is **not decoration—it is transmission**. A movement begins with an internal intention (**Dynamis**), is carried through the stylized bodywork and controlled breath of the performer (**Energeia**), and arrives through silence or gesture with full poetic impact (**Entelecheia**). Master Cheuk Fung's perspective reminds us that even a martial movement can follow the same arc.

Universal Yet Unique. These traditions may differ in culture, training, and aesthetics—but in each, the DEE Cycle serves as an energetic framework, guiding the performer from impulse to realization. It affirms that:

- The **body is not just expressive**—it is a transformer of energy.
- **Gesture is not random**—it is designed to carry meaning.

- The **audience does not just watch**—they feel the arc of energy moving through the space.

The Body as Universal Instrument. Across cultures, across time, and across disciplines, the DEE Cycle emerges as a quiet constant—a kind of energetic grammar embedded within the art of performance.

From the sacred slowness of Kutiyattam to the stylized boldness of Yakshagana, from mime's silent charge to Lessac's embodied voice, and through the elegant transmission of Kunqu, the arc is the same: **An inner impulse is shaped into expression, and that expression becomes shared meaning.**

What varies is the vocabulary. What remains is the **structure of energy**.

This is not just a convergence of styles—it is a convergence of **human understanding**. Each system, in its own way, acknowledges that the performer is not merely representing something. They are **channeling something**—from the invisible, through the body, into the space. It is in this act that the sacred lives.

The DEE Cycle is more than a theory. It is a truth that lives in the breath, in the spine, in the outstretched hand. It lives wherever **intention becomes movement**, and **movement becomes meaning**.

Part 3—Embodying the Future: From Lineage to Innovation

From Tradition to Transformation: The Path of Modern Theatre

As we move from the deep well of traditional practices into the terrain of modern theatre, the question arises: how do we carry forward the precision, presence, and energetic integrity found in these codified systems?

Contemporary performance often prioritizes innovation, breaking forms and challenging narratives—but in doing so, it sometimes risks losing connection to the **body as instrument**, the **gesture as language**, and the **breath as bridge**. This is not a call to return to past forms, but a call to recognize that **what is most ancient is often also what is most essential**.

The DEE Cycle offers a path—not backward, but **inward**. It does not prescribe a particular style or aesthetic. Instead, it invites the performer to attend to the **inner spark of intention**, the shaping of that energy through movement or sound, and the sacred moment when the audience receives and resonates with it.

In modern theatre, where text may be fragmented and stories abstract, this cycle becomes an anchor. It reminds us that no matter how experimental the form, the performer's **presence** is the heart of the exchange.

To embody the future of theatre means not discarding tradition, but transforming it—letting it live in the breath, the voice, and the charged stillness between movement and meaning. The DEE Cycle doesn't limit creativity. It **grounds** it.

FIGURE 3.20: Energy Through Time: The Performer as Bridge. A visual metaphor for the timeless flow of energy in performance. The performer stands between past and future, channeling ancient traditions into new expression. Here, the path of intention, movement, and transformation flows beyond culture and chronology. The body becomes not only a vessel—but a bridge between what was and what can be. AI-generated image created with OpenAI's DALL·E (via ChatGPT).

Final Reflections on the Chapter

This chapter has moved across continents and centuries, across techniques and philosophies, to reveal one simple truth: **the performer is an alchemist**. Not in the literal sense of turning metal into gold, but in the deeper sense of **turning intention into action**, and **action into shared experience** (see Figure 3.20).

In mime, Kunqu, Kutiyattam, Yakshagana, Lessac, and beyond, we've seen that performance is not merely about technique—it is about **energy in motion**. It is about knowing how to listen to the body, and how to let the body listen to the world.

The DEE Cycle offers a way to name what great performers already know in their bones. It speaks to the **transformational power of presence**—and the way a single breath, a single gesture, can shift the atmosphere of a room.

As we continue forward, we carry with us not only the knowledge of these traditions, but their pulse. Their rhythm. Their ability to awaken something sacred in both performer and audience.

The journey does not end here—it becomes even more alive.

NOTES

1. Kutiyattam, an ancient Sanskrit theatre form from Kerala, India, is recognized by UNESCO as a Masterpiece of the Oral and Intangible Heritage of Humanity. It blends ancient Sanskrit drama with local practices, reflecting the cultural synthesis of classical and regional influences. Performed in temple theatres called "Kuthampalams," Kutiyattam is traditionally enacted by the Chakyar and Nambiar communities. Elaborate costumes, makeup, and precise gestures are used in intricate acting styles involving detailed facial expressions and gestures that convey complex narratives from epic texts like the Ramayana and Mahabharata. Kutiyattam is unique for its integration of humor and ritualistic aspects, often including extended improvisations.
2. Gilda Navarra, a prominent figure in performing arts, dedicated her career to teaching physical expression and movement in performance. Her seminal work, *Cartilla de un oficio: Abecedario de un actor-mimo*, is a comprehensive guide for actors, especially mimes, outlining fundamental techniques, methodologies, and philosophical underpinnings of mime performance. It emphasizes the importance of body language and physicality in conveying emotions and narratives without spoken words.
3. Established in 1945, UNESCO, a UN specialized agency, promotes international cooperation in education, sciences, culture, and communication. Its mission is to ensure global peace and security through quality education, cultural preservation, scientific research, and global understanding through communication and information sharing. Key initiatives include literacy promotion, cultural heritage site protection, and empowering educational programs.
4. Chi (氣) is the romanization preferred by Master Cheuk Fung, aligning with widespread English usage in martial arts terms such as "Tai Chi." In modern pinyin, the same character is rendered as Qi. Both forms refer to the same concept of vital energy or life force.

SECTION 2

CONTEMPORARY APPLICATIONS AND PERSPECTIVES

Chapter 4

The Energetic Body: Performing from Within

4

The Energetic Body: Performing from Within

Part 1—Tracing the Evolution of Artistic Decodification

Energy in Motion: Modern Artists, Ancient Impulses

In this chapter, we move into the **body itself**—not as a neutral vehicle, but as a **living, energetic instrument**, shaped by memory, breath, tension, and intention. If previous chapters traced energy through theory, history, and tradition, here we step **inside the body**, to witness how energy arises and transforms from within the modern performer.

The DEE Cycle—**Dynamis, Energeia, Entelecheia**—continues to guide our exploration. But this time, it is not revealed through classical systems or historical echoes. Instead, we meet **contemporary artists** who activate energy through movement, voice, memory, ritual, and form. Their practices are varied, yet they share a commitment to **energetic presence** and **embodied expression**—to performing not from the surface, but from the **core**.

In this space, the body is more than a tool—it becomes a **threshold** between inner impulse and outer transmission. And the artists we're about to encounter embody that principle in action.

This chapter is not just a chronicle of methods—it is a lived testimony of theatrical alchemy. The human is at the center: vulnerable, powerful, incomplete, and radiant with potential.

> In the stillness of the performer's breath, the story begins—before language, before movement, before form.
>
> (from the author)

FIGURE 4.0: Axis of Being. Along the body's central axis, presence gathers. The spine becomes the conductor through which movement, breath, and intention align. AI-generated image created with OpenAI's DALL·E (via ChatGPT).

Todd Farley, Father of Modern Christian Mime

From Hawaii to the World Stage: The Birth of a Mime

Todd Farley's journey into performance began not with words, but with silence—specifically, the silence of mime. Growing up in Hilo, Hawaii, Farley spoke *pidgin English*,[1] a simplified form of the language developed to facilitate communication between people of different native tongues. When he moved to the US mainland, he encountered cultural and linguistic barriers. Traditional spoken language, especially for the purposes of expressing his Christian faith, felt limiting.

FIGURE 4.1: Todd Farley: Father of Modern Christian Mime. A pivotal figure in the evolution of contemporary mime, Todd Farley brought together sacred storytelling and embodied expression to create a spiritually charged performance language. His work reframed mime not just as entertainment, but as transmission of presence, faith, and breath-made-visible.

> The Rainbow Players gave me my first public outlet to the community through the art of mime, which was significant for me as I was still adjusting to Mainland USA and its culture having spent my childhood in Hilo, Hawaii where I spoke pidgin English. Mime was a way to communicate my faith and thoughts without the trouble of language. It also taught me how to turn a weakness into a strength.
>
> (Farley 2017: n.pag.)

The Rainbow Players—a mime ministry troupe touring Washington, Oregon, and California from 1978 to 1980—became Farley's first expressive laboratory (see **Figure 4.1**).

Developing Mimeistry: A Spiritual Technique

Farley's creative language evolved into something deeply personal and spiritual: *Mimeistry*. Rooted in classical techniques—particularly those of Étienne Decroux[2] and Marcel Marceau[3]—Mimeistry was Farley's fusion of physical theatre and Christian narrative.

Unlike conventional mime, Farley's performances integrated music, sometimes with lyrics, crafting a multimedia language of gesture and sound. He developed codified guidelines for "miming with music and words"—an innovation that extended mime's boundaries without sacrificing its stylization.

> It differed from a lot of other styles because it used music with lyrics in the background to tell part of the story. However, because it was deeply rooted in Marceau and Decroux technique it was still highly stylized.
>
> (Farley 2017: n.pag.)

This duality—faith and form, tradition, and innovation—became the signature of Farley's practice.

Teaching and the Mastery of Mimodrame

Eventually recognized by Marceau himself with the title *Father of Modern Christian Mime*,[4] Farley took on the responsibility of training others. He authored the foundational series *Mastery of Mimodrame*, Volumes 1–4, integrating spiritual intention with technical clarity.

His technique helped performers channel their *Dynamis*—the inner emotional drive—through *Energeia*, the stylized and codified movements of the Mimeistry vocabulary. The result was *Entelecheia*—a fully embodied, transformative moment for both performer and viewer. The DEE Cycle was not merely a framework; it was lived practice in every gesture of his work.

In Mimeistry, **music is not a background element**—it is a **narrative partner**. He once described music as "*the invisible character onstage*," capable of shifting tone, holding silence, or accelerating emotion. Just as the performer's breath fuels their gestures, the music breathes through the piece, guiding rhythm, tone, and emotional progression.

This is a crucial part of the energetic transmission. Music supports the **DEE Cycle** in real time:

- It evokes **Dynamis** in the performer, stirring the internal impulse.
- It modulates **Energeia**, shaping the energy of movement and the emotional current.
- It contributes to **Entelecheia**, helping the gesture reach the audience with full resonance.

His approach to "mime with music and words" became a key pillar of Mimeistry: Choreography was not ornamental, but **energetically and emotionally aligned with message and moment.**

Beyond Language, Toward Impact

Performances like *Moses* (see **Figure 4.2**) became illustrative of Mimeistry's power: A biblical narrative conveyed not through speech, but through breath, movement, and music. The story was carried by posture, tension, and release, guided not just by choreography but by conviction.

FIGURE 4.2: Scan the QR code to watch *Moses*, a performance by Todd Farley that fuses mime and music to tell the story of divine encounter, transformation, and leadership. Farley's body becomes the text—where gesture, silence, and rhythm speak louder than words. AI-generated image created with OpenAI's DALL·E (via ChatGPT).

Yet Farley was acutely aware that context mattered. Biblical themes may not resonate with all audiences. Still, by prioritizing clarity in movement and emotional universality, Mimeistry became an example of codified performance that could reach across cultural lines, even as it honored its religious roots.

Beyond Faith: Mimeistry in Broader Context

Though deeply rooted in Christian narrative, Farley's technique is not limited to religious content. It is **methodological**, not dogmatic. This opened the door for my own exploration of Mimeistry, leading to original pieces such as *Silencio Ludico* and the *9/11 Attacks*. These works, while not religious in theme, utilize the same **energetic clarity and codified movement** that define Mimeistry. The result is performance that reaches beyond theology to touch broader audiences through shared human experiences—grief, silence, joy, play, memory.

These experiments showed that while **gesture codification** is powerful, it must also be **contextually legible**. In the piece of Javier, discussed earlier, I recall being **immersed in the atmosphere** and struck by the beauty of form—but not fully able to **decode the symbolism**. Without the cultural and scriptural background, certain gestures remained opaque. The DEE Cycle—so alive in the performer's body—could be felt, but not always fully understood. This is both the **power and the limitation** of tightly coded symbolic language: It resonates deeply within a specific group, but may need recontextualization to reach beyond.

My own performances became a response to this question. *Silencio Lúdico* (see **Figure 4.3**), for instance, used the physical grammar of Mimeistry but engaged themes of inner stillness and imagination—accessible to a wide audience. Likewise, my work reflecting on *9/11* employed the same clarity of movement and emotional structure but communicated collective trauma and memory, rather than scripture.

FIGURE 4.3: *Silencio Lúdico*: The Author's Embodied Inquiry. A personal offering from the author's ongoing exploration of Human Theatre—where silence, play, breath, and gesture converge into poetic form. *Silencio Lúdico* invites the viewer to experience performance as presence: wordless, resonant, alive. Scan the QR code to watch the full piece. AI-generated image created with OpenAI's DALL·E (via ChatGPT).

A Living Language of Faith and Form

Todd Farley's contribution lies not just in what he performed, but in what he **codified and passed on**. Mimeistry is a form of **energetic literacy**, one where gestures are charged with meaning, shaped with musicality, and delivered with sacred clarity. Through my own experimentation, I found that this clarity could serve stories both sacred and secular—because what's ultimately transmitted is not just the message, but presence. Mimeistry, at its core, is not performance—it is **transmission.**

Bridge to What Follows

Farley's contribution lies in how he blends **faith, form, and feeling**—how he carries the past (Decroux, Marceau) into the present moment, without letting go of the sacred. His work invites us to consider how energy, when guided by purpose and form, becomes not only expressive—but **transformative**.

In the artists that follow, we'll see this same pursuit—across different faiths, cultures, and disciplines. What unites them is not a single style, but a shared desire: to make energy visible, and to speak the unspeakable through the living instrument of the performer's body.

Gilda Navarra, Master of Silence

From Puerto Rico to the World Stage

FIGURE 4.4: Gilda Navarra: Master of Silence. A foundational figure in Puerto Rican performance history, Gilda Navarra channeled the power of stillness and presence into a language all her own. Her silence was not emptiness—it was energy held, emotion distilled, and transmission without words. In her work, the body did not speak—it resonated.

If Todd Farley opened the door to redefining Christian mime as a contemporary spiritual practice, **Gilda Navarra** (see **Figure 4.4**) stepped through it with grace, fire, and **profound stillness**. Trained in modern dance, mime, ballet, and Flamenco, Navarra was drawn to the **essence of gesture**, to the **emotional resonance** that lives in silence, and to the performer's **inner energy** as the true source of meaning.

Her work is a powerful example of **Energeia:** not in theatrical spectacle, but in the **invisible transmission** between body and audience. Navarra's performances were known for their quiet intensity. Audiences often described the sensation of being "held" by her gaze or "moved" by a shift in her breath. She worked with silence not as a void but as a space of **charged potential**—a deep **Dynamis** waiting to be released.

Navarra's gestures and movements arose slowly, sculpted by inner impulse and disciplined stillness. Every movement was intentional. Every pause was alive. These weren't moments of rest; they were moments of transformation—**Entelecheia**—where the performer and audience met in complete presence.

Navarra also believed deeply in the **spiritual nature** of performance—not as dogma, but as communion. Her performance could be described as a **prayer through the body**—a form of surrender where the performer becomes both vessel and flame.

Her legacy lives on not only in her work, but in her students, many of whom continue to carry forward her methodology of **gesture, breath, and interiority** as tools for truth.

Fusion of Flamenco and Theatre

FIGURE 4.5: Fusion of Theatre and Flamenco. A still that captures Navarra's synthesis of flamenco's emotional intensity with theatrical presence. Each movement is both narrative and pulse—gestural fire woven with breath. Theatre, here, is not structure—it is flamenco made visible in the body's silence and surge. Image from *Detrás del silencio* by Gilda Navarra and Jorge Rigau.

Gilda García Daubon, known professionally as Gilda Navarra, began her artistic journey as a flamenco dancer in Pamplona, Spain, where she trained in the intense and expressive tradition that would mark her physical discipline for life. Touring across Spain, France, Belgium, and Portugal, she absorbed the artistic energy of various European movements, enriching her embodied language with a diversity of forms and experiences.

Her deep understanding of posture, line, and emotional projection—core elements of flamenco (see **Figure 4.5**)—would later shape the unique theatrical language she developed in Puerto Rico. Flamenco's rigorous discipline, passionate expressiveness, and inner sense of core strength became the invisible scaffolding of her teaching. She transmitted not just a technique but a profound sensibility rooted in bodily control, emotion, and presence (see **Figure 4.6**).

In 1971, Navarra founded the Taller de Histriones (see **Figure 4.7**), a theatre company and laboratory space that fused mime, flamenco, ballet, music, and Commedia dell'Arte. Through this synthesis, she pioneered a new kind of theatrical expression in Puerto Rico. Navarra's performers trained to access their subconscious and embodied experience as tools for creation—uniting improvisation, stylized gesture, and emotional clarity to deliver messages that resonated beyond the limits of text.

Navarra's commitment to this embodied approach was both artistic and philosophical. She emphasized the power of silence, the expressiveness of stillness, and the clarity of movement as a communicative act. The Taller de Histriones became a space not only for innovation but for the evolution of Puerto Rican theatrical identity, positioning her as a precursor to the dance-theatre movement[5] that would influence later generations.

Her training with Étienne Decroux, Jacques Lecoq, Martha Graham,[6] and Jacques Copeau further enriched her vision, helping her to develop a unique voice grounded in movement but open to interpretation, emotion, and transformation. Gilda Navarra did not merely teach mime or flamenco—she created a living grammar of expression.

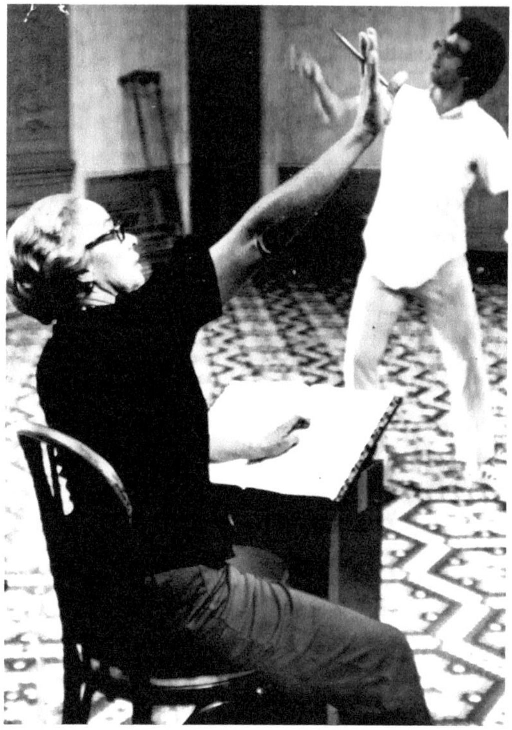

FIGURE 4.6: Gilda Navarra directing a rehearsal of *The Soldier's Tale*, 1971. An innovative space: Taller de Histriones. Image from *Detrás del silencio* by Gilda Navarra and Jorge Rigau.

A Shift Toward the Human: Theatre Rooted in the Performer

Her theatrical journey reveals a profound transition—from codified technique toward human-centered performance, where energy, embodiment, and emotional authenticity become the primary focus. This evolution is not an abstract notion in her work—it's lived, studied, and reimagined through the teachings of her masters.

Marcel Marceau: "Mime of Style"

After a rich career in flamenco and ballet, Navarra entered the world of mime, where her curiosity led her to connect with Marcel Marceau in 1960. She admired his genius, but also spoke with remarkable clarity about the limits of his approach for foundational training.

> Marcel Marceau develops the "Mime of Style." A disciple of Étienne Decroux, Marceau, through his genius, has created a unique and inimitable style that breaks all the rules and should not be taken as an example in the study or development of mime.
>
> (Navarra 2007: 24, author's translation)

While she admired Marceau's genius, Navarra was clear that his was a language of personal style—not foundational grammar.

FIGURE 4.7: Gilda Navarra's Taller de Histriones. More than a studio, Taller de Histriones was a space of initiation. A laboratory of embodiment, where Navarra trained performers to move not from style, but from truth. The body was not taught to imitate—it was taught to remember.

Jacques Copeau: Emptiness as Creative Space

Navarra's engagement with Copeau's lineage introduced her to the concept of the "nearly empty stage." For Copeau, simplicity was radical. By removing the weight of excessive scenography, he allowed the performer's body, breath, and intention to take center stage. In her own reflection, this idea is transformative. The body becomes the primary scenic element—capable of invoking landscapes, emotions, or entire stories. Copeau taught Navarra that creativity is found in emptiness, and that freedom begins when the performer claims the void with presence and intention.

Étienne Decroux: The Body as Language

Through Decroux (see **Figure 4.8**), she encountered a rigorous vocabulary of movement. His corporeal mime demanded a complete break from theatrical conventions: no props, no makeup, no spoken word. Instead, the performer speaks through physicality alone. Her documentation of this method reflects the power of silence as action. Decroux redefined acting as the act of making inner energy visible. This principle became foundational to her own work and to my exploration of the DEE Cycle—making it clear that Entelecheia is not the end of a gesture, but its transformation into meaning.

Jacques Lecoq: Gesture as Emotional Logic

From Lecoq,[7] she learned that movement isn't just form—it is logic, rhythm, and emotion. Lecoq emphasized that mime is not mimicry, but a language of impulses and reactions. She describes how Lecoq reconnected body and mind, allowing gesture to emerge from lived experience rather than predetermined forms. This shift was deeply humanizing: Lecoq's theatre was not about form for its own sake, but about rediscovering the roots of human expression. In her work, this resonates as the reclaiming of spontaneity—of letting Dynamis rise from within and organically unfold into expression.

Rather than just describing their teachings, her narrative embodies their fusion. She doesn't treat these masters as static references but as springboards toward her own discoveries. Through them, she began to dissolve the boundaries between acting and movement, between mime and dance, between discipline and instinct.

FIGURE 4.8: Gilda Navarra with classmates at Étienne Decroux's studio, New York, 1961. Image from *Detrás del silencio* by Gilda Navarra and Jorge Rigau.

This transformation is evident in her shift from technical precision to emotional truth, and from fixed styles to hybrid forms—where flamenco, mime, and contemporary dance coexist. The empty stage becomes a playground of inner energies. The body becomes not only an instrument but a voice.

Sensitivity in Motion

In an era when performance often leans toward spectacle, Gilda Navarra offers a quiet revolution—one grounded in **sensitivity**, **presence**, and the expressive intelligence of the body. Her methodology marks an evolution in theatrical language, one that prioritizes the **human experience** over aesthetic perfection or narrative illusion (see **Figure 4.9**).

Navarra's influence, as described by her student **Carmelo Santana Mojica**, is not merely technical but deeply emotional: "Gilda Navarra is a master of sensitivity who reaches not only those of us lucky enough to be her students but also everyone who manifests beauty in the movement of their body" (Mojica 2003: 93).

Her practice doesn't ask the performer to become someone else—it asks them to become **more deeply themselves**. Her legacy lies in how she trained bodies to feel, to listen, and to express—not from the mind, but from an **attuned and intuitive sensitivity**.

The Spirit in Motion: Connecting Energy and Expression

Navarra's teaching, rooted in her time with **Jacques Lecoq**, honors the **intimate elemental force** behind each gesture. She believed that movement is not merely a function of muscle or choreography, but the **physical echo of the soul's impulse**: "By identifying the 'intimate elemental force' of movement, one can create a physical expression charged with the fundamental energy of the human soul" (Navarra 2007: 25, author's translation).

This elemental force becomes, in her work, a **spiritualized Dynamis**—the internal capacity to create, to move, to act. In Navarra's view, the performer's spirit is not metaphorical—it is energetic. It initiates the **DEE Cycle**:

- **Dynamis** emerges from the spirit;
- **Energeia** expresses itself through trained, embodied movement; and
- **Entelecheia** is the presence that reaches the audience as something real and transformative.

FIGURE 4.9: Gilda Navarra *(left)* and Yaraní del Valle *(right)*. A rare and intimate image capturing a moment of shared sensitivity between mentor and student, presence and future. Here, gesture is transmission, and silence is teaching. Image courtesy of her friend and colleague, Prof. Rosa Luisa Márquez.

Her framing of energy as "belonging to the spirit" brings a poetic and philosophical depth to the DEE Cycle. It suggests that theatre, at its most alive, is not a repetition of rehearsed actions, but a **manifestation of inner truth.** For Navarra, every movement onstage is an **energetic act of the soul**—a ritual of becoming.

The Stillness That Speaks: Immobility as Movement

> When you realize that immobility is also a kind of movement, just as silence is also an expression ... only then will you truly understand what mime is.
>
> (Navarra 2006: 57, author's translation)

FIGURE 4.10: Gilda Navarra in *Asíntota: The Stillness That Speaks*. A moment from Navarra's *Asíntota*, where stillness becomes movement—not through gesture, but through breath, presence, and energetic charge. Her body holds the space like a tuning fork—vibrating with everything unspoken. Immobility, here, is not pause—it is power.

In Gilda Navarra's work, the body becomes a paradox—still, yet in motion; silent, yet resonant. Her teaching is grounded in the belief that **presence** alone, when fully inhabited, generates its own form of movement. She invites us to understand the **pause** not as absence, but as a charged container of potential—a form of **Dynamis** (see **Figure 4.10**).

In this view, a pause onstage is not a gap in the action—it is **the action**, suspended. It is **Energeia** condensed into stillness, a moment of complete awareness where breath, thought, and intention align. To hold space in this way is not passive—it is a voluntary act of construction, a conscious choreography of energy.

Navarra's work demands a particular kind of training—one that cultivates not just physical technique, but internal stillness and psychological clarity. In her world, every gesture that is withheld speaks as loudly as the ones expressed. Every pause must mean something. The performer becomes not only a mover, but a **witness** to the movement that lives within stillness.

The Evolution of Theatre and the Relevance of Stillness

Gilda Navarra's exploration of **immobility as movement** is not merely a stylistic choice—it is a **philosophical proposal** about the nature of performance and communication. It opens the door to a more **inclusive** and **attuned** kind of theatre—one that listens as much as it speaks, and that respects the power of quiet attention in a world overwhelmed by noise.

As we consider the trajectory of modern performance, Navarra's insights feel increasingly urgent. In a society saturated with motion and speed, the act of stopping—**truly stopping**—becomes radical. In that stop, in that held breath, something transformative happens: a space opens for reflection, for resonance, for connection. Stillness becomes the stage on which the deepest dramas unfold (see **Figure 4.11**).

The theatre of today and tomorrow must hold space for this kind of presence. As the world fragments and accelerates, the performing arts can remind us of the **depth in pause**, the **story in silence**, the **meaning in a gesture withheld.**

Gilda's teaching is not a method—it is a **way of being.** And in her work, we find not only a model of performance but a path for how to be more present in the world.

FIGURE 4.11: The Fundamental Energy of the Human Soul. A visual of Gilda Navarra's inner charge that influences Human Theatre—not action for its own sake, but presence rooted in silence. This image distills the essence of stillness as living energy: the soul's potential held, felt, and witnessed. Movement begins here—before the body moves, the spirit speaks. Image from *Detrás del silencio* by Gilda Navarra and Jorge Rigau.

FIGURE 4.12: Gilda Navarra, professor at the University of Puerto Rico and pioneer, guided her students in exploring the poetic power of silence and presence in performance. Image from *Detrás del silencio* by Gilda Navarra and Jorge Rigau.

Bridge to What Follows

While Gilda Navarra's work with silence allowed the performer to discover profound expression beyond words, her legacy also opens the door to a deeper inquiry (see

Figure 4.12): Can movement exist within stillness? This question is the cornerstone of **Fabio Mangolini's research.** His contributions pick up where Navarra's left off—pushing the boundaries of what constitutes "movement" in performance. Just as Navarra considered a pause to be a conscious act of communication, Mangolini considers immobility not as the absence of motion, but as **an active and intentional gesture**—a moment dense with potential energy.

FIGURE 4.13: Fabio Mangolini: Bearer of the Commedia dell'Arte. A contemporary master rooted in centuries of tradition, Fabio Mangolini embodies the energetic lineage of Commedia dell'Arte—where mask, breath, and rhythm converge into presence. In his work, tradition is not frozen—it is alive, improvisational, and vibrational. The performer becomes both history and now.

Fabio Mangolini, Bearer of the Commedia dell'Arte

From Italy to the World Stage

Fabio Mangolini is not merely a scholar or performer of **Commedia dell'Arte**—he is a living thread in its long, winding lineage (see **Figure 4.13**). With a background rooted in **philosophy, mask work, and movement,** Mangolini brings to this centuries-old form a sense of renewed presence and energetic clarity that resonates deeply with the DEE Cycle.

His professional career has left a significant mark on the contemporary theatre scene, known for his dynamic performances and his insightful teachings. After graduating from the University of Bologna in Italy, where he studied Philosophy, Mangolini decided to delve into the performing arts and participated in the Cantiere Internazionale d'Arte in Montepulciano (an international festival that promotes the performing arts and provides a space for experimentation and learning). It was during this time that Marcel Marceau, the renowned master of mime, invited Mangolini to his school, the École Internationale de Mimodrame in France.

Mangolini began his journey as a student in 1984, dedicating himself to directing, and later returned as a teacher in 1990. In Paris, he embarked on a career as a professional performer in Commedia dell'Arte and was fortunate to play the young Harlequin under the direction of Carlo Boso[8] in the company Les Scalzacani. Since then, his career has expanded, earning them global recognition as a "Bearer of the Commedia dell'Arte"—a leading advocate for this art form—becoming a worldwide reference through performances, lectures, and Commedia dell'Arte courses for aspiring performers. His methodical approach and passion have helped keep this rich theatrical tradition alive, resonating among new generations of artists.

The Tradition of the Mask

Commedia dell'Arte, with its masked characters and stylized physicality, is often misunderstood as a purely comedic or ornamental form. But for Mangolini, it is a **ritual of transformation**, where the actor disappears and the archetype breathes through the body. The **mask**, in this context, is not a cover—but a conductor. It demands that performers **amplify their energy**, make their impulses readable through physicalization, and allow their breath to guide action.

"You do not wear the mask," Mangolini often echoes. "You let the mask wear you."

In this practice, **Dynamis** arises the moment the mask meets the face: the performer's intention becomes charged with archetypal potential. **Energeia** unfolds as the body responds—each gesture larger than life, yet deeply honest. **Entelecheia** arrives when the audience no longer sees the actor, but a character who seems to exist beyond the performer's own identity. This is not imitation; it is **transmission**.

Ancestry in the Air

Watching Mangolini perform—even in rehearsal—is to witness the **air become thick with memory**. His movements are not casual. They are **ritualized responses** to a lineage of performance, carried in the very rhythm of his gait, the tilt of his torso, the elasticity of his gestures. What might appear stylized to the untrained eye is in fact **energetic precision**—a full embodiment of the DEE Cycle, shaped by hundreds of years of practice, discipline, and play.

He teaches not only how to move but how to **listen to the body** in the presence of form. The body, he reminds us, is not modern or ancient—it is **timeless**. And when trained to be energetically available, it becomes an antenna tuned to both history and immediacy.

The Mask as Portal

Through Mangolini's lens, the Commedia mask is more than a tool for performance—it is a **portal** (see **Figure 4.14**). It transforms the performer into a vessel for a story greater than themselves. It clarifies energy and requires presence, clarity, and surrender. Each archetype—be it Arlecchino, Pantalone, or Colombina—demands a different energetic texture. To play the mask is to **enter a specific frequency**, not merely a character.

In this way, Mangolini embodies the **DEE Cycle in full:**

- **Dynamis:** The archetypal charge that begins within.
- **Energeia:** The transformation of intention into rhythmic movement, vocal tone, and gestural shape.
- **Entelecheia:** The moment the mask transcends the performer and lands, fully alive, in the space between stage and audience.

FIGURE 4.14: The Mask as Portal: Crafted by the Sartori Legacy. Fabio Mangolini holds a mask created by Amleto and Donato Sartori, masters of the form whose work has shaped generations of performers. In his hands, the mask becomes more than an artifact—it becomes a portal. Through it, the performer sheds identity and becomes presence. It is not worn—it is entered. In the photograph: Fabio Mangolini.

Crossing the Bridge: Mangolini and Nomura Kosuke

Fabio Mangolini's journey took a decisive turn when he met **Nomura Kosuke,**[9] one of the foremost masters of *Kyōgen*, a traditional Japanese comedic form often performed alongside Nō.[10] Their relationship was more than mentorship—it was a cross-cultural dialogue in motion. In his seminal article "Commedia dell'Arte e Kyōgen: Due teatri agli estremi della Via della Seta" ("Commedia dell'Arte and Kyōgen: Two Theatres at Opposite Ends of the Silk Road"), Mangolini referred to Kosuke as *"the last direct descendant of* *the director of the Izumi School,*"[11] emphasizing the lineage and gravitas of his teacher.

Through Kosuke, Mangolini gained access not just to Kyōgen, but to **tamé**, the practice of holding and renewing energy onstage; **hakobi**, the flowing step that resists and glides; and **yūgen**, the subtle, mysterious beauty that lies beneath stillness. These ideas would deeply shape his own energetic vocabulary and the reinterpretation of Commedia as a codified but living system.

Koshi, Tamé, and Yūgen: A New Vocabulary for the Western Body

Mangolini's research into Japanese theatre introduced him to the concept of **koshi**, a dynamic center of gravity located at the base of the spine—what he would later describe as "**a tension that lifts the performer between heaven and earth**" (n.d.: n.pag.). In **Nō and Kyōgen**, koshi is not simply posture—it is **potential.** It is the **birthplace of movement**, where **Dynamis gathers and prepares for release.**

His doctoral thesis titled "**Attraversando il ponte**" ("Crossing the Bridge") details the importance of **tension in the performer's body** in relation to the dance of Nō Theatre, notable for its **slowed rhythm** and **stylization of movements.** Within this context, Mangolini highlights how **immobility onstage** can **sharpen stage presence.** This immobility, representing the **potential for explosive energy (Dynamis)**, is **carefully controlled and focused (Energeia)**, creating a **moment of intense anticipation for the audience (Entelecheia)**. While this technique may seem contrary to the idea of dynamic acting, he demonstrates that **immobility can, instead, be an act laden with tension and meaning.**

According to his research, mastery of the concept of koshi (see **Figure 4.15**) allows performers to achieve a balance that provides total control over their body. Koshi refers to the area around the hips and lower back, which is considered the center of gravity and the source of energy in Nō Theatre. This concept refers not only to a specific posture but is fundamental for manipulating energy. When applied correctly, it allows for the stylization of movements and gives the audience an impression of lightness and suspension. Through highly stylized movements, the artist can tell stories using gestures that are universal in their meaning, enabling communication without the need for words. Mangolini explains:

> The fundamental tension in the Nō actor's body lies in that area defined by the word koshi, the coccyx. It consists of creating muscular tension at the intersection of the lines that divide the body horizontally and vertically. Muscular tension at this point triggers a state of suspension between heaven and earth. The actor's weight moves forward, the axis of gravity passes through the front of the foot, creating a

> unique balance that leads the body into a stylized form, almost out of the ordinary. For the Nō actor, it is about starting from the koshi as a fundamental tension capable of completely transfiguring their body and voice.
>
> (Mangolini 2006: 57, author's translation)

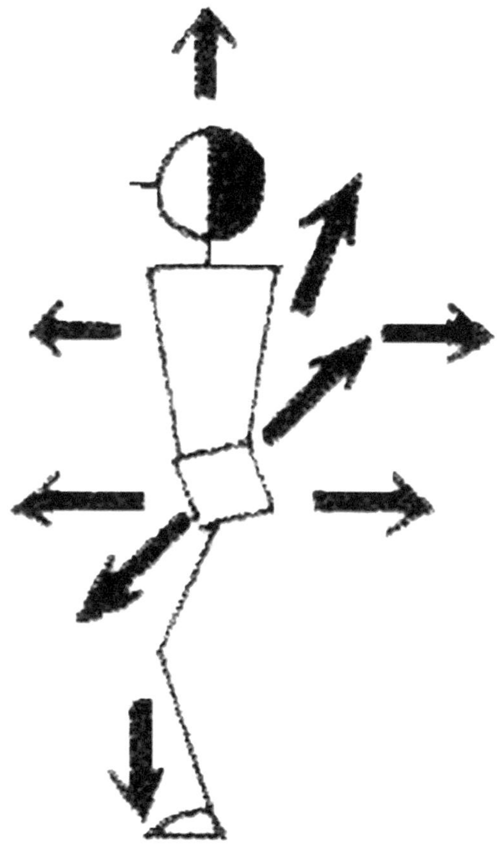

FIGURE 4.15: Mapping Koshi: Fabio Mangolini's *Diagram of Energetic Grounding* (from the doctoral thesis "Attraversando il ponte" ["Crossing the Bridge"]). This diagram, created by Fabio Mangolini, visualizes the internal forces at play in the concept of koshi—the pelvic center of energy in Nō theatre. More than anatomy, koshi is a gravitational axis, a spiritual root, and a source of power that rises through stillness. In Human Theatre, koshi is where presence begins.

When considering how this technique manifests in the expressiveness of the body, it becomes evident that control of the koshi creates an active intention that can be transferred to all movements executed by the performer. As Mangolini describes, tension in this part of the body facilitates explosive energy, which can create a powerful impact onstage. This principle is particularly enlightening when comparing Commedia dell'Arte, where energy can be extravagant and open, to the more introspective and subtle world of Nō Theatre. In Commedia dell'Arte, the potential for comedic energy (Dynamis) is unleashed through exaggerated movements and gestures (Energeia), resulting in a shared experience of laughter and joy for the audience (Entelecheia). In Nō Theatre, on the other hand, the potential for spiritual energy (Dynamis) is carefully contained and controlled (Energeia), resulting in a profound sense of awe and reverence for the audience (Entelecheia).

Reflecting on the DEE Cycle and the concept of koshi, it is essential to recognize that both are dynamic and constantly in motion. This process is called tamé, a concept studied by Mangolini during his training with Nomura, where performers control and renew their own energy to keep it alive onstage. This technique allows performers to showcase their art in a versatile manner, impacting the audience in ways that resonate long after the performance.

Mangolini emphasizes that while Commedia dell'Arte tends to be vibrant and direct, in Kyōgen, in contrast, the energy becomes more implosive. Here, the tension necessary to forge an otherworldly body is internalized, transforming into a force that invites the construction of yūgen—a Japanese term that describes aesthetic beauty deepening into subtlety and mystery. One aspect that distinguishes performers deriving from this approach is their ability to reach the intensity of energy required in a performance. Mangolini highlights that they invest a great deal of energy not only in physical movement but also in creating a meaningful connection with the audience.

The hakobi itself, or "flowing step," characteristic of Nō, is an example of the composition of vector contrasts. As the foot glides across the floor, an opposing movement pulls back, creating a resistance effect that gives a sense of fluidity and effort in movement. This tension between different vectors not only enriches the performance but also transforms it into a reflective experience for the viewer.

Mangolini posits that in Commedia dell'Arte, where energy is effusive and tends to create a close, direct relationship with the audience, the implosion in Nō Theatre produces a different effect. Both styles have their roots in the need for communication, but each uses energy uniquely to capture the attention and understanding of the spectator. One of Mangolini's contributions is the reinterpretation of the use of energy in Commedia dell'Arte, giving to the characters of the style new ways to be interpreted.

It is absolutely necessary to emphasize that skill in technique is not limited solely to physical abilities but requires systematic deepening and constant training. Throughout his career, Fabio Mangolini demonstrated that for a performer, evolution and adaptation to different forms of energy, the codes of each style, and the need to connect with the audience are fundamental. Mangolini's work reminds us that the most powerful performances are those that are rooted in both technical mastery and a deep understanding of the human condition.

Ultimately, this connection between physical work, energy, and emotional expression becomes the core of the performing arts. The exploration of energetic expression and movement allows the performer not only to tell stories but also to touch the souls of those who watch them. This form of expression reveals the power of the body as a communication tool; through its versatility, a performer can transcend words and deliver a message that resonates with a wide range of emotions.

Kyōgen and Commedia: Two Ends of the Silk Road

Kyōgen and Commedia dell'Arte may appear worlds apart—one rooted in Zen-like subtlety, the other in expressive physical comedy—but Mangolini saw a profound commonality between them. Both traditions rely on codified physicality, ancestral rhythm, and archetypal forms. Both require a connection between breath, rhythm, and character. And both demand from the actor a complete surrender to the present (see **Figure 4.16**).

Through his article and workshops, Mangolini positioned himself as a bridge between East and West, honoring tradition while seeking resonance through the DEE Cycle: from the inner intention (Dynamis), to embodied action (Energeia), to a lived, shared result (Entelecheia).

The Energetic Body in Practice

Mangolini's exploration of **emotional expression through physical expression** offers a vivid embodiment of the DEE Cycle in action. He does not simply speak about energy—he demonstrates how it flows, implodes, resists, and transforms (see **Figure 4.17**). His sessions emphasize:

- **Koshi** as the seat of grounded dynamism.
- **Tamé** as the stillness that gathers force.
- **Hakobi** as the channeling of that force.
- **Yūgen** as the invisible aura of depth.

Together, these elements shape a performer's ability to move with

FIGURE 4.16: The Alchemy of Presence: Fabio Mangolini in Motion. Inspired by Commedia dell'Arte, this image captures the dynamic interplay of posture, gesture, and mask in Mangolini's performance. Energy does not just flow—it is sculpted, refined, and offered. Humor becomes elegance, and theatrical presence becomes a form of embodied clarity. AI-generated image created with OpenAI's DALL·E (via ChatGPT).

intention, resonance, and clarity, qualities Mangolini insists are needed not just in theatre—but in life.

The importance of these teachings and their practical application highlight the need for every artist, whether in the field of mime, theatre, or any other form of performing art, to delve into mastering their body, the codification of their movements, and the energy they choose to project. In this lies the true magic of theatre: Its capacity to transform life through the pure expression of being.

FIGURE 4.17: Lineage in Motion: Mangolini and the Masters. Fabio Mangolini's teaching builds on the foundational work of Jacques Lecoq and Marcel Marceau, extending their philosophies into a practice rooted in energy, breath, and alignment. Here, tradition is not inherited passively it is activated, carried forward through the performer's body.

Mangolini's exploration of koshi in Nō Theatre provides a fascinating insight into the importance of core stability and energy flow. But is this concept unique to Japanese performance traditions? Let's explore how similar principles might be found in other cultures, examining evidence of koshi in popular artistic manifestations around the world.

Part 2—Awakened Ground: The Reemergence of Energetic Memory Across Cultures

Revisiting Grounding and Trembling: Foundations Reawakened

By this point in the journey, the themes introduced in **Grounding and Trembling** may no longer feel abstract. The trembling of the body—not as weakness but as **release**—now echoes the purposeful shaking of Japanese koshi practices or the subtle vibrations felt in somatic performance training.

In **Bioenergetic analysis**, trembling signals the **discharge of blocked energy**, the reawakening of aliveness. It is the body's way of unfreezing the past. In **koshi**, often seen in Japanese actor training, the performer begins with bent knees, open joints, and a subtle internal shake—not just to prepare physically, but to awaken an **energetic readiness**. What emerges is not theatrical tension but **vitality in flow**.

Both systems understand that energy must be **activated through the body**, not bypassed with mental control. They agree that the pathway to true expression begins **in the legs, in the gut, in the spine**—in the **unseen undercurrent of the performer's base**.

The trembling and the koshi, then, are not separate. They are **different languages for the same truth**: The body, when allowed to vibrate, to root, to open, becomes capable of transmitting more than form. It transmits **presence**.

Echoes of Koshi in Popular Artistic Manifestations in Other Cultures

The concept of **koshi**, often explored in Japanese theatre for its emphasis on core stability and energetic alignment, is not exclusive to the East. Traces of koshi—understood as a balance between posture, energy, and expression—can be seen in a variety of global performance traditions. This section explores how koshi manifests, consciously or not, in popular artistic forms such as **flamenco** and **Bomba Puertorriqueña**, reflecting its universal applicability as a tool of expressive power.

One such example is **Gilda Navarra**, a renowned flamenco dancer whose profound stage presence can be traced back to her foundational training. Flamenco, at its core, is an art form where posture, footwork, and emotional expressiveness are tightly interwoven. Even from the earliest lessons, students learn to work from their center—developing an intuitive sense of koshi. In her performance, Navarra unconsciously embodied the principles of koshi. As she danced with implosive intensity and refined body control, her posture served as both container and conduit for explosive energy (see **Figure 4.18**).

A particularly illustrative case can be found in the YouTube video titled "Amazing Flamenco," where a dancer demonstrates the delicate equilibrium of weight, posture, and gesture. The body moves with contained energy that pulses through the hips and spine—echoing koshi's essence of centered dynamism.

But flamenco is not alone in this. From the vibrant Caribbean, we turn to **Bomba Puertorriqueña,**[12] a dance rooted in Puerto Rico's African heritage. Bomba is not known for stylized movements, yet its expressiveness is born of rhythm and resistance. The dancers engage in a **call-and-response dialogue** with the drummers, relying on **fast, controlled footwork** and a relaxed but grounded upper body (see **Figure 4.19**). It is through this balance—effortless yet engaged—that a latent koshi emerges. Their **centered posture** and ability to maintain dynamic equilibrium reveal the same alignment and control discussed in traditional Asian practices.

FIGURE 4.18: Koshi Across Cultures: Flamenco and the Energetic Spine. Navarra and a flamenco dancer *(left and center)* grounded in the pelvis, rising through breath and spinal articulation, paired with a diagram of koshi *(right)*. Though born in distinct traditions, both embody the same energetic principle: movement begins in the center, radiates outward, and returns to stillness through rhythm and control.

Though less overt than in Japanese or Indian theatre, both flamenco and bomba demonstrate that the **energetic center of the body**, when trained and accessed, becomes a **universal principle of movement**. Koshi, then, is not bound by cultural borders—it is a **felt reality** in performers across the globe who have mastered the art of energy in motion.

FIGURE 4.19: Bomba and the Embodied Pulse of Koshi. In Bomba dance, explosive footwork meets the grace of upper-body release. The dancer channels power from the pelvis, balancing tension and flow. Here, ease and intensity coexist—koshi is not named, but it is deeply known in the body's intuitive intelligence. AI-generated image created with OpenAI's DALL·E (via ChatGPT).

This shows that the concept of koshi, though expressed differently, is a fundamental principle of movement that connects diverse cultures, from European to African and Caribbean, as well as Asian. As evidenced in the discussed theatrical traditions, this principle of alignment and weight distribution in the body becomes crucial for achieving powerful and authentic expression, regardless of the cultural context.

Spinal Intelligence: Energetic Alignment Across Traditions

Posture is more than a physical arrangement—it is an energetic gateway. In the work of **Gilda Navarra**, **Fabio Mangolini**, **Scott Putman**, and **Arthur Lessac**, posture becomes the spine of transformation. Though these practitioners come from different disciplines—mime, dance, and voice—they each recognize the central role of the **spine** in aligning energy and activating presence.

Having studied with all three, and holding certifications in both **EBAS (Elemental Body Alignment System)** and **Lessac's Kinesensic Training**, I have experienced firsthand how these systems—each in its own language—guide the performer toward a deeply aligned, energetically open state.

Despite their different vocabularies, these approaches share a common core:

- **Fabio Mangolini** works with the **coccyx** as a root of awareness—anchoring movement from the very end of the spine.
- **Scott Putman,**[13] through EBAS, centers the **sacrum** as a fulcrum of stability and kinetic intelligence.
- **Arthur Lessac** speaks of **C-Curve**, the natural curvature of the spine, as a source of buoyancy, breath, and vocal energy.

What connects these three is not only anatomical focus, but a shared **energetic intention**: to awaken the body's inner structure so that movement, breath, and sound arise from **effortless alignment** (see **Figure 4.20**). Each approach, in its own way, unlocks **Dynamis**—the dormant potential of the performer's body—channels it into **Energeia**—a clear and expressive flow—and culminates in **Entelecheia**—an embodied realization of presence and poise.

While they name and approach the spine differently, the **spinal axis** becomes a shared site of transformation: a central line where the **DEE Cycle** is physically, emotionally, and energetically embodied.

These traditions invite us to consider the spine not just as structure, but as **conduit**—where intention is translated into action, and the whole body becomes available to the moment.

As we continue, we turn now to the work of **Scott Putman** and **Arthur Lessac** to explore how this **energetic axis** reveals itself further through their engagement with the Japanese concept of **koshi**, and how it informs the expressive, embodied performer.

Scott Putman and Arthur Lessac: Benefits of Koshi for Everyone

In the continuous journey of decoding energy and movement, the insights of Scott Putman (see **Figure 4.21**) and Arthur Lessac converge remarkably through their distinct but complementary approaches. Both offer frameworks that echo the principle of koshi—the dynamic center from which expressive power radiates. Their work reveals that energy flow and alignment are not abstract concepts, but physical realities grounded in anatomical and experiential understanding.

Scott Putman, a renowned figure in dance and movement education, developed the Elemental Body Alignment System (EBAS), which he explains in *Aligning the Pathways Within*. His framework centers on the **Energy Triangles of the Body**, articulated through three interconnected principles:

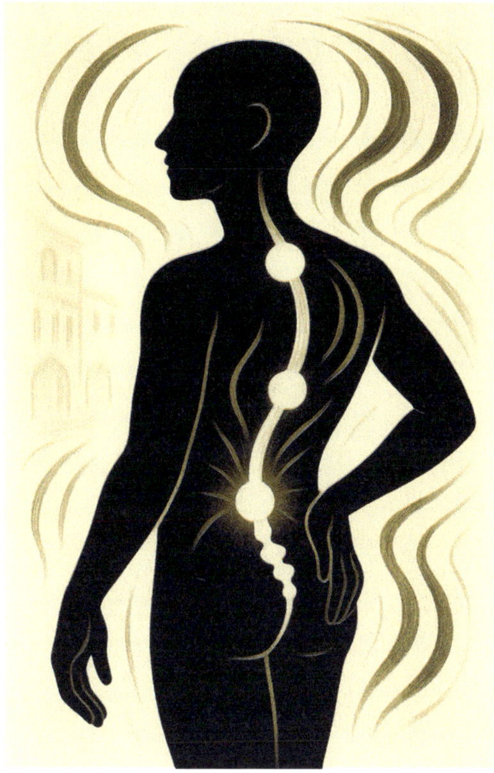

FIGURE 4.20: Awakening Inner Structure: Alignment as Energetic Source. This image evokes the moment when the body reorganizes from within—when movement, breath, and voice no longer emerge from control, but from alignment. In this state, presence becomes effortless, and expression arises not from force, but from flow. AI-generated image created with OpenAI's DALL·E (via ChatGPT).

1. **Centerline:** A vertical force of alignment passing through the body's center, beginning in the sacrum. It divides the body and provides an anchor for movement, mirroring the alignment cultivated through koshi awareness.
2. **Blood Flushing:** Also described as "energy circulation," this principle emphasizes the fluid movement of energy through the body to release tension and promote well-being.
3. **Triangulation:** This spatial principle orients the body around dynamically structured triangles, especially the **Triangle of the Sacred Source (Sacrum)**, which functions as a vortex stabilizing movement and allowing energy to flow vertically.

FIGURE 4.21: Scott Putman: Creator of EBAS and Architect of Spinal Flow. A pioneer of Elemental Body Alignment System (EBAS), Scott Putman brings breath, structure, and intuitive movement into alignment. His work echoes the principles of koshi and Energeia, centering the spine as a channel of flow rather than rigidity.

Together, these principles (see **Figure 4.22**) culminate in a system that, leading to expressive, efficient, and balanced movement—what we might describe through the DEE Cycle as the transformation of **Dynamis** into **Energeia**, reaching **Entelecheia** in performance.

In practice, both EBAS and Kinesensics guide the performer toward deeper self-awareness, control, and expressive freedom. Their combined wisdom highlights the universality of koshi—not just as a concept rooted in Japanese performance, but as a cross-disciplinary foundation for movement and expression.

From my own perspective, having experienced and trained in both methodologies, I affirm that there is no substantial difference in the alignment they aim to achieve. Whether accessed through Putman's triangles or Lessac's C-Curve: an integrated performer capable of channeling energy with presence, clarity, and authenticity.

Both researchers and performers (Mangolini and Putman) focus their work on finding tools that help artists from different fields achieve high levels of performance while reducing the likelihood of injuries.

In relation to this approach, Arthur Lessac identifies a similar posture called C-Curve, which derives from the Curvo-Linear Principle, offering both physical and mental benefits (Lessac 1990: 158). The C-Curve relates to koshi because it emphasizes the importance of spinal alignment and core stability. The Curvo-Linear Principle challenges the traditional conception of the spine. Lessac invites us to imagine it as an elongated arc ")" instead of a S-shaped curve. This approach is based on observing babies and their postures, who are naturally not influenced by rigid patterns or habits. Lessac also emphasizes that by exploring balance through the combination of breathing and the C-Curve of the back (see **Figure 4.23**), one experiences a sensation of falling with each movement; achieving to "live" in this posture allows the performer to

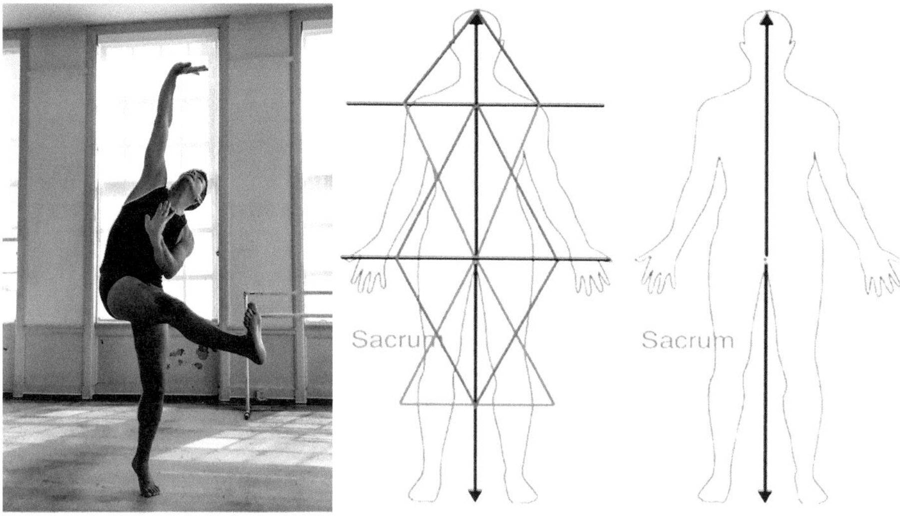

FIGURE 4.22: Koshi in Action: Scott Putman and the Architecture of Alignment. *(left)* Scott Putman in performance, embodying koshi-driven flow where breath, structure, and emotion converge. (Photo credit: Barbara Shore). *(center)* A visual representation of Triangulation—the body's ability to find support through dynamic spatial awareness. *(right)* A diagram of Centerline—illustrating vertical alignment from koshi to crown, the axis of energetic balance in movement and stillness.

be present onstage. The sensation of falling, doesn't this echo the "Grounding and Trembling" we encountered in Bioenergetics?

In Lessac's book, we can observe that the sensation of the C-Curve is not just about elongating the spine toward the sky but also about the posture of the spine arising as a result of bent knees. The description of "bending the knees" serves as a common point among the three physical postures proposed by the researchers. Bent knees allow for movement and control of the pelvis, coccyx, and sacrum. The sensation of rising completes the posture. Both Lessac and Mangolini recognize the positive influence of this sensation on the voice. In fact, Lessac extended his training to voice work starting from a simple exercise that recalls the C-Curve and connects it with breathing (Lessac 1997).

Reflection: A Shared Center, a Shared Breath

Whether expressed through Putman's sacred triangles, Lessac's C-Curve, or the koshi of Japanese performance, what emerges is a shared understanding:

The **body is not merely an instrument of movement, but a center of energetic intelligence**. In all three systems, energy originates in the **sacral axis**—a place of instinct, emotion, and potential. And from there, it rises. This is not metaphor but **somatic reality**. The subtle shift of the pelvis, the soft bend of the knees, the elongation of the spine—these are not technical corrections. They are gateways. Gateways to breathe, to voice, to presence. To **Energeia**.

And in each of these systems, we also find the echo of **trembling and grounding**—the body alive, charged, present, yet humble. Lessac's falling sensation, Putman's vortex of triangulation, and Mangolini's anatomical awareness all point to the same truth: **Expression is born from balance**, not tension. These methods do more than teach alignment—they **reveal how alignment awakens energy** (see **Figure 4.24**).

As we transition from these embodied frameworks into the work of **Eugenio Barba**, we move from internal architecture to external theatrical tradition. Yet what remains constant is the same inquiry: How can the performer stand onstage and become a **living conduit of transformation**?

FIGURE 4.23: Arthur Lessac demonstrating the C-Curve, a core element of his body training rooted in the curvo-lineal principle. His softly bent knees and rounded spine reflect dynamic alignment—supporting energetic flow, breath resonance, and a grounded yet mobile presence. Image courtesy of Deborah Kinghorn and Lessac Institute; archival details not provided.

Part 3—Reframing Tradition: Barba's Anthropology and the Pitfalls of Orientalism

The Premise of Barba's Inquiry

As we transition from embodied frameworks into the work of Eugenio Barba, we shift from internal architecture to external theatrical tradition. Yet the central question remains: How can the performer stand onstage and become a living conduit of transformation?

Barba, a towering figure in contemporary theatre theory, offers a compelling yet contested approach to this question. His foundational text, *The Secret Art of the Performer* (1982), and the establishment of the International School of Theatre Anthropology (ISTA) marked a global turn in performance studies. Rooted in cross-cultural comparison, Barba's work seeks to identify the universal principles of theatrical behavior. But this very ambition invites critical scrutiny, particularly when these universals emerge from frameworks that risk simplifying or misrepresenting cultural specificity.

FIGURE 4.24: A Luminous Body in Motion: Grounded Radiance. This figure embodies the union of alignment and expression, breath and balance, presence and transformation. Grounded in the sacrum, energy radiates from within—revealing that true movement begins not at the surface, but at the center. The body becomes light, not by reaching—but by remembering. AI-generated image created with OpenAI's DALL·E (via ChatGPT).

The Genesis of Theatre Anthropology

Barba's exploration began in 1963 with his immersion in Indian Kathakali and continued through the creation of Odin Teatret (1964) and ISTA (1979). His vision fused performer training with anthropological insight, leading to a hybrid model he termed "Theatre Anthropology": the study of extra-daily behavior across global performance traditions.

ISTA's publications, filled with over 700 images alongside text, develop a compelling visual grammar that codifies performer behavior through global analogies. However, this comparative method often relies on surface similarities without fully interrogating the cultural, spiritual, and technical depth of each form. They are designs, structures, and movements that repeat and seem to have a common origin, but this does not imply that we can make such a broad assertion about the principles that regulate stage behavior.

Codification and the Risk of Omission

A major feature of Barba's theory is the concept of *extra-daily* techniques—stylized, intentional behaviors that depart from ordinary movement. He credits Asian traditions like Nō, Kathakali, and Chinese Opera with embodying these codified forms and positions Etienne Decroux as the only Western analogue.

Conspicuously absent are foundational Western contributors such as François Delsarte, **Rudolf von Laban**,[14] and Jacques Copeau. Delsarte's *System of Expression*, Laban's effort theory and spatial movement analysis, and Copeau's influence on corporeal mime present a rich, codified Western lineage. Gilda Navarra, for instance, identified Copeau as the first practitioner she witnessed using expressive systems.

By omitting these figures, Barba constructs a dichotomy: the East is structured and sacred, while the West is spontaneous and lacking. This false binary not only erases Western rigor but also exoticizes eastern traditions, obscuring their complexity in favor of symbolic utility.

Why does Barba not include the work and analysis of Delsarte or Laban in his work? This omission is significant when tracing the lineage of expressive systems.

Misreading the *Natyashastra*: Lokadharmi and Natyadharmi

Barba frequently cites the *Natyashastra*[15] book by Bharata Muni,[16] interpreting Lokadharmi and Natyadharmi as behaviors of the same actor inside and outside of performance. Indian scholars have firmly challenged this. Dr. Smt. Shukla[17] (2013) clarifies that these terms denote two distinct theatrical forms: Lokadharmi represents naturalistic presentation; Natyadharmi refers to stylized and symbolic performance.

> The Hindu theorist [referring to Bharata Muni] from the earliest days conceived plays in terms of two types of production: Lokadharmi-realistic, that is the reproduction of human behavior on stage and the natural presentation of objects, and Natyadharmi-conventional, which is the presentation of a play through the use of stylized gestures and symbolism and was considered more artistic than the realistic mode.
>
> (Shukla 2013: n.pag.)

Dr. Manomohan Ghosh,[18] whose 1951 English translation of the *Natyashastra* remains definitive, supports this reading:

> The practice of representation (dharml) 1 in a dramatic performance has two aspects: realistic (lokadharmi, lit. popular) and conventional (natyadharmi, lit. theatrical).
> (Muni 1951: n.pag.)

The misinterpretation stems in part from Barba's reliance on anecdotal definitions, such as those offered by Indian dancer Sanjukta Panigrahi, rather than academic consensus. Barba is not referring to a type of theatrical production, but rather to an ordinary person outside the theatre. This argument has been refuted by the last two Indian scholars.

Energy Lost in Translation: Entelecheia versus Exertion

Barba often contrasts "Western waste" with "Eastern efficiency" in energy use, yet paradoxically praises the latter for its excess. His definition of energy as "muscular and nervous strength" deviates from both Aristotle's concept of *Energeia* and traditional Eastern frameworks like the Yi–Chi–Li (Intention–Energy–Manifestation) cycle.

Fabio Mangolini, Scott Putman, Arthur Lessac, and others offer a more accurate application: energy is dynamic yet focused, sourced from koshi or the sacral spine, rising through alignment and breath. Mangolini's integration of *koshi* avoids Barba's reduction of the term to "hips" and challenges his claim that locking joints produces presence. Instead, energy arises from flow, not friction (see **Figure 4.25**).

Energeia is internal coherence, not external display. Presence emerges through subtlety, not tension. Barba's interpretation conflates Energeia with Entelecheia, creating confusion for students and perpetuating reductive techniques that prioritize effort over attunement.

Kung Fu Master Cheuk Fung offers clarity (n.d.: n.pag.):

> Chi is just a concept, just a word used to represent the energy that is truly there ... From a Western

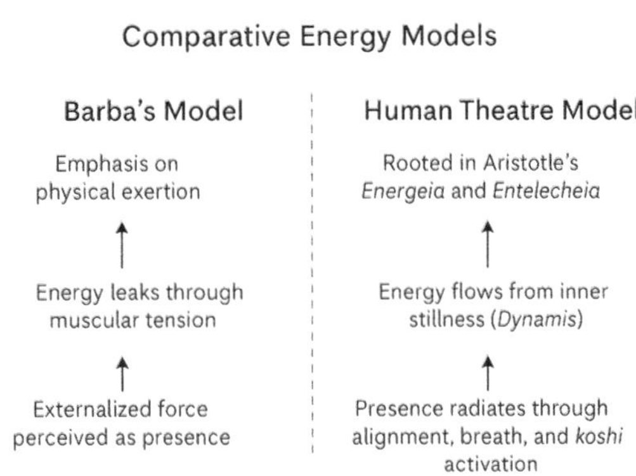

FIGURE 4.25: Two Energies, Two Paradigms: Exertion versus Entelecheia. This diagram contrasts Barba's model of performance energy—defined by external tension, muscular control, and visible effort—with the Entelecheia-based flow of Human Theatre, where energy arises from alignment, intention, and inner coherence. These are not merely styles—they are different understandings of how presence is generated, received, and sustained. AI-generated image created with OpenAI's DALL·E (via ChatGPT).

> perspective, you could say it's like that conservation thing ... we are studying how intention directs human potential energy to transform into bioelectric nervous system energy and ultimately into mechanical energy in muscles.

Energetic presence, in the Human Theatre approach, emerges not from exaggerated gesture but from inner stillness and concentrated intent.

Convergence or Confusion? Visual Analogies and Universal Codes

In *L'arte segreta dell'attore* (*The Secret Art of the Performer*), Barba includes numerous visual comparisons to argue for transcultural similarity—placing side by side Aztec dancers, Odissi performers, and Commedia dell'Arte actors. However, these comparisons often rest solely on posture and aesthetic composition, without engaging the deep training, purpose, or energetic mechanisms behind them.

This raises the issue of what might be termed **convergence of movement**: the recurring appearance of certain forms or gestures across different traditions not because of shared origins, but because those forms serve functional needs. Just as wings evolved independently in birds and bats (convergent evolution[19]), so too might similar theatrical postures arise across cultures for practical reasons—not from a universal code.

These stylizations of actions are present in different art styles for religious, political, or social reasons, but not for common universal principles. The similarity in the execution of a stylized action does not mean that those principles are the same.

Barba's attempts to universalize based on visual similarities often ignore these deeper energetic principles. For example, Mangolini and others emphasize that true presence arises from energetic preparation and inner alignment, not outward mimicry. Barba's own diagrams, while suggestive, risk being reductive when used to imply shared meaning across disparate practices.

The DEE Cycle, which integrates intention, internal flow, and physical manifestation, offers a more comprehensive lens for comparison. Through this model, one can distinguish between superficial similarities and genuine common ground rooted in embodied experience.

Reframing Presence, Balance, and Suspension

Barba's model equates presence with micro-tensions and displacement. In contrast, traditional forms such as Japanese Nō and Indian dance generate presence through stillness, alignment, and inner resonance. The Human Theatre approach, informed by Mangolini and others, sees presence as *Energeia*: focused, intentional, and energetically sustained.

Balance, in Barba's view, is something to be disrupted for dramatic effect. But many traditions treat balance as a spiritual and functional center—a state of harmony, not instability. Suspension, likewise, is misunderstood: not muscular arrest, but breath-driven pause, where movement is held in potential, not forced into rigidity.

An actor standing feet firmly on the stage can be much more present than someone striking certain poses. Presence is not in the posture alone—it is in the energetic intention that animates it.

Orientalism in Theory and Practice

Edward[20] Said's *Orientalism* (1978) critiques how the West constructs the East as mystical, exotic, and inferior, creating a cultural imbalance that justified colonial dominance. Barba, despite his admiration for Asian forms, falls into this very trap. Barba, while inspired by the East, risks reproducing this exoticism.

Statements like "the Western actor lacks rules" reinforce a stereotype of Western spontaneity versus Eastern discipline. Barba praises Asian traditions for codification but simplifies their diversity. Scholars like Diego Pellecchia[21] and Prado Bernat Castany[22] caution that this contributes to epistemic distortion: future scholars might inherit a mythologized, misleading canon.

> Barba tends to idealize Zeami when, as Zarrilli has suggested, he does not acknowledge that even in Asian traditions there are many practitioners who certainly do not reach the highest peaks in the "presence" to which Barba is fascinated.
>
> (Pellecchia 2011: 170)

Pellecchia questions whether Barba possesses the tools to accurately assess the quality of performers invited to ISTA symposiums—an issue reminiscent of Mnouchkine's reflections after viewing Kabuki actors during her trip to Japan. Following Bourdieu's theory of art reception as contextually bound and socio-historically situated, Pellecchia suggests that Barba and Mnouchkine risk overstepping their jurisdiction by passing artistic judgment on forms whose cultural codes they may not fully understand.

It is worth noting that Pellecchia's critique refers to an earlier 1988 edition of Barba's work. In the 2011 edition of *The Secret Art of the Performer*—the version referenced in this study—Barba does recognize that not every Asian performer reaches the highest standards of technical and energetic mastery. However, the work continues to mix these discussions with cultural and spiritual generalizations. Notably, Barba's persistent attempts to define "energy" in theatrical terms remain interwoven with culturally and religiously specific concepts, reinforcing a universalist view that glosses over critical nuances.

This confusion extends to Barba's conceptualization of "everyday" and "non-everyday" techniques. Barba defines "everyday techniques" as the minimal use of energy conditioned by culture, profession, and social status, while "non-everyday techniques" are marked by a "waste of energy." However, equating cultural embodiment with trained technique misrepresents how cultural patterns shape unconscious behaviors rather than rehearsed skills. Culture does not train; it inscribes—deeply, subtly, and variably. This misunderstanding muddies the energetic clarity proposed by traditions such as those outlined by Mangolini, Putnam, Navarra, and Lessac.

Further, Barba's definition of energy—centered on muscular and nervous strength—reduces energy to biomechanical effort. This view conflicts with the Dynamis → Energeia → Entelecheia (DEE) Cycle, which defines energy as the intention that becomes action through a controlled internal process. Kung Fu Master Cheuk Fung affirms this energetic process using Eastern terminology: Yi (intention) as Dynamis, Chi as Energeia (nervous/bioelectric activity), and Li as Entelecheia (muscular manifestation). The DEE and YCL cycles offer a meeting point between Eastern and Western views, grounded in both experience and philosophy. Energeia, then, is not what is seen—it is what animates what is seen.

Barba's failure to distinguish between Energeia and Entelecheia leads to misinterpretation. Mangolini, after exposure to Nō Theatre in Japan, recognized this problem early: energy is not theatrical exaggeration but internal coherence and radiance. The danger lies in how these misunderstandings are handed down to students, as seen in the thesis of Maria Alessia Sini, who reproduces Barba's formulations without critically engaging his assumptions. She affirms Barba's claim that Oriental actors expend great energy to achieve presence, even in simple gestures—a view contradicting energy-efficient, breath-centered practices in many traditions.

Ultimately, Barba's universalism imposes a conceptual uniformity onto theatrical practices deeply rooted in localized ritual, history, and sacred expression. Castany, in *Edward W. Said: Orientalismo* (*Edward W. Said: Orientalism*), underscores this risk: Portraying Eastern theatre as static or monolithic undermines its evolution and complexity.

Final Reflections on the Chapter

In this chapter, we have critically explored the **energetic body** through the contributions of various thinkers and practitioners, highlighting not only technical insights but also epistemological risks in how we frame and transmit embodied knowledge.

We began with **Todd Farley**, whose Mimeistry technique exemplifies codified movement infused with spiritual intentionality. From there, we examined **Gilda Navarra**, a visionary artist who fused mime, ballet, Physical Theatre and flamenco within Puerto Rican theatre, showing how hybrid languages can emerge from deep cultural integration. **Fabio Mangolini**, building on European and Asian traditions, gave us tools to perceive balance not as stillness or display but as a living dynamic between **koshi** (tension) and **Energeia** (directed energy), forming part of the DEE Cycle. These voices offer more than techniques—they offer systems of embodied knowledge grounded in cultural and personal specificity.

We then turned to **Eugenio Barba**, whose legacy in Theatre Anthropology is undeniably influential. However, his universalist framing and selective use of sources raise vital questions about **representation, cultural appropriation, and Orientalism**. Through the analysis of his terminology—*extra-daily*, *energy*, *presence*, and more—we encountered a pattern of generalization that risks flattening the richness of non-Western traditions into consumable theory. This critique was not aimed at rejecting Barba's contribution, but rather at refining and contextualizing it within a broader, more responsible understanding of intercultural exchange.

Where Barba sees codification as a mark of the "Orient," this chapter has reclaimed codification as a **choice**, not a cultural essence. Codification becomes a **tool**, not a prison—a way to focus intention, not to restrict freedom. Through the lenses of **Putman**, **Lessac**, and **Kung Fu Master Cheuk Fung**, we see energy not as exertion or theatricality, but as the transmission of intention (Dynamis) through the body (Energeia) into realized presence (Entelecheia).

Ultimately, this chapter does not simply critique—it offers a reorientation. The energetic body, as understood here, is not just a theatrical instrument. It is a **site of dialogue** between traditions, a **vessel of intention**, and a **bridge between cultures** when treated with care, accuracy, and embodied knowledge. As such, the responsibility of the performer, teacher, and scholar is not to universalize, but to **contextualize**—to honor both tradition and innovation, theory and practice, presence and principle.

NOTES

1. Pidgin English refers to a simplified form of language that develops as a means of communication between groups who do not share a common language. It typically blends elements of English with local languages and emerges in contexts of trade, colonization, or migration. While often viewed as "broken" English, pidgins follow consistent grammatical rules and can evolve into fully developed creole languages over time.
2. Étienne Decroux, a prominent figure in the evolution of modern mime, is often referred to as the "father of modern mime." Born in Paris, Decroux studied at Jacques Copeau's École du Vieux-Colombier, where he developed a profound fascination with corporeal mime. This passion led him to shape it into a rigorous art form distinct from traditional pantomime. Decroux's approach emphasized natural movements and controlled physical

actions, resulting in a unique vocabulary and philosophy centered on the significance of the body in theatrical expression. His teachings resonated with many, including the legendary mime Marcel Marceau, and his influence spread globally. In 1940, Decroux established a mime school in Paris and conducted workshops across Europe and New York. His legacy continues to profoundly impact physical theatre and mime in the present day.

3. Marcel Marceau (1923–2007), a legendary French mime artist and actor, revolutionized the art of mime, bringing it to a global audience. His iconic character, Bip the Clown, with its white face paint, striped shirt, and top hat, embodied humor and poignant storytelling. Marceau's work transcended language, using physicality and expressive gestures to convey complex emotions and narratives. He performed in theatres, films, and television, and taught mime, elevating it to a respected artistic expression.
4. Christian mime as it would be referred to in this case would be mime performed in a Christian context with a Christian worldview. "Christian mime" is consider "Christian" when performed by a believing Christian, on a topic accepted as a "Christian" topic (i.e., a Biblical story or Truth, a Christian moral, a story of Christian faith or Christian life and engagement in this world) (Farley 2017).
5. Dance-theatre movement blends dance and theatre to tell stories and express emotions through physicality, gesture, and space, creating powerful, embodied narratives.
6. Martha Graham, a pioneer of modern dance, revolutionized movement with her expressive technique and bold themes drawn from mythology, literature, and history. Founder of the Martha Graham Dance Company, her influence continues to shape dance and the performing arts worldwide.
7. Jacques Lecoq, a renowned French actor, teacher, and director, pioneered physical theatre and actor training. He founded the École Internationale de Théâtre Jacques Lecoq in Paris, emphasizing movement, improvisation, and the physical body in performance. Lecoq explored play dynamics, the actor-audience relationship, and integrating mime, masks, and storytelling. His methodologies encouraged actors to express themselves physically, fostering creativity and spontaneity. Lecoq's influence globally impacts performers, directors, and theatre practitioners, and his teachings continue to resonate in contemporary theatre arts.
8. Carlo Boso, an acclaimed Italian actor, director, and teacher, founded Les Scalzacani, a performance company that explores traditional theatre forms with contemporary elements. Under his direction, Les Scalzacani's vibrant productions celebrate Commedia dell'Arte through innovative storytelling, dynamic characters, and improvisational techniques. The company emphasizes physicality, humor, and audience interaction, creating an immersive experience that honors the roots of Commedia dell'Arte while making it accessible to modern audiences. Boso's work inspires new generations of performers and theatre enthusiasts, celebrating Commedia dell'Arte's enduring appeal.
9. Nomura Kosuke, a distinguished Japanese actor, is a leading figure in Kyōgen, a Japanese comic theatre, dating back to the fourteenth century, that developed alongside the more

solemn and stylized Nō drama. While Nō often explores themes of spirituality, memory, and ritual, Kyogen offers a contrasting tone—lighthearted, humorous, and grounded in everyday human behavior. Typically performed between Nō plays, Kyogen serves both as a counterbalance and a complement, emphasizing rhythm, vocal clarity, and codified gesture in ways that align with the principles of energetic performance. As a leading figure in Kyōgen, Kosuke has contributed to its preservation and modernization, performing traditional and contemporary plays, teaching, and promoting it internationally, ensuring its relevance in the global theatre landscape.

10. Nō Theatre is a traditional form of Japanese performance that combines stylized movement, music, and chant to explore spiritual and emotional themes. Originating in the fourteenth century, it emphasizes minimalism, symbolic gestures, and the use of masks to express universal human experiences.
11. Izumi School, a prominent Kyōgen school, has preserved and promoted this unique theatrical art form. It emphasizes traditional techniques, expressive physicality, and comedic nuances. Under Kosuke's leadership, the school performs classic Kyōgen plays and educates new actors in its principles and practices. By balancing tradition with innovation, the Izumi School revitalizes and appreciates Kyōgen in japan and internationally.
12. Bomba Puertorriqueña is a traditional Puerto Rican music and dance genre that originated from African's slaves cultural influences and is characterized by its vibrant rhythms and improvisational nature. It typically features live drumming, with the dancers responding to the beat in a call-and-response fashion, creating a dynamic interaction between the musicians and performers. The dance reflects the rich cultural heritage of Puerto Rico, expressing themes of resistance, celebration, and community identity. Bomba is not only a form of entertainment but also a way to connect with the island's history and heritage, often performed during festivals and cultural gatherings. Its energetic movements and rhythms make it an effective practice for releasing pent-up emotions and promoting joy and physical expression.
13. Scott Putman, a respected figure in dance and movement training, developed the EBAS (Elemental Body Alignment System) method. EBAS exercises improve structural integrity and range of motion. Through anchoring and initiating movements via the pelvis, the body learns efficient movement through experiential anatomy. The system enhances students' understanding of movement origins, body alignment, and physical consciousness of energy pathways. It overrides the central nervous system, creating new neuromuscular firings that support a greater understanding of sensorial technique.
14. Rudolf von Laban was a Hungarian choreographer, movement theorist, and one of the most influential figures in the development of modern dance and physical theatre. He created Laban Movement Analysis (LMA) and the Effort Theory, systems that decode the qualitative and spatial dimensions of human movement. Laban's work laid the groundwork for movement training across dance, theatre, therapy, and education—emphasizing the expressive and communicative potential of the body. His system continues to inform actor training programs and somatic practices worldwide.

15. *Natyashastra*, an ancient Indian treatise attributed to the sage Bharata Muni, dates back to 200 BCE to 200 CE. It's a foundational text for classical Indian dance and theatre, detailing performance principles like gestures, facial expressions, rhythm, and music. The *Natyashastra* teaches storytelling through movement and expression, emphasizing the fusion of drama, dance, and music to evoke emotions. It preserves traditional Indian arts and underscores the spiritual and cultural significance of performance as a means of connecting to the divine and expressing human experience.
16. Bharata Muni, revered in Indian cultural history, is traditionally credited with writing the *Natyashastra*, an ancient Sanskrit text on performing arts. Believed to have lived between 200 BCE and 200 CE, he's often called the "father of Indian dramaturgy." His work systematically codifies performance principles, aesthetics, and storytelling power, shaping classical Indian theatre and dance. Bharata Muni's insights into emotions (RASA) and art's role in society continue to resonate in contemporary Indian and global artistic practices and studies.
17. Dr. Shukla, a distinguished scholar and educator, founded the *Rupkatha Journal on Interdisciplinary Studies in Humanities*, a peer-reviewed academic journal that promotes dialogue and research across various disciplines. Her work emphasizes the importance of interdisciplinary approaches in understanding complex social and cultural phenomena, encouraging scholars to integrate diverse perspectives. Dr. Shukla's commitment to academic excellence and innovation has significantly impacted the scholarly community.
18. Dr. Manomohan Ghosh, a distinguished Indian sanskritist, historian, and literary translator, made significant scholarly contributions to classical Indian literature and performing arts. His most notable work is the translation of the *Natyashastra*, an ancient treatise on Hindu dramaturgy and histrionics by Bharata Muni, published in 1951 by the Asiatic Society of Bengal. This translation provided the first complete English version of the foundational text, outlining essential principles of performance. Dr. Ghosh also authored numerous historical writings and translations, including *Abhinayadarpanam* by Nandikeshwar, a manual on hindu dance and drama, and *Glimpses of Sexual Life in Nanda-Maurya India*, a translation of the Caturbhāṇī. He also wrote *A History of Cambodia from the Earliest Times to the End of the French Protectorate* and *Contributions to the History of the Hindu Drama*. Dr. Ghosh's academic rigor and expertise made his work invaluable, and his article "On the Source of the Old-Javanese Ramayana Kakawin" is often cited by scholars, further establishing his impact on the study of Sanskrit literature and performing arts.
19. Convergent evolution is a biological phenomenon in which species that are not closely related independently evolve similar traits or behaviors in response to comparable environmental pressures or ecological conditions. Though evolutionarily distant, organisms living in similar environments may develop analogous adaptations—nature "replicates" advantageous structures because, over time, biological systems with traits beneficial to survival and reproduction tend to prevail. This process, driven by genetic variability and natural selection, not only explains specific adaptations but also accounts for the emergence

of similar solutions across different evolutionary paths. In a broader conceptual sense, it can also describe how similar methods or practices emerge in different artistic, cultural, or theoretical traditions despite distinct origins.

20. Edward Said was a Palestinian-American literary theorist and cultural critic. His seminal work *Orientalism* (1978) critiques the West's historical representations of the East, arguing that Western depictions of "the Orient" served to justify colonial domination by constructing the East as exotic, backward, and inferior. the book launched postcolonial studies as a critical field and continues to influence scholarship in literature, history, and cultural theory.
21. Diego Pellecchia, a renowned scholar and researcher in theatre studies, particularly in the field of traditional Japanese Nō Theatre, has made significant contributions to the study of its reception and interpretation in Western contexts. His work, titled *Aesthetics and Ethics in the Reception of Nō Theatre in the West*, delves into the intricate interplay between aesthetic appreciation and ethical considerations in how Nō Theatre has been received and adapted by Western audiences and practitioners. Pellecchia's analysis goes beyond mere surface-level observations, exploring the cultural nuances and philosophical underpinnings of Nō, shedding light on its unique qualities and the challenges inherent in translating its cultural significance across diverse artistic traditions. Through his scholarship, Pellecchia enriches the discourse surrounding the global appreciation of traditional theatre forms and contributes to a deeper understanding of the profound impact of cultural exchange on performance art.
22. Prado Bernat Castany, a prominent scholar and critic, has made significant contributions to literary and cultural studies, particularly postcolonial theory. His most notable work, *Edward W. Said: Orientalismo*, analyzes Said's groundbreaking text, *Orientalism.* In this seminal work, Said critiques the Western portrayal of Eastern societies and explores the implications of these representations on cultural perceptions and power dynamics. Castany's analysis provides valuable insights into said's arguments and the enduring influence of orientalism on literature and social thought. His scholarship contributes to a deeper understanding of cultural interactions and the responsibility of representation in the global context.

Chapter 5

The Energetic Performer: From Within to Without

5

The Energetic Performer: From Within to Without

Part 1—Towards an Organic Entelecheia

The Foundations of Organic Presence

In theatre, behavior must not be acted—it must be lived. The performer who dominates the DEE Cycle, who truly embodies Desire, channels Energeia, and produces a clear Effect, will not merely imitate life—they will generate it. When this internal cycle is fully understood and correctly activated, the result is an organic performance: a sequence of actions and reactions that feel real, fluid, and spontaneous, even within the highly structured context of the stage.

The term *organic* has often been used to describe this kind of authenticity, yet its true meaning remains elusive unless understood through the energetic mechanics behind it. An organic performance is not one that mimics reality, but one that emerges from within the performer's lived experience, emotional memory, and physical impulse. It is a result of training, awareness, and the conscious application of techniques that, once absorbed into the subconscious, allow the performer to respond truthfully in real time.

Here, we re-enter the body not as a passive recipient of codified rules, but as a living field of dynamic transformation. The DEE Cycle—Dynamis → Energeia → Entelecheia—is no longer a philosophical abstraction but a roadmap to presence. The body, trained not to perform but to *listen*, begins to register subtle shifts in tension, breath, and energetic radiance. This is the journey **from within to without**: from internal decision (Dynamis), through electric activation (Energeia), toward complete, organic action (Entelecheia).

FIGURE 5.0: Gesture Becoming Form. From somatic sensation, the hand emerges to speak. Gesture becomes form—the visible trace of the performer's inner landscape. AI-generated image created with OpenAI's DALL·E (via ChatGPT).

Actors become a vessel of pure communication. They respond not from forced intention, but from internal necessity, allowing their actions to resonate deeply with the audience. This state of responsiveness—the ability to receive, process, and return energy through action—is at the heart of both the DEE Cycle and what we call organic theatre.

The Organic Performer: Where Technique Becomes Instinct

Technique, in this context, does not mean repetition. It means refinement. The organic performer is not someone who follows rules, but someone who has internalized principles so completely that they become **instinctual responses**. Like a martial artist responding to movement or a musician flowing through improvisation, the performer becomes an embodied intelligence.

This is the space in which the performer's **presence becomes radiant**. Not because of external effort, but because of internal coherence. The koshi grounds the spine, breath flows through the torso, and the mind is no longer separate from the body—it is felt as part of the gesture. The audience doesn't just see movement—they *feel* intention.

This chapter will explore the foundations of this concept, beginning with the work of **Konstantin Stanislavski**. He was the first to advocate for a theatre rooted in lived emotion and real behavior, laying the groundwork for a lineage of practitioners—from André Casaca to Alexander Lowen—who would expand this idea across physical, psychological, and philosophical dimensions. Together, we will examine how the organic actor is not born, but cultivated through a process of inner discovery, disciplined training, and a deep reconnection with instinct.

Let us now trace the origins of this organic approach, and revisit Stanislavski—not only as a director or method founder, but also as the initiator of a performance philosophy grounded in the living essence of human truth.

Konstantin Stanislavski: Founder of the Idea of an Organic Theatre

Konstantin Stanislavski was a Russian actor, director, and theatre theorist who transformed the art of performance and laid the foundations for what we now consider modern, psychologically grounded acting. Dissatisfied with the stylized, declamatory traditions of the nineteenth century, Stanislavski developed a comprehensive system for actors to create truthful, emotionally resonant performances. His approach emphasized **"living the part"**—not merely imitating or demonstrating emotion, but experiencing it sincerely and organically through the body, breath, and imagination.

At the core of Stanislavski's system was the principle that **internal impulses and physical actions are inseparable**. His techniques—including the use of affective memory, the "magic if," and a rigorous attention to physical and psychological preparation—shifted the actor's work from external mimicry to internal authenticity. He believed the actor's task was not to represent a character, but to embody it truthfully within the given circumstances of the play. This vision laid the groundwork for later schools of thought in both Europe and the United States, including Method Acting and many contemporary somatic approaches to performance.

Despite his revolutionary insights, however, Stanislavski's concept of "experiencing" (*perezhivanie*) has often been misunderstood as a purely psychological process, downplaying the **energetic and embodied dimensions** that enable a performer to truly live onstage. Scholar and practitioner **Alberto Castañeda** addresses this limitation by reframing perezhivanie[1] (living through, see **Figure 5.1**) in somatic terms. For Castañeda, the actor does not merely experience emotion intellectually, but engages the body as a vital site of memory, imagination, and transformation. To fully grasp Stanislavski's method, he argues, we must consider both emotional memory and **kinesthetic intelligence**.

This reevaluation aligns Stanislavski more closely with what we now understand through the **DEE Cycle**. What begins as internal impulse (**Dynamis**) gathers momentum through emotional resonance and body awareness (**Energeia**), culminating in expressive, embodied action (**Entelecheia**). Rather than viewing Stanislavski's system as outdated or overly psychological, Castañeda repositions it as an early articulation of what we now call **energetic presence**.

Adding complexity to this discussion is **Eugenio Barba**'s interpretation of organic theatre, which attempts to distinguish "organic" behavior from codified or mechanical performance. However, Barba tends to use the term ambiguously, often associating it with instinctual or non-Western behaviors, yet failing to define the energetic mechanisms underlying them. In this way, Barba's vision overlaps with—but also diverges from—the integrative

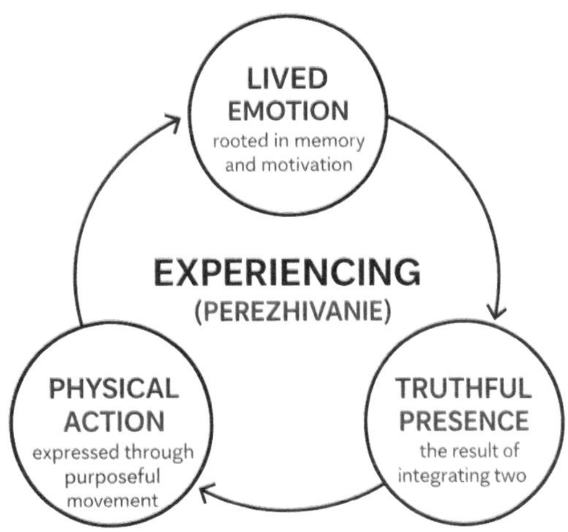

FIGURE 5.1: Stanislavski's Organic Cycle: Perezhivanie in Motion. This diagram illustrates Stanislavski's concept of perezhivanie—a cyclical process in which lived emotion, physical action, and truthful presence feed one another to generate authentic behavior onstage. In this model, performance is not representation but transformation: emotion becomes motion, and motion awakens meaning. AI-generated image created with OpenAI's DALL·E (via ChatGPT).

approach traced in this chapter. Where Castañeda emphasizes the body as the **thinking-feeling source** of experience, Barba leans toward external manifestations of presence, at times risking a return to the surface-level codification that Stanislavski sought to move beyond.

By placing Stanislavski in conversation with both Castañeda and Barba, we begin to see the emergence of a **deeper framework**—one that understands organic acting not as mystery or style, but as a tangible, trainable interplay of **impulse, energy, and embodied clarity**.

Konstantin Stanislavski revolutionized modern acting by shifting its foundation from artificial gesture and declamation to lived behavior and psychological truth. He proposed that an actor's role was not to simulate emotion but to genuinely experience and embody it onstage. This transformation laid the groundwork for what we now recognize as *organic performance*—a state in which the actor does not act, but exists truthfully within the circumstances of the role (see **Figure 5.2**).

At the core of Stanislavski's system is the belief that physical actions and internal impulses are inextricably linked. His notion of "experiencing" a role meant that actors had to draw from personal memory, bodily awareness, and emotional truth. Rather than project a rehearsed persona, the performer must live *in the moment*, discovering each action anew through what he called the *magic if*—a technique that asks: "What would I do if I were in this situation?"

This approach marked a profound departure from the formalized theatrical traditions of his time, aligning instead with an emerging understanding of the body as a responsive, intelligent system. Stanislavski's emphasis on relaxation, concentration, and the unity of physical and psychological life finds direct resonance with modern ideas such as the DEE Cycle. The actor begins with *Dynamis*—a motivation or desire that initiates energetic focus

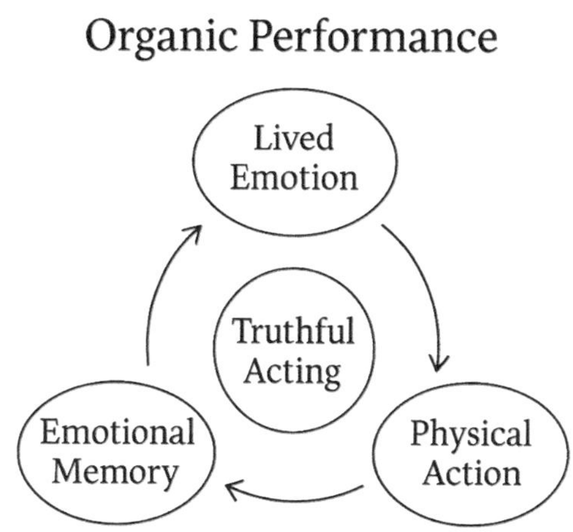

FIGURE 5.2: Stanislavski's Inner Web: Emotion, Memory, and Action. This diagram visualizes Stanislavski's view of organic performance as a triad of lived emotion, emotional memory, and physical action—each element feeding the others to produce truthful, embodied expression. Memory is not a tool for imitation—it is a current of lived resonance that animates the body from within. AI-generated image created with OpenAI's DALL·E (via ChatGPT).

(*Energeia*), and through integrated action, this focus finds expression as *Entelecheia*—an embodied result, clear and purposeful.

Although Stanislavski did not use the terminology of Aristotle or modern somatics, his work **prefigures** these ideas. He was, fundamentally, calling for a performance grounded in what we now call **presence**—not a technique to be imposed from the outside, but a state of openness cultivated from within—a **state of embodied awareness.**

His legacy is more than historical—it is foundational. Across continents and generations, Stanislavski's call for an organic actor still echoes: **A performer who does not act, but lives.** Stanislavski's organic approach continues to influence performers who seek to unify mind, body, and spirit in their creative work. In the sections that follow, we will see how other practitioners have expanded on this vision, offering tools to deepen our understanding of what it means to perform not through artifice, but through authenticity.

André Casaca: Instinct, Play, and the Poetics of the Body

Building upon Stanislavski's commitment to inner truth and lived emotion, André Casaca introduces a theatrical language rooted in instinct, vulnerability, and the logic of play. While Stanislavski sought psychological truth through internal motivation, Casaca dives into the physical intelligence of the body—where impulse precedes thought, and expression is born from presence rather than planning (see **Figure 5.3**).

Born in **Tambaù, São Paulo (Brazil) in 1972,** Casaca developed his research on actor preparation at **LUME Teatro** within the Department of Research at the University of Campinas. He later trained in Italy at the International Centre of Theatre "L'Albero" under Yves Lebreton, eventually becoming his assistant. Settled in Italy since 1995, Casaca has since become a **leading figure in clown, physical theatre, and relational pedagogy**, serving as the founder and artistic director of **Teatro C'art Comic Education.**

FIGURE 5.3: André Casaca, founder of Teatro C'art and creator of Comical-Relational Education—a visionary in physical theatre who invites performers to rediscover presence through instinct, play, and poetic simplicity.

Casaca's work emphasizes a return to **playfulness** as a core creative tool. Drawing from the tradition of clown and physical theatre,

FIGURE 5.4: André Casaca's Embodied Approach: Where Vulnerability Becomes Expression. This image interprets Casaca's theatrical language, where vulnerability, play, and spontaneity do not oppose structure—they become it. Through the body, these forces intersect to generate organic, instinctual expression. Presence, here, is not rehearsed—it is revealed.

he constructs a space in which performers do not hide behind a role but reveals their deepest self through the simplicity of action. In this framework, failure is not an obstacle—it is a source of beauty, discovery, and authenticity. The performer is not expected to control every moment, but to **surrender to the moment as it unfolds** (see **Figure 5.4**).

This surrender is not passive. On the contrary, it requires profound sensitivity and inner readiness. Casaca's approach demands that the performer awaken to their **sensations, impulses**, and inner **rhythms.** It is here that his work intersects with the DEE Cycle: The performer's **Dynamis** arises as instinct or impulse, **Energeia** manifests through spontaneous physical reaction, and **Entelecheia** appears in the coherent gesture or embodied expression that results.

Casaca redefines technique as something that grows organically from the performer's vulnerability. His pedagogy—known as **Comical-Relational Education**—invites performers to explore breath, rhythm, and poetic image not to act, but to be. Like Stanislavski, he proposes not a system to be mastered but a **sensibility to be awakened** (see **Figure 5.5**).

His work extends beyond the stage: His method has reached **over 15,000 children and teenagers in Italy**, and has been applied in **schools, therapeutic settings,**

and international cooperation projects in Cape Verde, Ethiopia, Israel, Palestine, and Brazil. His performances, including *Tranquilli!!!* and *Felici per sempre*, have received wide acclaim, and in 2008, Casaca was honored at the **World Creativity Festival in Sanremo.**

In this way, Casaca continues the **organic lineage** of performer-centered theatre. He restores play to its rightful place as both process and product, reminding us that **behind every truthful gesture lies a body tuned to the present**—a performer willing to be seen not for who they pretend to be, but for who they truly are in the act of becoming.

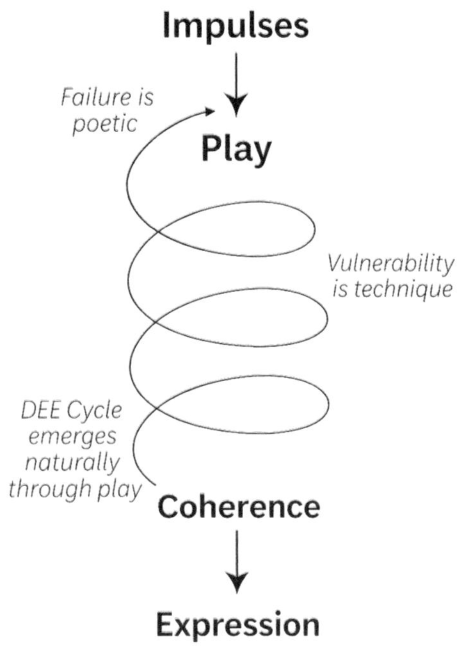

FIGURE 5.5: The Casaca Spiral: Presence Through Instinct, Play, and Embodied Poetics. This visual captures André Casaca's spiral model—a dynamic flow of presence that emerges not from formality, but from instinct, spontaneity, and physical poetry. Here, the body doesn't perform—it plays. And in that play, presence arises: wild, rhythmic, true. AI-generated image created with OpenAI's DALL·E (via ChatGPT).

Alexander Lowen: The Body as the Seat of Truth

While Casaca embraces spontaneity and play, Alexander Lowen offers a complementary path rooted in embodiment and bioenergetic awareness. A student of Wilhelm Reich, Lowen developed *Bioenergetic Analysis* as a method of reconnecting individuals with the expressive capacity of their bodies. Though not a theatre practitioner in the traditional sense, Lowen's work has had profound implications for performance, particularly in understanding how energy, posture, and emotional memory interact (see **Figure 5.6**).

Lowen proposed that our physical structure mirrors our emotional history. Chronic muscular tension, or "body armor," forms in response to unresolved experiences, inhibiting both movement and expression. In performance, this translates to blocked impulses, disembodied presence, and mechanical delivery. For Lowen, freeing the performer meant freeing the body—restoring its capacity to feel, move, and express without inhibition.

His practices include grounding (establishing strong contact with the earth through the feet), breathwork, vocal release, and physical tremor. These are not aesthetic choices, but energetic clearings. As the actor releases tension, they gain access to deeper levels of emotional and energetic truth. In DEE Cycle terms, Lowen's work supports the transition from **Dynamis** to **Energeia** by ensuring that the body is open enough to channel the impulse and generate responsive, coherent action (**Entelecheia**).

Where Stanislavski built an internal psychology of action and Casaca framed the body as a poetic instrument, Lowen provides the physiological and therapeutic bridge. He reminds us that presence is not only felt—it is also **unblocked**. His emphasis on the emotional history of the body encourages people to become conscious of the physical habits that limit their expressivity and to develop practices that liberate the full range of their energy.

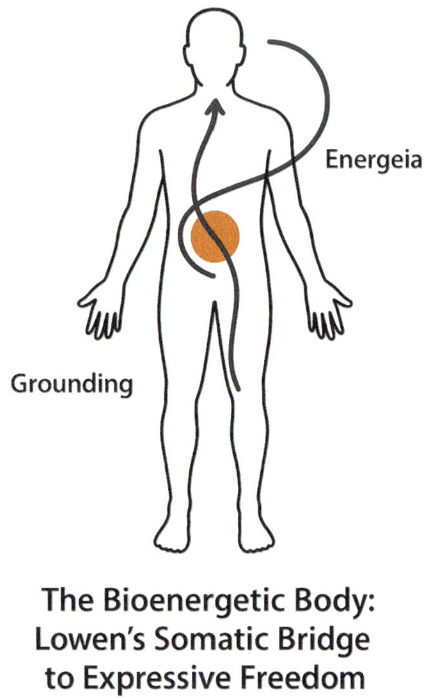

FIGURE 5.6: The Bioenergetic Body: Lowen's Somatic Bridge to Expressive Freedom. This visual captures Alexander Lowen's model of the body—not as instrument, but as archive, access point, and amplifier of truth. Grounded in breath, tremor, and release, the bioenergetic body reconnects sensation and expression, creating a foundation where emotional truth and theatrical presence begin as one. AI-generated image created with OpenAI's DALL·E (via ChatGPT).

Thus, Lowen expands the organic paradigm from an artistic choice to a **somatic necessity**. One of the key contributions of Bioenergetic Analysis is the concept of the **channels of communication**[2]—pathways through which the body expresses and receives emotional and energetic information. These channels include the eyes, voice, breath, posture, and movement. For Lowen, these are not merely expressive tools but diagnostic indicators of where energy flows freely or where it is blocked. Performers' capacity to engage these channels with awareness directly influences their presence, authenticity, and expressive power onstage.

By treating the body as the seat of truth, he empowers performers to embody characters not through external mimicry but through a fully felt, internally resonant physicality. In this, his legacy merges with that of Stanislavski and Casaca to form a holistic vision: the organic performer as an awakened, embodied, and expressive being. He restores play to its rightful place as both process and product, and reminds us that behind every truthful gesture lies a body tuned to the present, a performer willing to be seen not for who they pretend to be, but for who they are in the act of becoming.

Part 2—Tension: Our Modern Obstacle and Fundamental Tool

Awakening the Organic Performer

In the modern performer's journey toward organic presence, **tension** appears both as a primary obstacle and as an indispensable tool. Unconscious, chronic tension restricts breath, inhibits flow, and fractures the performer's energy. But when consciously engaged, **tension becomes a threshold**—a bridge between internal impulse and external action.

This section introduces a vital evolution in our energetic framework: the integration of **Tension** into the DEE Cycle—**Dynamis → Energeia → Entelecheia**—reimagined now as a spiraling model: **Tension → Dynamis → Tension → Energeia → Tension → Entelecheia**—TDTETE.

This model shifts our understanding of energy from linear to cyclical. Tension isn't simply something to eliminate—it becomes part of the performer's natural rhythm. Energy doesn't just travel forward; it **builds, holds, releases, and renews**. Tension is what **precedes each expressive phase**, sharpening presence and amplifying intention.

Let's break this down:

- **Before Dynamis:** A desire or emotional need gathers—it vibrates beneath awareness.
- **Before Energeia:** The body organizes this inner charge—muscles align, breath focuses.
- **Before Entelecheia:** A pause, a gathering—tension holds the energy just before release.

Think of it like a **wave:** Energy builds, crests, then crashes into motion. Or like the breath: **Tension is the inhale**—a swelling of potential. **Expression is the exhale**—the letting go, the transformation into presence.

Through this lens, the **organic performer** no longer avoids tension—they **enter it, feel it, and ride its rhythm.** Tension becomes not the opposite of freedom, but the **precondition of it.** Performance becomes a series of spirals, not steps—a dance between stillness and impulse, breath and action, silence and sound (see **Figure 5.7**).

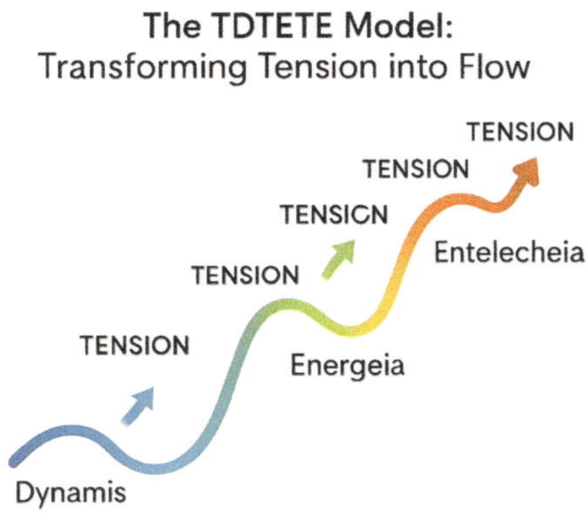

FIGURE 5.7: The TDTETE Model: Tension as Rhythmic Catalyst in the Energetic Cycle. This diagram reimagines tension not as obstruction, but as an integral pulse in the performer's expressive rhythm. At each phase—before Dynamis, before Energeia, before Entelecheia—tension gathers, focuses, and releases energy. The model reveals a spiraling structure where presence arises not despite tension, but through it. AI-generated image created with OpenAI's DALL·E (via ChatGPT).

The TDTETE Model: Mapping Energy Through Tension

In the traditional **DEE Cycle,** energy flows linearly: from internal impulse (**Dynamis**) to activation (**Energeia**) to realization (**Entelecheia**). But lived experience—especially in performance—is rarely that clean, or that straight.

The **TDTETE model** offers a more accurate, more embodied map. It reveals energy not as a line, but as a **spiral**—a rhythmic sequence where **tension** appears between each phase like a **checkpoint or surge**, guiding the performer through transformation.

This spiral shows how energy moves in cycles, not straight paths. At every turn, tension appears—not as interruption, but as **rhythmic reset**. It is what sharpens awareness, prepares release, and deepens presence.

- **Before Dynamis**, tension emerges as the **inner need**—the spark of discomfort or desire that sets the cycle in motion.
- **Before Energeia**, tension organizes energy—**alignment before action**, restraint that clarifies the surge.
- **Before Entelecheia**, tension holds space—**the pause before the gesture**, the stillness before impact.

Think of it like **music**—tension is the beat that creates rhythm, not noise. Or like **waves**—tension is the crest that gathers just before it crashes into expression.

This reframing does not romanticize tension—it **invites the performer to engage it consciously**. Tension is not merely resistance—it is **potential.** Each moment of contraction contains the seed of expansion. The performer who learns to feel, ride, and release these waves does not perform with effort, but with **radiant, grounded presence**.

This contrasts with externalist models, such as **Barba**'s, which emphasize surface perception over internal awareness. But can performers truly connect with an audience without mastering their own internal terrain? This model suggests: **no**.

Instead, **TDTETE** becomes a **map of mastery**—not over technique, but over self: breath, rhythm, alignment, and release (see **Figure 5.8**).

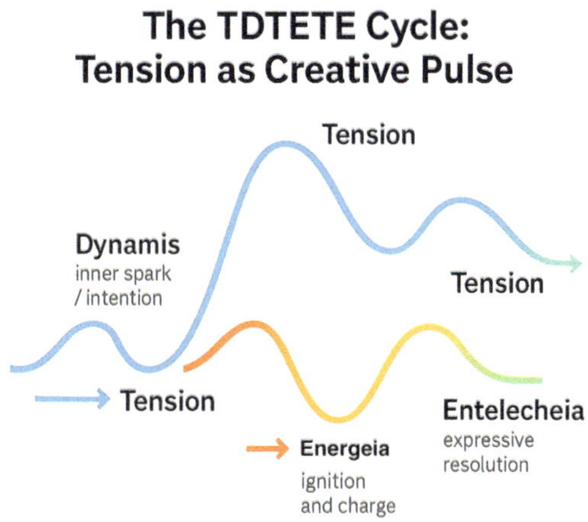

FIGURE 5.8: The TDTETE Spiral: Tension as Rhythmic Reset. This diagram visualizes the cyclical energy flow of the TDTETE model, where tension punctuates and powers each phase: before Dynamis, before Energeia, before Entelecheia. Tension is no longer seen as obstruction—it becomes a creative pressure point, giving shape, rhythm, and strength to expression. AI-generated image created with OpenAI's DALL·E (via ChatGPT).

The Koshi Principle and Its Applications

The concept of **koshi**—a term rooted in Japanese performance traditions, particularly Nō Theatre—represents a central axis of physical and energetic control. While often translated simply as "hips," koshi extends far beyond anatomy. It refers to a **center of gravity** in the body that governs balance, stability, and expressive power. When activated properly, koshi serves as the **energetic fulcrum** from which intention is grounded and released.

In practice, **Farley** and **Navarra** offer two complementary understandings of tension that help illuminate this principle:

- **Navarra**, drawing from her background in flamenco and ballet, emphasizes tension as a **state of muscular activation**—a stretch between opposing forces that energizes movement.
- **Farley**, rooted in mime and spiritual tradition, views tension more as an **aesthetic power**—a way of suspending the body in heightened rhythm, transcending the ordinary through control and lightness.

By integrating both perspectives, we begin to see koshi not only as a physical center but as a **dynamic point of energetic alignment**: Muscular intensity (Navarra) combined with buoyant spiritual clarity (Farley).

Mangolini, who studied traditional Japanese theatre directly with masters like Nomura, clarifies that in Nō, the koshi is activated through subtle, internalized effort that radiates **presence without excess**. The actor becomes like a tree deeply rooted, yet flexible—projecting strength not through external force, but through **calm, internal pressure.**

Koshi in Modern Performance Practice

The term **koshi**, while deeply rooted in Japanese theatrical and martial traditions, describes more than just a physical point in the body. It refers to an integrated center of **grounding, balance, and energetic initiation**—a nexus where **intention meets structure**, and from which expressive action flows. In contemporary performance practice, this principle appears—sometimes implicitly—in the work of artists and theorists like **Arthur Lessac** and **Scott Putman.**

Arthur Lessac's approach to movement and voice is based on sensory awareness and internal experience. He emphasizes *tonal and structural energy*, drawing attention to the **resonance of the spine**, breath, and body in space. This connects closely with koshi as an axis of vertical integrity and embodied alignment. Lessac helps performers awaken internal vibratory awareness, enabling speech and movement to originate from a grounded, energized body.

In **Scott Putman**'s movement pedagogy, although the term "koshi" is not explicitly used, a similar logic is present. His approach emphasizes **expressive movement initiated from inner awareness**, breath coordination, and physical responsiveness. My understanding of Putman's teaching suggests a focus on movement that arises from **internal intention** rather than external force—an idea that harmonizes with the koshi concept, even if it is not formally labeled as such.

This understanding reinforces a broader idea: **Stage movement and everyday movement are not separate**. Instead, they share a **common energetic root.** Whether in performance, teaching, or personal life, the activation of koshi enhances **ease, power, and communication.** The benefits of koshi are not reserved for elite performers—they are available to all who learn to inhabit their bodies with conscious attention and responsive energy.

This internal organization becomes especially vital in distinguishing between **lifeless technique** and **embodied performance**. Without a stable koshi center—without the energetic balance of **Dynamis, Energeia, and Entelecheia**—even highly trained artists risk becoming disconnected or performative. Presence becomes strained, gestures lack intention, and expression feels mechanical.

Performers who cultivate koshi not only move with **greater expressiveness and strength**, but also sustain **clarity, control, and groundedness** under pressure. Their bodies serve as vessels of communication—where voice, gaze, and gesture are not imposed, but **emerge naturally** from a coherent internal source.

Presence, in this view, is not built from the outside in—it rises from within, centered in koshi and expressed through alignment, intention, and flow.

Together, these diagrams suggest a dual map: vertical presence through koshi (**Figures 5.9** and **5.10**), and horizontal resilience through tension awareness (**Figure 5.11**). One roots the performer; the other teaches how not to fall.

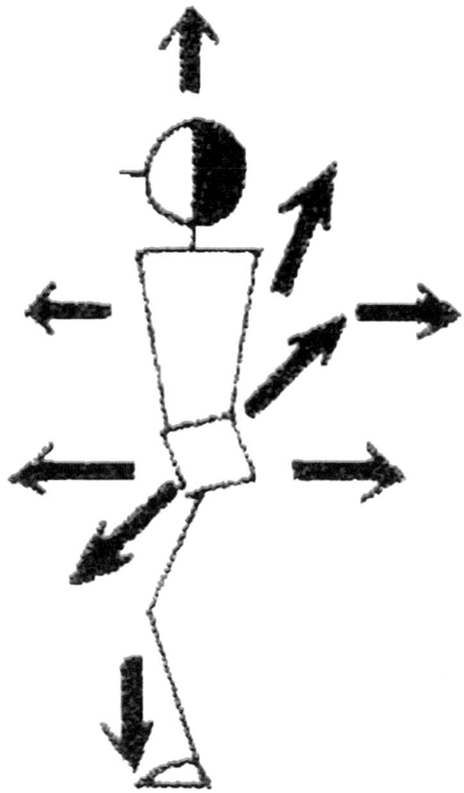

FIGURE 5.9: Koshi as Energetic Axis: Diagram by Fabio Mangolini. Previously introduced, this diagram is revisited here to explore practical applications of koshi across traditions. The image highlights the grounding forces and vertical alignment that underlie presence, balance, and expressive flow in Human Theatre. Here, koshi becomes more than anatomical—it becomes pedagogical, performative, and energetic.

The Adaptive Cycle of Tension

The evolving challenge for performers is not merely to eliminate tension, but to **recognize, navigate, and harness it**. Tension, when unconscious, can block expression and dull presence. But when consciously observed, it becomes a **reservoir of energy**, offering the performer intensity without rigidity and power without strain.

This challenge, of course, is not unique to performers. Every human being experiences **daily stress**, but performers, by the nature of their work, must amplify emotional and physical states while remaining open and responsive. This amplifies the **energetic load** they must carry—and the importance of developing tools to manage it.

To understand how the body adapts to prolonged tension, we turn to **Alexander Lowen**, who defined tension as:

> The consequence of the imposition of a force or pressure on the organism, which reacts by mobilizing its energy. Naturally, if the body manages to escape that force, it is not subject to any tension.
>
> (Lowen 2012: 193, author's translation)

This concept reveals a crucial truth: **tension is a response.** It is not a flaw, but a **defense mechanism**, a way the body mobilizes energy in the face of stress or pressure. However, when tension is chronic—when the body cannot discharge it—it begins to **consume energy** rather than channel it.

Lowen outlines this process through **three distinct phases of adaptation:**

1. **Alarm Reaction:** When the body encounters acute tension, it releases **adrenaline**, mobilizing energy to confront the stressor. If the threat passes and the energy is discharged, the body returns to a state of balance.
2. **Adaptation Phase:** If the pressure persists, the body enters a holding pattern. It produces anti-inflammatory hormones to manage stress internally. However, this adaptation is energetically expensive—like a cold war between the body's defense system and the unresolved force.
3. **Exhaustion Phase:** When adaptation continues without resolution, the body becomes depleted. Chronic tension crystallizes into **rigid muscles, blocked breath,** or **emotional numbness,** impairing not only performance but health and self-expression.

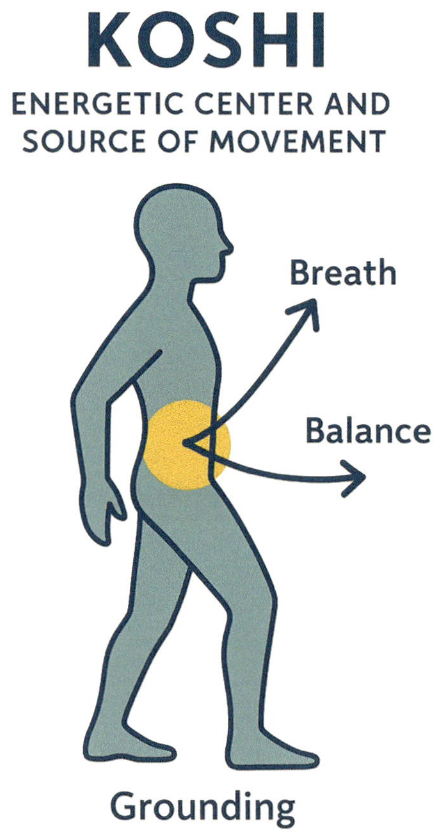

FIGURE 5.10: Koshi serves as the performer's core axis—integrating breath, alignment, and intention. From this center, energy rises through the spine and radiates through movement and voice, enabling power without strain, expression without excess. Presence here is both rooted and expansive—a balance of stillness and flow. AI-generated image created with OpenAI's DALL·E (via ChatGPT).

In performance, these stages are often invisible but deeply felt: a once-vibrant actor appears **flat, mechanical,** or **overly strained.** What we interpret as a lack of talent or effort is often the **symptom of accumulated tension**—of a body caught in the exhaustion phase.

This model gives us a framework not only for understanding **why performers "burn out,"** but also for recognizing the **early signs of tension dysregulation.**[3] By becoming aware of how the body reacts, holds, and compensates under pressure, the performer begins the journey back to organic presence—not by eliminating tension, but by **riding its arc** before it calcifies.

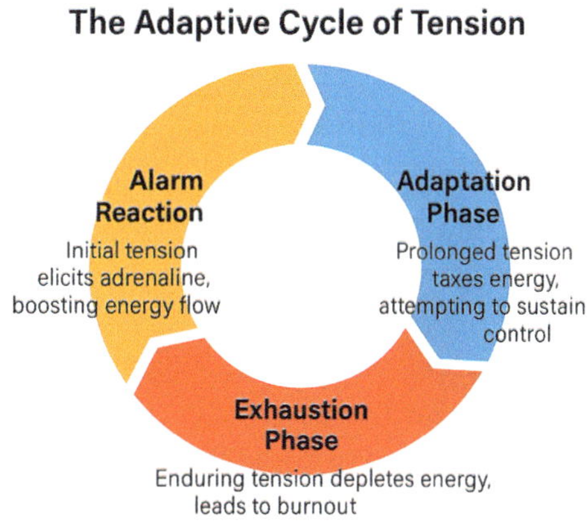

FIGURE 5.11: Lowen's Adaptive Cycle of Tension: From Mobilization to Exhaustion. This diagram illustrates how the body responds to prolonged stress—beginning with mobilization, passing through adaptation, and potentially collapsing into energetic depletion. For performers, recognizing this cycle is crucial: it reveals how tension, when ignored, leads to burnout—yet when consciously interrupted, can be transformed into sustainable, expressive energy. AI-generated image created with OpenAI's DALL·E (via ChatGPT).

Cultural Conditioning and Tension

Our physical form is not shaped in isolation. Culture, society, and upbringing deeply influence how we move, breathe, and hold ourselves. These influences often manifest as **unconscious tensions**—habitual postures, gestures, or muscular patterns that were once adaptive, but now function as energetic blocks (see **Figure 5.12**).

Alexander Lowen identified this cultural imprinting as a key source of chronic tension. For example, familiar phrases like "shoulders back," "chest out," or "belly in" reflect societal norms around posture and presentation. While these commands may appear harmless, they often compel the body into **unnatural shapes** that restrict breath, reduce mobility, and **consume energy**.

These so-called "corrections" become **energy consumers:** physical patterns that drain vitality rather than support expression. Over time, they lead to a **disconnect between intention and action**, making it difficult for performers to access genuine expression or fluid movement.

Arthur Lessac's work helps illuminate a path beyond this conditioning. His approach focuses on **awareness and internal sensing**—inviting performers to rediscover natural posture, resonant voice, and free breath. Rather than imposing alignment from the outside, Lessac encourages students to explore movement from the **inside out**.

Gilda Navarra, Fabio Mangolini, and Scott Putman also emphasize the need to question these inherited postures and tensions. Their work suggests that the body must become **conscious of itself**, unlearning cultural patterns that stifle spontaneity and replacing them with energetic clarity and personal awareness (see **Figure 5.13**).

In this light, **tension is not just physical—it is ideological.** It is shaped by the values of the society we grow up in. And so, part of becoming an organic performer is learning to recognize which tensions belong to the role, and which were inherited unconsciously from culture (see **Figure 5.14**).

This process is not just about acting—it's about healing. Reclaiming the body from cultural stiffness opens the door to **renewed communication, freedom, and presence.** The performer doesn't simply learn to move better; they learn to exist more fully—onstage and in life.

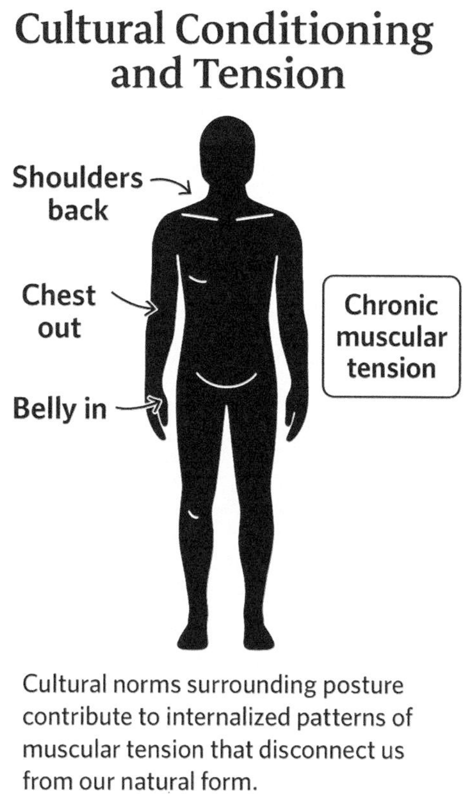

FIGURE 5.12: Cultural Conditioning and Tension: Habit, Posture, and the Path Back to Flow. This visual comparison reveals how habitual postural patterns, shaped by culture, education, and social expectation, can interfere with breath, block energy, and fragment expression. By recognizing and releasing these imprints, the performer reclaims organic alignment and somatic truth—where movement, voice, and presence arise naturally. AI-generated image created with OpenAI's DALL·E (via ChatGPT).

The Impact of Tension on Communication

Tension doesn't just affect movement—it disrupts **communication at its core.** When energy is blocked, our ability to express ourselves authentically becomes compromised. The actor's voice may falter, the body may feel stiff, and the eyes may no longer transmit truth. In this way, **tension becomes a barrier between intention and expression.**

At the heart of communication lies an internal process: the transmission of **thought into intention,** and intention into action. But when this chain is interrupted—by fear, chronic stress, or muscular contraction—the message becomes **distorted**. We may say one thing, while our body communicates something else entirely.

Alexander Lowen explored this phenomenon in depth, noting that many of his patients experienced **low energy levels linked to emotional repression or depression**. In these states, the breath becomes shallow, the voice muted, and the eyes disconnected. Yet, as energy is restored—often through **breathing, vocal release, or movement**—emotions may suddenly emerge. A throat once constricted may open into sobs or laughter, not as performance, but as **release**.

FIGURE 5.13: Unconscious Tension in the Performing Body. This image captures how subtle muscular contractions—rooted in cultural or emotional memory—can shape an actor's posture and movement. Tension becomes visible before it becomes conscious, offering both obstacle and opportunity in the creation of presence. AI-generated image created with OpenAI's DALL·E (via ChatGPT).

Lowen noted that when the **desire to express is weaker than the fear of expressing**, the result is **numbness**. In this case, tension has hardened into armor. But with awareness, even this can be softened. Once muscle tensions—particularly in the **throat, chest,** and **jaw**—are released, energy begins to flow again. The actor, once blocked, becomes **available**—to themselves, to the audience, and to the moment.

In performance, these patterns are subtle yet profound. An actor may speak clearly but feel disconnected. Another may move fluidly but leave no emotional trace. In both cases, **tension has severed the link between energy and intention**. Reconnecting that link is not a technical correction—it is an **energetic awakening**.

Organic performers learn to listen: not just to text or cues, but to the **resistance within their own body**. Through breath, posture, and vocal resonance, they re-establish the natural channels through which energy moves and meaning is shared. In this space, communication is no longer something to project—it becomes something to **allow**.

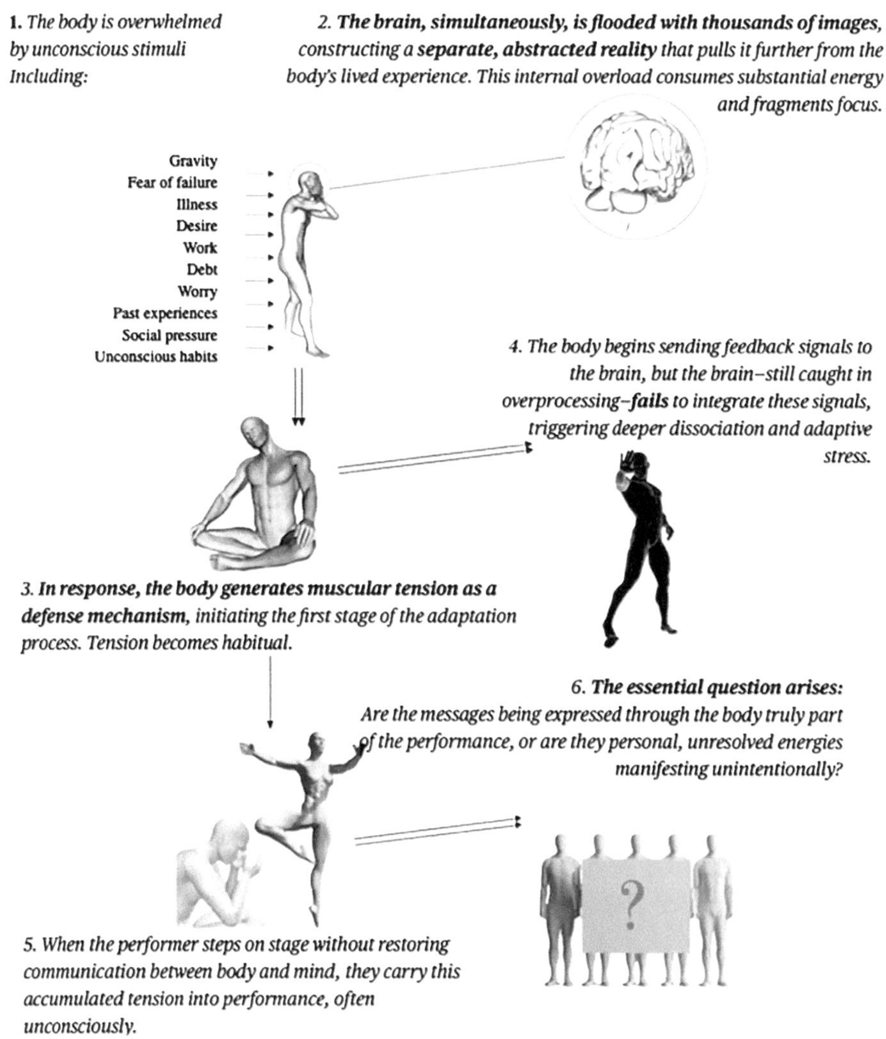

FIGURE 5.14: Tension as Embodied Narrative. The performer's body externalizes internal conflict, often without intention. These habitual patterns carry stories—of fear, protection, conditioning—and once seen, they can be transformed into channels of authentic communication.

The Mind–Body Divide

One of the most pervasive obstacles to organic presence is the **disconnect between the mind and the body**. In modern life, we are conditioned to live from the neck up—consumed by screens, information, and mental noise (see **Figure 5.15**). This imbalance causes performers to operate from intellectual intention rather than somatic awareness, fragmenting their ability to embody truth.

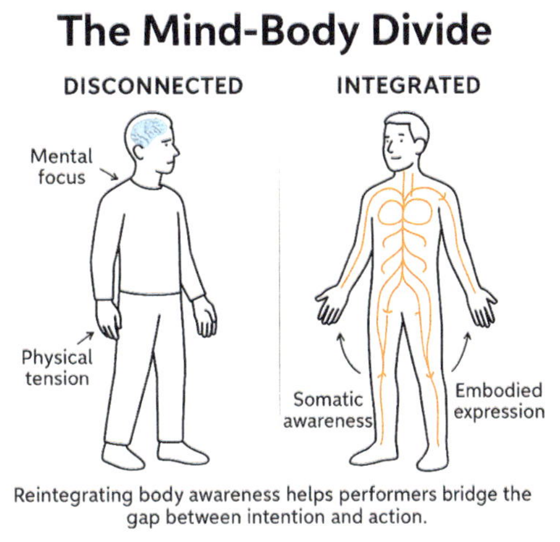

FIGURE 5.15: The Mind–Body Divide: From Fragmentation to Integration. This visual comparison reveals how modern cultural conditioning favors control over connection, resulting in disembodied presence and fragmented expression. By restoring the body's felt sense—its breath, rhythm, and intuitive knowing—the performer reclaims unity between inner impulse and outward presence, dissolving the split between mind and body. AI-generated image created with OpenAI's DALL·E (via ChatGPT).

Alexander Lowen draws attention to this split, especially in his observation that many modern teaching methods prioritize cognitive data over experiential knowledge. He emphasizes that **true understanding occurs only when the body is involved.** Until an idea is physically sensed—through movement, breath, or emotional reaction—it remains abstract and disconnected from lived reality.

This insight is especially relevant in training performers. Many actors memorize text or choreograph their movements without ever allowing their **nervous system** to integrate the material. The result is a performance that feels **calculated rather than alive.** The actor may speak fluently, but their body betrays tension. The gesture may be clean, but it lacks resonance. This is the signature of a mind–body divide.

In the visually saturated world we live in, where aesthetics are often emphasized over internal feeling, performers may unconsciously prioritize **how things look** over how things **feel.** This orientation leads to disconnected performances—external accuracy without internal necessity.

To repair this divide, performers must learn to **listen to their bodies as much as they listen to their thoughts.** Tension patterns, postural habits, and even breathing rhythms offer feedback about what is truly happening beneath the surface. When these signals are acknowledged, the body begins to rejoin the expressive process—not as a tool, but as a **partner in creation.**

As Lowen suggests, the body is the **first site of learning.** It holds not only memory and trauma but also instinct, creativity, and intelligence. The path to reconnection begins with **awareness**, and it is through awareness that the performer reclaims the **organic integration of energy, intention, and expression.**

Part 3—Expressive Alignment and the Performer's Intent

Communicating Our Intentions with Our Energy

Our bodies are expressive instruments—but only when the energy within them is aligned with clear and honest intention. As we've seen throughout this chapter, **intention is the driver of energy flow**. When it is distorted by fear, self-doubt, or unconscious tension, the result is a misalignment: a forced smile when we're sad, a shaky voice when we want to project confidence. These inconsistencies weaken presence, both onstage and in life (see **Figure 5.16**). This idea connects directly to the work of **Alexander Lowen**, who argued that the **heart is the seat of expression**. If its rhythm is disturbed, our entire communicative ability falters. Similarly, **Antonio Núñez Partido**[4] notes: "Our heart is the most sensitive organ in our body. Our life depends on its rhythmic and constant activity. When this rhythm is altered, even momentarily, we experience an anxiety that reaches deep into our being" (Partido 2009: 9, author's translation).

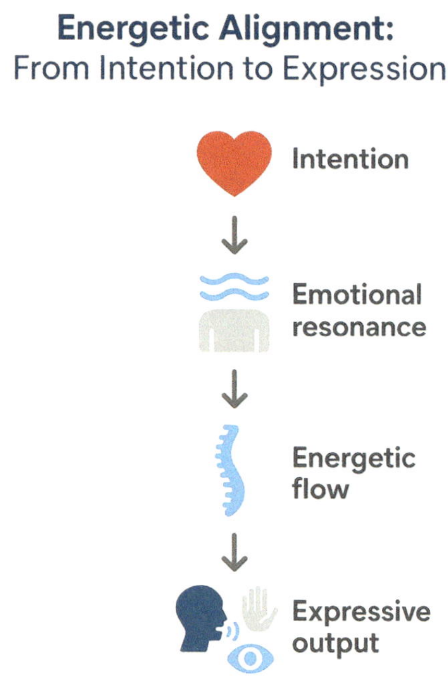

FIGURE 5.16: Energetic Alignment: From Intention to Expression. This diagram visualizes the journey of authentic performance: beginning with inner intention, resonating through emotional awareness, flowing along the spinal axis, and finally manifesting in gesture, voice, and gaze. Here, the body becomes a channel—not for effort, but for attuned, embodied communication. AI-generated image created with OpenAI's DALL·E (via ChatGPT).

Such anxiety may manifest in subtle or invisible ways—**a blocked breath, stiff posture, or internal hesitation.** But even when we aren't aware of it, our audience often is.

Communication begins before words are spoken, in the resonance of breath, body, and presence.

Lowen believed that **all living beings carry an innate desire to express**—not only through speech, but through the whole body. Every movement, posture, and glance sends a message. Even the color of our skin, the way we breathe, the energy in our eyes becomes part of the communicative field. This is especially true for performers.

In the theatre, these signals are magnified. A director might cast based on visual impressions—body type, posture, presence—but if the performer's **energy does not support the image**, the illusion crumbles. The organic performer transcends appearance by projecting from within. **When energy is coherent**, it overrides aesthetic bias and draws the audience into authentic connection.

To achieve this coherence, actors must train not just their voice and movement, but their **intention**. Spontaneity and self-trust are crucial. As Lowen notes (inspired by Abraham Maslow's *The Creative Attitude*), **spontaneity guarantees sincerity**. It reflects a performer in free function—honest, unforced, and alive.

In DEE terms, intention (Dynamis) fuels energetic engagement (Energeia), which emerges as expressive result (Entelecheia). When intention is fragmented or unacknowledged, the cycle stalls. But when the actor's inner drive is **felt, owned, and physically supported**, the cycle flows—seamlessly, powerfully, and truthfully.

This section reminds us that the greatest performances do not come from control. They come from **alignment**. Performers in energetic coherence do not need to fake emotion. Their body becomes the message. And the message resonates.

Communication Channels

Alexander Lowen believed that physical tensions often block our emotions, **disrupting our ability to communicate authentically**. This leads us to the concept of **communication channels**: energetic and expressive pathways—such as the **eyes, voice, breath, posture, and movement**—through which emotion, intention, and vitality flow. When these are obstructed by chronic tension or unconscious holding patterns, true expression is compromised.

Communication, at its core, is the **external expression of an internal state**. In the DEE framework, our potential for expression (**Dynamis**) is shaped and transmitted through the body (**Energeia**) and ultimately made manifest in outward gesture and voice (**Entelecheia**). When communication channels are open and responsive, this flow is clear. But when blocked, even sincere intentions can appear forced, disconnected, or inauthentic.

Lowen explains that **the voice**, in particular, reflects the state of the heart. When the emotional center is open, the voice flows freely. But when fear or tension dominates, **"constriction rings"** can form in the body, most often in three key areas:

- The **mouth and jaw** (clenched lips, locked jaw).
- The **junction of the head and neck** (where voluntary and involuntary control meet).
- The **chest** (emotional containment or shutdown).

Each of these rings can hinder emotional expression, and many actors are intimately familiar with this: the shaky voice before a performance, the dry throat during an intense scene, the locked ribcage under pressure. These are not just physical sensations—they are signs of **blocked energy** (see **Figure 5.17**).

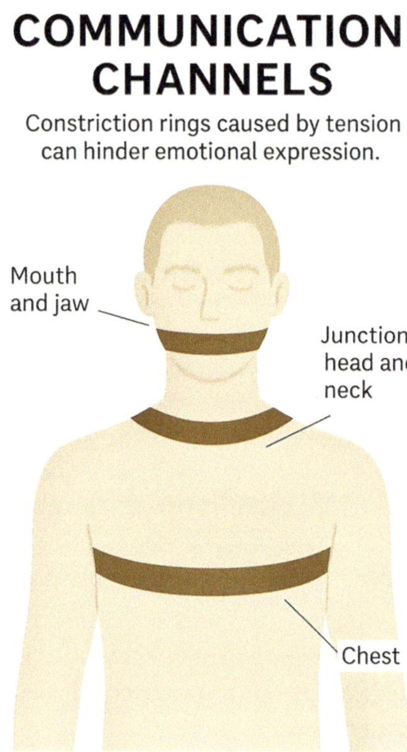

FIGURE 5.17: Communication Channels: Releasing the Constriction Rings. This diagram illustrates how chronic tension forms energetic "rings" around the mouth, throat, and chest—zones essential for vocal and emotional authenticity. These constrictions don't just inhibit sound—they distort intention. Releasing them restores the performer's ability to transmit inner truth with presence, resonance, and clarity. AI-generated image created with OpenAI's DALL·E (via ChatGPT).

When released through **bioenergetic exercises, breathwork, or techniques like Lessac's Kinesensics**, these blocks can dissolve, allowing energy to **resonate** through the performer. Authentic emotion becomes possible—not because it is "acted," but because it is truly felt and embodied.

The result is not simply clearer speech or stronger movement—it is **transformational presence**. The performer connects not only with the audience, but with themselves, engaging the stage as a channel for genuine human experience.

In this way, communication channels are not just physical—they are **energetic bridges between the inner world and outer expression.** Learning to clear and inhabit them is not only essential for the actor—it is essential for the human being behind the role.

The Importance of Spontaneity

To truly captivate an audience, a performer's expression must be **spontaneous**. It must feel genuine, not rehearsed—authentic, not contrived. Spontaneity, in this sense, is not the opposite of preparation; rather, it is the result of deep preparation that has become **fully integrated**. It is what happens when performers are so aligned with their characters and inner state that expression emerges naturally, without force (see **Figure 5.18**).

Alexander Lowen, drawing from **Abraham Maslow**'s *The Creative Attitude*, defines spontaneity as:

> The guarantee of the sincere expression of the nature and style of a being in free functioning and its uniqueness. Both words, spontaneity and expressiveness, imply sincerity, naturalness, truthfulness, absence of affectation, lack of desire to imitate others, etc.
>
> (Lowen 2012: 226, author's translation)

This definition echoes the core of **organic performance**: A presence that is alive, reactive, and unique in every moment. Spontaneity ensures that each performance is not merely a repetition, but a re-creation—fresh, full of possibility, and rooted in honest impulse.

In terms of the **DEE Cycle**, spontaneity occurs when the performer's *Dynamis* (inner desire) rises unimpeded, and *Energeia* (activation) moves fluidly through the body, culminating in *Entelecheia*—the expressive result that radiates presence and truth.

Lowen suggests that **"achieving the spontaneity of a person"** requires unlocking the unconscious. Repressed impulses, when liberated, lead to embodied actions that feel

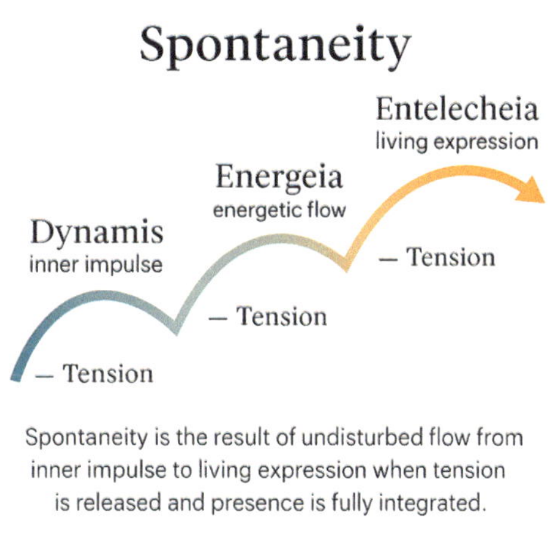

FIGURE 5.18: Spontaneity as Energetic Freedom. This image captures a moment of full DEE activation—where the cycle flows without resistance, and the performer moves with instinctive ease. Impulse becomes action, action becomes presence. In this state, energy doesn't need to be forced—it arrives, alive and aligned. AI-generated image created with OpenAI's DALL·E (via ChatGPT).

honest and alive. This does not mean abandoning craft or discipline. On the contrary, it means creating the internal conditions for authenticity to thrive. Performers' task becomes one of **removing resistance**—mental, emotional, or physical—that might block their energetic expression.

This also connects with the work of Stanislavski, whose method of *experiencing* emphasized not "playing" a character, but **being**—living truthfully under imaginary circumstances. When spontaneity is present, the audience does not simply witness technique. They witness **a living moment**, born in real time.

Importantly, spontaneity also allows for **pleasure**. When performers are fully present, their joy, tension, vulnerability, and playfulness are transmitted energetically. This pleasure is not egotistical—it is magnetic. It draws the audience in and transforms performance into shared experience.

Ultimately, spontaneity is not a goal to be achieved—it is a state to be **allowed.** It arises when performers have cultivated awareness, released tension, and trained their instrument to respond freely. It is the **expression of freedom through form**—and it is what makes a performance unforgettable.

Study of Communication Channels

To further explore the idea of communication as energetic transmission, we turn to the work of **Scott P. Phillips**,[5] a multidisciplinary practitioner whose background in theatre, martial arts, and qigong offers a compelling lens through which to view the performer's expressive capacity. Since 1977, Phillips has cultivated a practice rooted in Chinese martial disciplines and ritual movement, emphasizing how breath, intention, and presence form a unified system of communication.

In his article, "Theatre, Ritual, and Exorcism in Chinese Martial Arts," Phillips outlines how performance traditions drawn from martial training can be applied to theatrical craft. His insights help us understand how the body becomes both transmitter and receiver of energy, operating through channels of intention, breath, movement, and gaze.

1. **Calisthenics and Breath: Building Body Awareness**
   Phillips notes that while the **Shaolin Temple** is not a theatre school, its rigorous physical training—including calisthenics and **daoyin** (an early form of qigong)—has long influenced the aesthetics of performance. These practices enhance **grace, coordination, and expressive fluidity**, training the body to move with clarity and focus.
2. **Yi and Shen: Intention and Spirit**
   Central to Phillips' synthesis is the concept of **Yi** (**intention**) and **Shen** (**spirit**). In martial and theatrical movement alike, clarity of intention is paramount.

Performers' internal focus (Yi) shapes their outward expression (Shen), allowing for movement that is not only efficient but emotionally charged. This mirrors the DEE Cycle: **Dynamis becomes focused intention (Yi), which channels Energeia through embodied presence, ultimately manifesting in Entelecheia—the expressive result.**

3. **Gaze as a Communicative Tool**
   Training the **gaze**—how and where the eyes focus—plays a critical role in both martial arts and theatre. Phillips explains that in traditional practice, the eyes are trained not to telegraph movement in advance, but to hold intention with subtlety and precision. This creates tension, mystery, and connection—qualities central to stage presence. As **Lowen** puts it: "The eyes are the mirrors of the soul" (1975: 241–44), conveying energetic truth whether or not words are spoken.
4. **Codification and Emotional Authenticity**
   Drawing on the legacy of **Mei Lanfang**, a master of Beijing Opera, Phillips highlights that while physical expression may be codified, it must still be **emotionally inhabited**. Codified gestures are not shortcuts to emotion; they are frameworks within which genuine feeling must arise. This principle reminds us that technique, no matter how refined, must remain a vessel for authentic energetic transmission.

Ultimately, Phillips' cross-cultural analysis reinforces the central premise of this chapter: **The body is the primary medium of communication**, and its expressive power is directly tied to its energetic clarity. By cultivating internal alignment, breath control, and intentional movement, the performer transforms from an interpreter of ideas into a **conduit of experience**.

Energy flows not only through the limbs but through every channel of awareness—eyes, voice, breath, and stillness. When these channels are open and the performer is fully present, the result is not only powerful performance but **transformative connection**—the true aim of organic theatre.

Part 4—Energetic Alchemy of the Performer: Healing Through Presence

Antonin Artaud: Cruelty as a Language of the Heart

Antonin Artaud remains one of the most radical and influential voices in the history of modern performance. His concept of "cruelty" has often been misunderstood as violence or brutality. Yet for Artaud, cruelty was not aggression—it was **necessity**, **rigor**, and a relentless commitment to truth. It was about tearing away theatrical illusion and touching the **raw heart of human experience**.

Artaud envisioned a theatre that bypasses reason and strikes directly at the nervous system. His performances were not designed to explain but to **awaken**—to shake audiences into visceral awareness. For him, theatre had a role similar to that of dreams or rituals: it existed to disrupt the conscious mind and **release repressed forces.** In this sense, *cruelty* becomes a **language of the heart**, one that does not soothe, but confronts, disturbs, and liberates.

> The plague unleashes conflicts, releases forces, and triggers possibilities. If these forces are dark, it's not the plague's fault nor the theatre's, but life's. Theatre, like the plague, helps us bring out those moral and social conflicts.
>
> (Artaud 2015: 38, author's translation)

FIGURE 5.19: Artaud's Vision: Theatre as Plague—A Sacred Confrontation. This image echoes Antonin Artaud's belief that theatre, like the plague, unleashes repressed forces—emotional, psychic, and spiritual. It bypasses intellect, shocks the senses, and awakens presence through rupture. For Artaud, performance is not entertainment—it is ritual exorcism, a sacred disruption that makes the invisible visible. AI-generated image created with OpenAI's DALL·E (via ChatGPT).

This quote illuminates his vision of theatre as a **purging fire**—a space that does not avoid pain or chaos, but exposes it so that healing and transformation can occur. Artaud did not seek catharsis[6] in the Aristotelian sense. His aim was not emotional cleansing through identification, but energetic **revolution** through confrontation.

This radical perspective aligns deeply with the principles explored throughout this chapter. Just as the DEE and TDTETE models emphasize embodied energy and internal impulse, Artaud's theatre calls for **presence without filter**, action born not of technique, but of **existential urgency**. His vision echoes in every performer who dares to enter the stage not with a mask, but with **an open wound turned toward the light** (see **Figure 5.19**).

In placing Artaud here, at the opening of *Energetic Alchemy of the Performer*, we acknowledge that healing often begins in disruption. That sometimes, the most honest expression is the one that shakes us loose from comfort and reminds us what it means to **feel fully and speak truly**—even if through screams, silence, or shadows.

Catharsis Reimagined: A Multifaceted Legacy

The concept of **catharsis** is among the most enduring and debated in theatrical history. Originating in Aristotle's *Poetics*, catharsis traditionally refers to the **purification or cleansing** of the audience's emotions—particularly pity and fear—through its vicarious engagement with dramatic action. But what exactly is being "cleansed," and how? Is catharsis a moral release, a psychological unburdening, or an energetic transformation?

In modern contexts, catharsis has taken on **multiple meanings** depending on the lens through which it is viewed (see **Figure 5.20**):

- In **psychoanalysis**, Freud and Breuer described catharsis as the emotional discharge that occurs when repressed material is brought to consciousness and expressed.
- In **performance studies**, catharsis is often interpreted as a **psychophysical phenomenon**, experienced by either the audience or the actor—or both—as a result of intense emotional or energetic engagement.
- In **trauma therapy**, catharsis might refer to the process by which deeply held emotional wounds begin to release through embodied expression.

Each of these interpretations highlights a different aspect of the phenomenon, and yet they all circle the same core truth: **Something locked is unlocked**. Whether it is the spectator weeping in the dark, the actor trembling in full-body release, or the child reenacting an internal struggle through play, catharsis marks the **moment when emotion becomes motion**—when energy once bound by silence or suppression is liberated.

Importantly, catharsis does not always arrive as relief. Sometimes it is painful, disorienting, or even destabilizing. This is why Antonin Artaud reimagined catharsis not as an emotional purge but as an **existential confrontation**—a breaking open of the self, a wound through which clarity might eventually enter. For Artaud, catharsis was not about empathy or identification but about **shock**, presence, and the raw encounter with **life's inner forces**.

In the context of energetic performance, catharsis becomes a **somatic threshold**: a point at which stored tension or unconscious memory is discharged through the body's expressive systems. This is not "acting out" emotion but **moving through** it with awareness. Whether the experience is ritualistic, therapeutic, or artistic, the key mechanism is always the same—**the unlocking of blocked energy** and its reorganization into clarity, flow, and presence.

Thus, catharsis is not a singular effect but a **multifaceted legacy**, living at the intersection of theatre, therapy, and transformation. It belongs not only to

Aristotle or Artaud but to every performer who has wept, screamed, or stood still onstage and felt something deep inside begin to move.

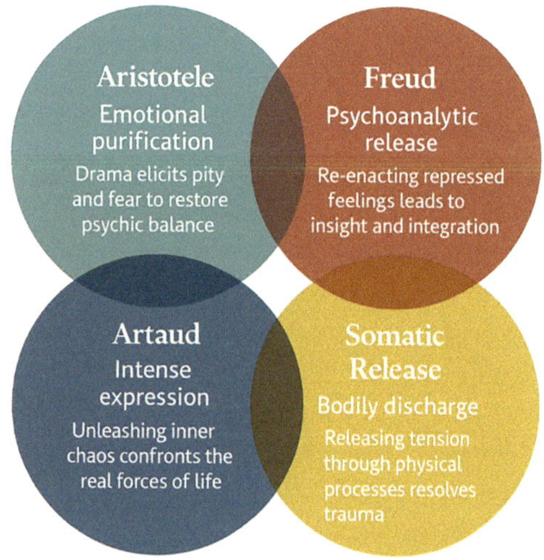

FIGURE 5.20: Models of Catharsis: A Legacy in Four Voices. This comparative diagram maps four major interpretations of **catharsis** across time and tradition: **Aristotle**, who framed it as emotional purification through tragedy; **Freud**, who reimagined it as psychological release through unburdening; **Artaud**, who viewed it as a violent energetic rupture that breaks through repression; and **Somatic Practice**, which integrates the body and nervous system—treating catharsis as a **gradual release of stored tension** and a return to expressive freedom. Together, these voices trace catharsis from classical poetics to **embodied transformation**. AI-generated image created with OpenAI's DALL·E (via ChatGPT).

Artaud's Catharsis: Direct, Unfiltered, Transformative

If Aristotle's catharsis was meant to soothe, Antonin Artaud's version seeks to **ignite**. Artaud did not envision catharsis as a gentle moral or emotional purge but as an **energetic rupture**—a direct confrontation between the performer's raw inner world and the audience's senses. For Artaud, true theatrical power lies not in representation, but in *real transmission*—of pain, conflict, joy, and unresolved psychic tension.

In this light, catharsis becomes not a conclusion but a **violent opening** (see **Figure 5.21**). It is an **unfiltered discharge** of experience that arises in the moment—not as something constructed or rehearsed, but as something channeled. In Artaud's view, the stage must serve as a **ritual space** for the exposure and transformation of inner realities. Language becomes gesture, thought becomes sound, and emotion becomes vibration. Performers, fully immersed, allow their body to become a conduit for forces that cannot be articulated through words alone.

Unlike classical catharsis, which purges pity and fear through empathetic observation, Artaud's model demands **somatic participation**—a direct hit to the nervous system. This aligns with the energetic frameworks presented in this book, particularly the DEE and TDTETE cycles. Artaud's approach bypasses *Dynamis* → *Energeia* → *Entelecheia* in a linear fashion and instead thrusts the performer and audience into an **explosive Energeia**, one that triggers and reshapes perception.

He believed that this raw engagement revealed the hidden structures of trauma, repression, and unspoken desire. The catharsis was not simply emotional—it was **existential**, a tearing open of the self. Through this exposure, transformation was possible. Artaud wanted theatre to awaken forces the audience didn't know they carried—to act as a *mirror and a wound*, reflecting what lies beneath the surface.

FIGURE 5.21: Artaud's Energetic Catharsis: Inner Forces Unleashed. This image embodies Artaud's vision of theatre as a **raw**, **unfiltered transmission of psychic energy**. Presence becomes **eruption**—a somatic explosion that bypasses logic, confronts the unconscious, and opens a portal to transformation. Here, performance is not crafted—it is channeled. AI-generated image created with OpenAI's DALL·E (via ChatGPT).

This is why Artaud's cruelty, and his catharsis, are not techniques in the traditional sense—they are **acts of necessity**. They rely on performers' willingness to surrender control, to trust that their body knows more than their intellect, and that truth, no matter how disruptive, can be healing.

In many ways, this anticipates the somatic practices explored later in this chapter. Artaud's legacy is not just aesthetic—it is energetic, visceral, and **spiritually radical**. He shows us that catharsis, when pursued not as spectacle but as transformation, becomes one of the most **direct paths to presence and healing**.

From Tensions in Our Bodies to Trauma

Tension, as explored earlier, is not only a physical barrier to expressive flow—it can also be a **symptom of unresolved trauma**. In performance, the body often becomes the **repository for emotional history**: memories that are not accessible through conscious thought may still live in breath, gesture, posture, and muscular patterning. These embodied imprints affect presence, communication, and the performer's energetic alignment.

For some, these imprints are subtle—manifesting as a clenched jaw, collapsed chest, or stiff spine. For others, especially those with more profound or chronic trauma, these signals can become disruptive or even debilitating, severing the bridge between intention and expression. As trauma researcher **Bessel van der**

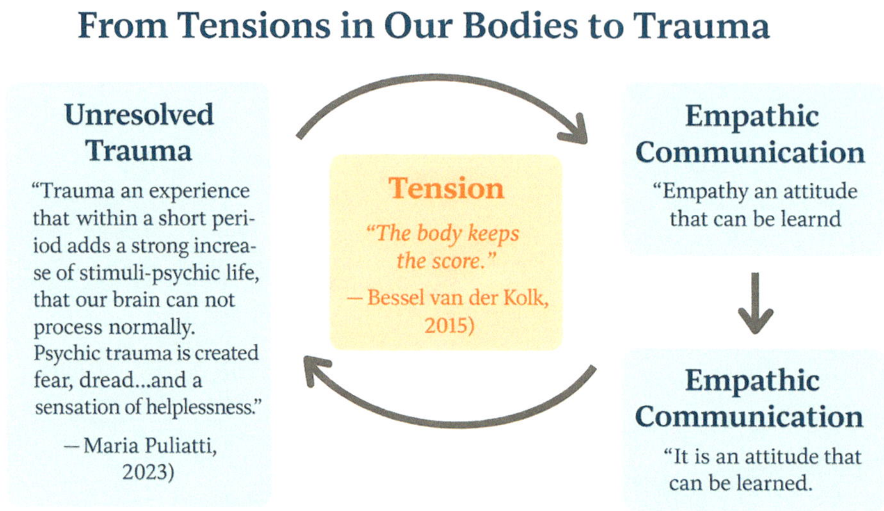

FIGURE 5.22: From Tension to Transformation: Trauma's Journey Through the Performer's Body. This flowchart visualizes how unresolved trauma manifests as chronic muscular tension, blocking the flow of energy and limiting expressiveness onstage. Drawing on the work of Puliatti, van der Kolk, and ArtSocial, the model traces a path from overwhelm to defense, and ultimately to release—through awareness and internal empathic communication. Empathy becomes both a mirror and a bridge—first offered externally, then cultivated inwardly by the performer to reclaim coherence and presence. AI-generated image created with OpenAI's DALL·E (via ChatGPT).

Kolk[7] has observed, "The body keeps the score" (van der Kolk 2015: 3). What we have not processed, the body continues to carry—and eventually, to express.

Psychotherapist and trauma therapy expert **Maria Puliatti**[8] defines trauma as:

> An experience that within a short period adds a strong increase of stimuli to psychic life that our brain cannot process normally. Psychic trauma is the consequence of serious events, of short or long duration, outside normal human experience. These overwhelming events create fear, dread, and a sensation of helplessness.
>
> (Puliatti 2023: 39, author's translation)

This understanding reframes performance training. The aim is not simply to shape external behaviors, but to **liberate blocked energy**, to make space for truth to flow again (see **Figure 5.22**). When the performer begins to notice habitual tensions, emotional triggers, or dissociative states, they are not signs of failure—they are signals. Invitations. Entry points into deeper awareness and, potentially, healing.

The organization **ArtSocial** from Spain reinforces this connection between trauma, presence, and empathy:

> Empathic communication is not only important in helping relationships but also in any work and social environment ... Empathy means understanding another person's feelings and thoughts without making them your own. Empathetic communication is an attitude that some have naturally or can be learned.
>
> (ArtSocial n.d.: n.pag, author's translation)

When gently acknowledged and consciously integrated, trauma becomes a **powerful source of depth, empathy, and presence**. Through breath, movement, and vocalization, the actor can transmute what was once frozen or fragmented into **coherent, radiant energy**.

This transition—from mechanical training to somatic sensitivity—is part of what makes **energetic alchemy** possible. It is where actors stop acting and begin to **listen** to their body, becoming both the subject and the instrument of transformation. In this space, the performer no longer forces performance to happen—they allow it to emerge.

This is not therapy—it is theatre with **therapeutic potential**. A sacred act of presence. A stage not for pretending, but for becoming.

Disclaimer

The following sections draw from my personal experiences and reflections in confronting trauma and emotional tension. My aim is to share these real-life accounts to illustrate a performer's journey of releasing physical blockages, enhancing energy awareness through the DEE Cycle, and cultivating empathetic communication. This path has allowed me to deepen my connection with myself and, from that foundation, connect more meaningfully with audiences—inviting them into the nuanced inner worlds of the characters I embody.

Please understand that what follows is not intended as advice or instruction to confront your own traumas, nor is it a substitute for professional mental health care. Everyone's readiness and path are different. If parts of my story resonate with you, I encourage you to consider reaching out to a qualified therapist or counselor. Your well-being is paramount, and professional support can provide the tools and safety needed for healing and growth.

Complex Post-Traumatic Stress Disorder (CPTSD) and Dissociation

As I mentioned, I'm going to share some of my personal traumas with you. The reason I do this is because I've done deep work on myself to understand the roots of each of my emotional blocks, and I came to realize that every one of those traumas left behind a physical tension—something that affected me not only as a person, but also as a performer. This journey revealed to me the direct connection between who I am as a human being, who I am as a performer, and how I communicate.

It's precisely through this process that the idea of Human Theatre was born. A theatre where the performer's personal history is not hidden but embraced, where the emotional memory becomes a source of truth and transformation onstage. Human Theatre is not about performing trauma—it's about understanding how it shapes the body, the voice, and the energy we carry into the space. It is a space where healing, authenticity, and expression meet.

That's why I've chosen to share my life experiences—to illustrate how trauma can affect our ability to connect with our bodies, manage our energy, and communicate authentically. These concepts have been explored by thinkers like Stanislavski and Lowen, and I've seen firsthand how they manifest in life and in art. Often dismissed as distant or insignificant, these internal tensions profoundly shape who we are. But I've also learned that theatre can be a powerful tool for healing, for reconnection, and for rediscovering ourselves—both onstage and off.

Then, what are CPTSD and Dissociation?

Complex Post-Traumatic Stress Disorder (CPTSD): This is a condition that can develop after prolonged or repeated trauma, such as ongoing abuse or neglect. It's similar to PTSD but includes additional symptoms like difficulty with emotional regulation, distorted self-perception, and relationship problems.

Dissociation: This is a mental process where you feel disconnected from your thoughts, feelings, memories, or sense of self. It can be a way of coping with overwhelming trauma (see **Figure 5.23**).

Personal Reflections and Traumatic Memories

Identity and Isolation

I was born in Chicago, Illinois, and before I turned one, I was living in Puerto Rico. My identity was shaped by a tension that followed me everywhere—a name split in two: Richard, Anglo-Saxon, and Martínez, undeniably Hispanic. In Puerto Rico, I was "el Americano." In the United States, "the Latino" or "the Hispanic." Neither one, entirely. My life became a question whispered beneath every introduction: *Do I belong here? Am I American, Puerto Rican, both—or neither?*

That question haunted me, especially at school. In Puerto Rico, it's customary to use both the father's and the mother's surnames—something rarely done in the United States. I remember people asking, "Don't you have a mother?" Or feeling the pressure to use only my mother's surname to blend in, despite the confusion it caused with legal documents. These small moments weren't small at all. They built into a persistent sense of estrangement, echoing colonial legacies I couldn't yet name, but deeply felt.

Over time, I found relief through the theatre mask—its ability to strip away social identity and access something more raw, more real. It wasn't about hiding. It was about becoming. The mask helped me bypass who I thought I was, and reach into who I truly felt myself to be.

Family Dysfunction and Abuse

Violence surrounded me from a young age. Alcohol and drug abuse at home normalized chaos. Fights. Yelling. Being thrown to the ground. I didn't know life could feel any different. Between the ages of four and eight, I was sexually abused by a close relative. I also witnessed the same person abuse someone else. My response was to disconnect—to shut down my mind while my body endured.

Fragments of those memories still come and go, ghostlike. They fractured my emotional development and left me with defense mechanisms I couldn't understand. Years later, it was dance—especially flamenco—that began to reawaken me. Its raw, grounded expression gave shape to my fury. Every stomp was a declaration: *I am still here.*

Natural Disasters

I still remember Hurricane Georges. The eerie stillness of the eye. The winds shifting directions and tearing through everything. The sound of roofs being ripped off, trees bending, and windows exploding. The next morning: devastation. Rubble. Silence. Grief.

Experiencing this as a child etched a primal fear in my body. It wasn't just about the loss of material things. It was the terror of not being safe—anywhere. It added to the layers of trauma I already carried. Only much later, through the Lessac method, did I find a way to calm that inner storm. Breath became my anchor. My return.

Witnessing Extreme Violence

In my teenage years, violence became more vivid, more immediate. One afternoon at a pizzeria, I saw a man on a motorcycle shoot another driver point-blank. I can still hear the shot, feel my body freeze, see the blood trail behind a passenger trying to crawl away. The sound of his head hitting the sidewalk, the way the street seemed to hold its breath in horror—it never left me.

Soon after, near my student apartment, another murder scene. Another life erased. These images made my body a home for tension and vigilance. But later, Commedia dell'Arte and Buffoons gave me a way to externalize this violence—to tell its truth without being consumed by it.

Struggle and Overcoming
In middle school, I found refuge in books, research, and study. Learning was my survival. Still, I was bullied—especially for my perceived femininity. I felt increasingly isolated, despite my academic achievements.

I didn't yet have theatre tools to process what I was holding. My brain, trying to protect me, encoded deep muscular tension that froze my movements and made my body feel like a cage.

Dissociation
My first dissociative episode came during an oratory competition. I was speaking, but I wasn't there. I watched myself from a distance, executing the speech perfectly—but when it ended, I was confused and detached. People applauded. I didn't understand why. That pattern continued: In moments of stress, I'd vanish inside myself. It took years of somatic practice and movement work to begin unraveling this split.

Music and Theatre as Refuge
Through it all, music and theatre were safe havens. My grandparents introduced me to jíbara music[9] and Puerto Rican traditions, offering me a sense of

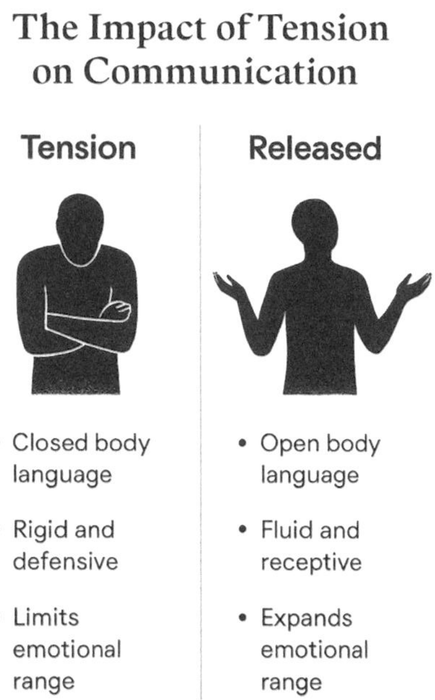

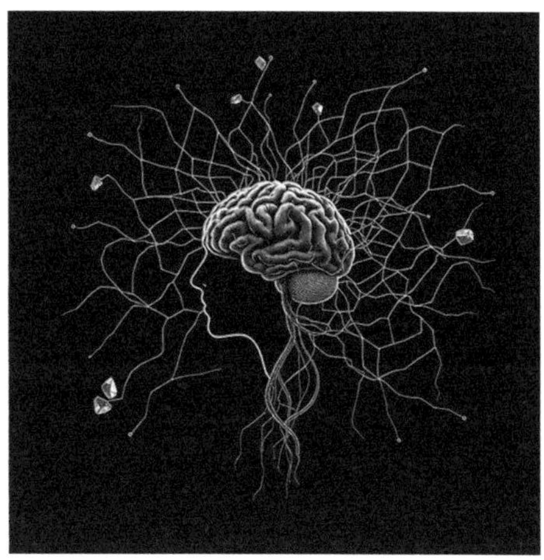

FIGURE 5.23: The Body as Tapestry: Trauma as Energetic Memory. Intense experiences can weave themselves into the body—layer by layer—forming a tapestry of unresolved tensions through which new experiences are filtered. This embodied archive shapes how we move, breathe, speak, and connect. Healing begins not by erasing, but by learning to read and reweave the thread. AI-generated image created with OpenAI's DALL·E (via ChatGPT).

cultural grounding. Their stories and melodies helped me express pain I couldn't yet name—and joy I didn't know I was allowed to feel.

My secondary school theatre teacher nurtured my passion further. That same year, a Specialized High School in Fine Arts opened. It became a sanctuary where art wasn't just expression—it was survival. Even though I still dissociated onstage, each rehearsal was a way home.

University and the Immigrant Body

The loss of my grandfather shook me. Grief triggered dissociative states again, especially during performances. I was also navigating sociopolitical instability, and violence on campus added to the stress. One day, police clashed with students outside my classroom. I froze. Sweat dripped down my spine as I forgot how to breathe.

After finishing my bachelor's, I moved to the United States and worked at a bank. I became the only fluent Spanish speaker in the teller line, and customers naturally gravitated toward me. It created connection—but also separation. When I struggled to explain credit card systems, I felt like I was failing everyone.

Eventually, I immigrated again—this time to Italy, drawn by a university program aligned with my vision. But migration comes with loss: of roots, of familiarity, of language. It brings constant pressure to prove yourself in unknown territory. It makes you question where you truly belong.

The Pandemic and a Breaking Point

When the pandemic hit, everything collapsed. Theatre disappeared. My lifeline—my release—was gone. Isolation in Italy was filled with grief, fear, and overwhelming empathy. Every global crisis felt personal. Every emotion too big to hold.

I told my therapist: "I feel everything in an unbearable, gigantic way." That was the moment I began the work of unravelling—of facing the traumas that had shaped me.

A New Beginning in Theatre

Therapy helped me reconnect body and mind. But it was theatre that brought me back to myself. Movement gave voice to what words couldn't say. Masks allowed me to express without judgment—to step beyond the self and become something truer.

It wasn't easy. The scars of abuse, disaster, and death run deep. But each moment onstage became part of my healing. I found strength not in erasing the past, but in transforming it.

The Essence of Human Theatre

Today, I use theatre to connect, to listen, and to tell stories that might help others find words they don't yet have. I've learned that art isn't about performance—it's about presence. We all carry pain. We all carry resilience. Theatre is where those truths meet.

This is the origin of *Human Theatre*.

Not a technique.

But a return.

To the breath.

To the body.

To each other.

The Mask as a Therapeutic Instrument

The mask has long been used in theatre to explore identity, archetypes, and presence. But for performers navigating trauma or struggling with self-expression, the mask becomes something more: a **therapeutic instrument.** It offers paradoxical liberation—by concealing the face, it frees the body. By masking identity, it reveals deeper truths (see **Figure 5.24**).

In my own experience, my masks became a vital bridge between dissociation and embodiment. They allowed me to step outside myself—not in the numbing, protective way trauma enforces, but in an intentional, exploratory way. Wearing the mask, I could become "another." In that safe distance, I began to revisit emotional memories without being overwhelmed by them. Over time, I noticed something remarkable: the masks were working on me even when I didn't expect it. Without realizing it, I was engaging in a kind of **somatic therapy**—reconnecting my body and mind through movement, breath, and presence.

This realization echoed the work of Maria Puliatti, who suggests that trauma can be addressed through psychomotor stimuli—movements and physical experiences that reopen blocked pathways of internal communication. I came to understand how training methods like **Lessac** also served a healing function for me. They were more than performance techniques; they were ways of restoring inner dialogue and helping my fragmented parts communicate. This became crucial not just for recovery—but for accessing truth in performance.

The **mask suspends judgment**. When worn, it bypasses ego, social constructs, and ingrained defense mechanisms. This enables performers to move beyond self-consciousness and enter a state of **playful experimentation**. Physical impulses become clearer. Movement becomes intuitive. We begin to listen to the body's expression without filtering it through narrative or identity.

In therapeutic or training contexts, mask work can:

- **Reignite spontaneity** and playfulness in movement.
- **Release muscular holding patterns** by shifting focus from facial expression to full-body articulation.

- **Create distance from personal trauma,** allowing the performer to observe, express, and reframe emotional memory.
- **Build expressive range** by allowing the performer to embody archetypal or abstract energies that expand beyond personal identity.

The power of the mask lies also in the **heightened state of awareness** it demands. Because it limits or shifts the senses, it compels performers to reorient their attention and adapt their presence:

- **Vision:** The mask's limited eye openings narrow visual fields, forcing intense focus and awareness of space and others.
- **Breathing:** Breathing must be regulated. Rhythmic, controlled breaths become essential to avoid fatigue, increase oxygenation, and maintain energy.
- **Hearing:** With partial auditory blockage, listening intensifies. Performers must rely more on sound cues and deepen auditory awareness.
- **Touch:** While not blocked, the sense of touch becomes more pronounced—used to convey clarity, precision, and emotional honesty.

Disciplines such as **Commedia dell'Arte, Larval Mask,** and **Neutral Mask** offer powerful tools for exploring these states. Presence arises not from personality, but from intention and stillness. The body becomes the voice.

FIGURE 5.24: Suspension Before Expression: Masks from the Author's Collection. These masks are not costumes—they are thresholds. Chosen for their capacity to quiet identity and amplify presence, they embody the poetic pause before emergence—a moment where expression is held in suspension, charged with breath and potential.

FIGURE 5.25: Mask as Mirror: A Student's Therapeutic Exploration. In this exercise by student D. at Teatro Umano, the mask becomes a tool for uncovering, not concealing. Through play, silence, and embodied stillness, the student confronts internal rhythm and emotion—allowing masked presence to reveal unspoken truths.

As I trained further, the mask taught me to deconstruct and reassemble each movement, making every choice precise and conscious. I gained greater control over the **DEE Cycle**, both physically and mentally. I learned to trust my body, to listen to it, and to let it lead. I found that as I controlled and synchronized breath and body, I began unlocking vocal blockages and emotional tension stored for years. Breathing no longer served only my technique—it gave me back vitality, presence, and emotional clarity.

These transformations weren't unique to me. I've witnessed others—some who weren't even trauma survivors—benefit from mask work in surprising and profound ways.

> ***Student Reflection: D's Journey with the Mask*** [see **Figure 5.25**] *The mask gave me the illusion of protection, but it did not hide me—it exposed me. It forced me to communicate through my body, to control my breath, and to reclaim the space. Over time, I stopped fearing the audience. The mask became a warm embrace that helped me overcome my fear of being seen.* (D, student at Teatro Umano)

This power lies at the heart of **Human Theatre**: The belief that personal history, when embraced with skill and sensitivity, becomes a wellspring for performance, authenticity, and connection.

In Human Theatre, the mask is not a tool for escape—it is an **invitation to return**. To return to the breath. To energy. To sensation. To truth. Through the mask, we create a space to **express, transform, and heal**.

Part 5—Theatre and Trauma: Bridging Performance and Healing

Theatre as Healing Practice

Theatre has long been a space for reflection, transformation, and catharsis—but can it go further? Can it become a true instrument for healing trauma?

For me, the answer is yes. But with a necessary clarification: Theatre is not therapy. It cannot replace psychological or medical care, especially for those in acute need. What it can offer, however, is a space of reconnection—a place where embodied presence, creative exploration, and emotional truth intersect to support personal transformation.

Theatre allows the performer to explore identity, relationships, and emotion in a context that is structured but freeing, imaginary but deeply real. When a person engages in performance work rooted in the body, breath, and impulse—such as what I've proposed in Human Theatre—they begin to recognize the physical traces of trauma: shallow breath, chronic tension, disconnect from sensation, and an inability to feel or express.

In theatre, we train to breathe fully, move with intention, speak with resonance, and listen with the whole body. These are not only tools for performance—they are skills for survival and self-repair.

In my own journey, theatre gave me the container to face emotions I couldn't yet name. When trauma had silenced me, theatre helped me find expression through the body. When fear made me withdraw, rehearsal spaces encouraged me to take up space, to be seen. When dissociation kept me fragmented, exercises in energy, voice, and presence reminded me that I was still here.

Theatre doesn't ask us to relive trauma—but it allows us to reclaim agency over our story. And sometimes, that's the first step in healing.

This potential is not just anecdotal. Increasingly, psychologists and somatic therapists recognize the value of embodied arts in trauma recovery. Practices that combine movement, rhythm, voice, and safe interaction support what researchers call "bottom-up healing"—change that begins not with words, but with the nervous system and the body.

Thus, theatre—especially when approached with sensitivity, somatic awareness, and emotional intelligence—can become more than expression. It becomes alchemy.

It transforms:

- Fear into focus.
- Tension into tone.
- Dissociation into presence.
- Silence into story.

This is not about performing pain. It's about transmuting it into energy, and using that energy to build connection—with ourselves, with our scene partners, and with the audience.

In Human Theatre, this is central. We don't perform trauma—we learn from it, move through it, and use the body as a site of memory and resilience. We engage theatrical tools like the DEE Cycle, mask work, breathwork, rhythm, and character transformation to not only create art—but to restore integrity to the self.

In that sense, yes—theatre can be an instrument for trauma treatment. Not by acting out pain, but by learning to listen to it, to hold it safely, and to transform it into presence.

EMDR and the Performer's Body: Bridging Somatic Healing and Theatre

In *Il Trattamento dei Traumi* ("The Treatment of Trauma"), psychologist Maria Puliatti outlines how EMDR therapy—traditionally used to treat psychological trauma—can be enriched through body-based practices. She integrates **mindfulness**, **sensorimotor psychology**, **somatic psychotherapy**, and **psychomotor techniques** to help individuals reconnect with their bodies and regulate emotions. Surprisingly, while reading her work, I noticed how many of her observations echoed my own discoveries as a performer—particularly through my training in **Lessac Kinesensics** and **Human Theatre**.

Although I am not a psychologist, I have spent years exploring the link between trauma, the body, and artistic practice. My personal experiences and professional training—especially during my time at the Lessac Institute (2012–14)—taught me that **embodied preparation** for performance often mirrors the **preparatory phase of trauma treatment**.

Both EMDR and theatrical training ask the individual to:

- Cultivate body awareness;
- Identify physical and emotional responses;
- Regulate nervous system activation; and
- Use sensory and imaginative tools to build resilience.

Let's unpack some of these shared principles and see how they resonate in the performer's body.

Stability and Regulation of the Nervous System

A fundamental step in both EMDR therapy and performance training is cultivating the ability to **remain centered**—even while navigating emotionally charged material.

In therapy, this is often referred to as **emotional regulation** or the ability to stay within the "window of tolerance." A person who has experienced trauma may easily slip into states of hyperactivation (anxiety, panic) or hypoactivation (numbness, dissociation). EMDR therapists help clients identify these states and develop tools to return to stability.

In Lessac training, we do something similar—though the context is different. We train performers to recognize **energetic fluctuations** in the body, breath, and voice. We become aware of when tension overrides intention, or when the breath becomes shallow and disconnected. We learn to return to a **grounded, sensory state** where full-body communication becomes possible again.

This is not just about technique. It's about cultivating **nervous system intelligence**.

In both settings, **somatic awareness** becomes the first tool for healing and expression:

- "Where is my breath right now?"
- "What sensations am I noticing?"
- "What is my baseline when I'm calm? When I'm overwhelmed?"

For the performer, this training builds emotional agility onstage. We can access grief, joy, rage, or vulnerability—and just as importantly, **return to center** once the scene ends.

For me, this ability to regulate was transformative. After years of living in a state of **hypervigilance**, I began to reclaim my baseline—learning that I didn't always need to be on guard. Through performance and breath-based training, I experienced what safety felt like in my body for the first time in years.

Training and Tools: EMDR Meets Lessac

Both EMDR therapy and the Lessac method share a somatic foundation. They begin with the **body**, not the intellect. They seek to build regulation, resilience, and presence through specific tools—tools that allow individuals to reconnect with themselves in safe, embodied ways.

In **EMDR**, tools like **bilateral stimulation**, **orienting techniques**, and **mindful awareness** guide the individual into a balanced state. The therapist helps clients become aware of their breath, sensations, and emotional responses—tracking what brings discomfort and what brings relief.

In **Lessac**, the performer engages the same kind of tracking. We explore:

- Breath sensation: How does breath feel in the body? Where does it want to go?
- Body alignment and balance: What parts are holding tension? Where is release possible?
- Sensory engagement: What sensations are available in the voice, movement, and presence?

Both approaches emphasize **attunement**—to the self, to sensations, to the environment.

In my own case, training in the Lessac method gave me tools I didn't know I needed. When trauma made me feel scattered or out of control, returning to breath, tone, or simple alignment cues provided a sense of structure and safety. These weren't just performance techniques—they were lifelines.

Through repetition and sensory exploration, I began to regain control over the basic mechanisms of expression. The body remembered. And with that memory came relief, presence, and a growing sense of personal power.

Imagination and the Mind-Body Connection

Both **EMDR** and the **Lessac** method place a deep trust in the **imaginative** and **sensory** capacities of the body. While they work from different foundations—clinical therapy and theatrical training—each uses **imagination** not to escape reality, but to reconnect with it more fully, somatically, and safely.

In EMDR therapy, clients often **visualize inner states, memories**, or **supportive symbols** while engaging in bilateral stimulation. These images are not arbitrary—they are drawn from the body's stored experiences and can bring emotional release or insight when processed intentionally.

In Lessac's work, imagination activates the **senses**. We don't just "breathe"—we **"breath-sense."** We don't just walk—we **tone-walk**, **feel-weight**, **hum-vibrate**. Every action is an invitation to sense, to imagine, and to transform.

This sensory imagination becomes a tool for:

- Accessing emotions without being overwhelmed.
- Discovering movement patterns that align with feeling states.
- Cultivating a deeper sense of **self-compassion**, often through the metaphor of the "inner child."

In my own practice, imagination was never separate from healing. At times when I couldn't find words for my emotions, visualizing breath as light or tone as a wave gave me an entry point. The Lessac method helped me **transform a freeze response into flow**, not through analysis, but through **playful somatic exploration**.

This playful approach mirrors aspects of EMDR's resourcing phase, where clients create and rehearse **safe spaces**, **anchoring images**, and **supportive figures**. The body begins to **trust** again—not because it is told to, but because it is **shown**, gently and repeatedly, that safety and expression can coexist.

Proprioception and Interoception: How We Connect with Our Body

One of the most revealing parallels between EMDR therapy and Human Theatre lies in the **sensory intelligence** of the body—especially in the twin faculties of **proprioception** and **interoception**.

Proprioception is the body's internal GPS. It allows you to know the position of your limbs without needing to look at them. It's what lets a dancer turn in space with precision or a performer find balance in a complex stage picture. In trauma recovery, this sense helps anchor people back into their bodies after moments of dissociation.

Interoception, on the other hand, is how we perceive our **internal sensations**—heartbeat, breath, digestion, even the subtle fluctuations of emotion as felt in the body. It tells us when we're anxious or calm, cold or warm, grounded or out of sync. For trauma survivors, this sense often gets numbed or distorted. But when recovered, it becomes a powerful tool for **emotional regulation** and self-awareness.

Both EMDR and Lessac training (and, by extension, Human Theatre) involve **sensory re-education**:

- Exercises that bring awareness to **internal temperature, postural alignment**, or **vibration in the bones**.
- Practices that **retrain the nervous system** to perceive the body safely and accurately.
- A focus on **fine-tuning attention**—to breath, to movement, to felt rhythm.

In my case, learning to listen to my inner world was one of the most challenging and healing steps. There were times I didn't recognize hunger or fatigue until I collapsed. Other times, a racing heart would trigger spirals of fear. But by reconnecting with these inner signals—through breath-sensing, body awareness, and vocal tone—I gradually rebuilt my trust in my own body.

As performers, this connection is not optional—it is the bedrock of presence. A performer with finely tuned proprioception and interoception can shift energy in real time, adjust tone with intention, and remain alive to the smallest impulse.

More importantly, they can recognize when tension is functional ... and when it's a symptom of something unresolved.

In trauma healing, these same skills help widen the **window of tolerance**—the zone in which we can feel, process, and respond without shutting down or becoming overwhelmed. That, in essence, is the shared ground between EMDR and Human Theatre: a return to **embodied awareness** as a source of strength, safety, and transformation.

Levels of Nervous System Activation

When preparing for trauma therapy, a crucial element is understanding how the **nervous system** responds to threat. The same understanding is valuable for performers—especially those who are engaging deeply with their personal histories or with emotionally charged material.

There are two dominant nervous system responses to trauma:

- **Hyperactivation:** The body remains stuck in a state of high alert. Muscles tense, breath becomes shallow, and the mind constantly scans for danger.
- **Hypoactivation:** The system shuts down. Energy drops. The performer may feel numb, disconnected, or frozen, unable to act or express.

Both responses reflect a nervous system that has gone outside its **window of tolerance**—the zone in which a person can engage with emotional material without becoming overwhelmed.

In EMDR, the therapist helps guide the client **back into that window**, using tools like bilateral stimulation and somatic tracking to regulate physiological arousal. In Human Theatre, we do something similar through embodied training: **Breath, grounding, vocal tone, and physical orientation** become the actor's tools for staying present, even amid powerful material.

I've personally lived in a state of hyperactivation for years—unaware that my body had developed an automatic alarm system. Even in moments of calm, my mind rehearsed escape routes. For example, when my partner was cooking with professional knives, I wasn't thinking about the meal—I was planning how to flee in case something went wrong. It wasn't logical. It wasn't conscious. But it was real.

Another trigger was **language**. As an immigrant, the constant effort of expressing myself in a foreign tongue—onstage or in everyday life—could feel like a threat. My brain translated small social exchanges into danger. Even as I stood in a scene, part of me would be bracing for exclusion, failure, or exposure. My gestures became tight. My breath, restricted. My presence, fractured.

These are the unconscious patterns we carry to the stage.

But here's the good news: **These patterns can be transformed.** Both EMDR and performance training offer pathways back into regulation—into safety, into awareness, into energy. The key lies in understanding the **language of the body**, and in cultivating the tools to listen and respond with compassion.

Benefits of Regulation: The Performer's Toolkit

In both EMDR and Human Theatre, the goal is not to suppress emotion—but to meet it with **presence and control**. Regulation is the bridge between activation and expression.

For the performer, this means cultivating skills that allow intense emotional states to **move through the body without overwhelming it**. The same tools used in trauma therapy—such as breath regulation, sensory awareness, and grounding—become instruments for energetic clarity onstage.

Here are some core benefits of nervous system regulation that apply directly to the performer's work:

- **Attention Regulation**: The ability to stay focused amid distraction. This is essential in performance, where split attention can cause disconnection from the scene or partner.
- **Body State Regulation**: Awareness of physical needs—hunger, fatigue, temperature—and the ability to care for them ensures the body remains a safe and available instrument.
- **Sensory Regulation**: Knowing how to use and respond to sensory input (sound, light, touch) helps the performer stay rooted in the environment without being hijacked by it.
- **Energy Regulation**: The capacity to adapt energy to the demands of the moment. It prevents collapse in moments of stillness or explosive release in moments of subtlety.
- **Emotional Regulation**: The skill of expressing emotion without being overtaken by it—a hallmark of mature performance.

As an actor, I learned that emotional power **does not depend on losing control**, but on channeling internal impulses through breath, body, and presence. When I began to practice Lessac's work with awareness of these principles, I noticed a shift: not only was I more expressive—I was more alive. Less reactive. More grounded.

Both EMDR and Lessac recognize that the **body is not separate from the story—it is the first storyteller**. By aligning physical training with emotional tracking, both methods allow for transformation without re-traumatization.

Tension in the Pelvic Area: The Ground Beneath Presence

One of the lesser-discussed—but crucial—physical areas impacted by trauma is the **pelvic region**, including the **gluteal and perianal muscles** (see **Figure 5.26**). According to Maria Puliatti, persistent tension in this area can significantly disrupt one's ability to feel **grounded**—both physically and emotionally. And for the performer, that lack of grounding undermines presence.

When we're disconnected from the base of our bodies, we lose our **sense of stability**. We may feel top-heavy, tense, or disconnected from the floor. Our breath gets shallower. Our knees lock. Our gestures become disjointed.

I've experienced this personally. There were times in my life when anxiety or trauma made me feel like I was floating just above my body, unanchored. I could be onstage, speaking lines, and still feel like my feet weren't fully touching the ground. I only began to recover that sense of grounding when I trained to **release pelvic tension consciously**, using techniques from the **Lessac method, koshi alignment**, and **somatic work.**

This area of the body is intimately linked with:

- Postural alignment.
- The flow of energy between the upper and lower body.
- Emotional safety and sexual identity.
- Our ability to rest into stillness without collapse.

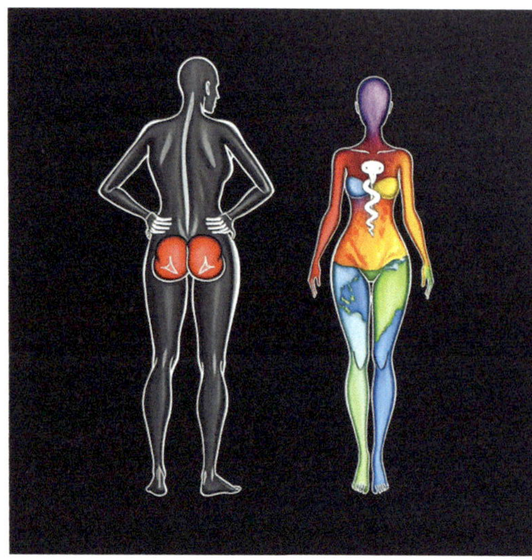

FIGURE 5.26: Grounded versus Ungrounded: Tension in the Pelvic Floor. This diagram compares a body holding unconscious tension in the gluteal and perianal region *(left)* with one that is released and grounded *(right)*. Pelvic tension disrupts alignment, breath, and energetic flow—while release restores connection to the earth, enabling true presence from the base upward. AI-generated image created with OpenAI's DALL·E (via ChatGPT).

The **C-Curve** from Lessac, along with the Japanese concept of **koshi** (researched and adapted by Mangolini), focuses precisely on this center. So does Putnam's **energetic triangle model**. All of these point to one truth: **The base of the body is not just structural—it's energetic.**

When this base is tense, rigid, or numb, energy cannot rise. The performer loses **verticality**, and with it, expressive power. But when it is engaged, aligned, and alive, a powerful transformation occurs: movement becomes connected, voice becomes supported, and presence radiates upward from the ground.

By integrating somatic awareness with theatrical technique, performers can develop not only a greater command of movement, but also a deeper **trust in their own bodies**. This trust is essential for healing, for connection, and for truly transformative performance.

From Potential to Presence: Reclaiming the DEE Cycle

What we've explored so far—from nervous system regulation and sensory awareness to somatic engagement and expressive tools—brings us back to a core structure of this book: the DEE Cycle: Dynamis → Energeia → Entelecheia.

These stages describe how potential becomes action, and how action leads to fulfillment or expression. But when viewed through the lens of trauma and healing, this cycle gains new significance.

Dynamis (Potential): In trauma recovery, this is the moment when stored tension, emotion, or story begins to stir. It is the internal urge—the desire to act, to speak, to be seen.

Energeia (Activation): This is the energetic ignition. In both EMDR and theatre, it's where the impulse moves into breath, voice, or gesture. It's the beginning of externalization.

Entelecheia (Expression): This is completion. Not perfection, but the release of held energy into something seen, heard, or embodied. Onstage, it's when presence becomes palpable. In therapy, it's when insight or emotional clarity emerges.

What struck me in my own healing journey was that I was already moving through these phases in my training—long before I understood their therapeutic dimension. The DEE Cycle wasn't just a performance tool. It was a natural process for **moving through trauma**.

In performance:

- We connect with inner potential (Dynamis).
- We activate the body and voice (Energeia).
- We complete the act through presence and impact (Entelecheia).

In healing:

- We acknowledge stored emotional energy.
- We engage breath, sensation, and imagination to move it.
- We release it through voice, gesture, or shared understanding.

This is the essence of Human Theatre. A space where art and healing overlap, where expression follows sensation, and where the DEE Cycle becomes a bridge between past wounds and present vitality.

Rediscovering this cycle through a therapeutic lens deepened my respect for its power. It reminded me that energy, when blocked, becomes tension—but when honored and expressed, becomes transformation.

Against Mannerism: The Call for Authentic Expression

In the pursuit of beauty, precision, or virtuosity, theatre can sometimes veer into **mannerism**[10]—a kind of stylized performance that emphasizes external form at the expense of emotional depth. The term, rooted in the Italian *maniera*, originally described an elegant style of art. But over time, it came to represent a certain **excess**: where aesthetic flourishes overshadow meaning, and where performance becomes ornate, even hollow.

We see this in theatre that prioritizes the perfect gesture, the ideal image, the dazzling technique—without anchoring it to human truth. Everything may look flawless, but something essential is missing. There is no heartbeat. No message. No communication.

For me, this realization didn't arise from theory—it came from experience. I've been onstages where every movement was technically impeccable, yet I felt disconnected. I've worked with performers who could mimic every emotion, yet never truly revealed themselves. In these moments, theatre became spectacle—but not connection.

This is the danger of mannerism: It seduces us into performance without presence.

In contrast, **Human Theatre** demands something different. It asks not for perfection, but for **authenticity**. It's not about suppressing technique, but about using it to serve expression. When our gestures emerge from sensation, when our breath is alive with meaning, when our voice carries the memory of experience—then we communicate.

This is where the DEE Cycle becomes vital again:

- **Dynamis** provides the internal motivation—real, felt, lived.
- **Energeia** transforms that impulse into action.
- **Entelecheia** completes it with expressive presence.

A performance that honors this cycle is never mannered. It is embodied. It is alive.

As I worked through my own healing process, I became increasingly attuned to this distinction. I could feel when I was acting "from the outside in"—performing a version of myself that was polished, controlled, but emotionally disconnected. And I could feel when I was rooted—when my body, breath, and story aligned.

The difference was not subtle. It was transformational.

Authentic expression is not about being raw or exposed for its own sake. It is about alignment—between what we feel, what we do, and what we communicate. When that alignment occurs, performance becomes a human act, not just an artistic one.

This is the call of Human Theatre. Not to abandon form, but to **infuse it with life**. Not to reject style, but to **anchor it in truth**. Not to seek applause, but to **invite recognition**—that moment when the audience sees not just the character, but the humanity beneath.

Against mannerism, we offer presence. Against artifice, we offer energy. Against perfection, we offer empathy.

Because in the end, the most powerful performance is the one that moves not only bodies, but hearts.

Survey Reflections: Lessac and the Healing Power of Presence

To understand whether the benefits I experienced through Lessac training were shared by others, I partnered with the Lessac Institute to distribute a questionnaire to practitioners, instructors, and Master Teachers of the method. My goal was to learn how this voice-body-energy approach supported personal and professional growth, and more specifically, whether it had any therapeutic or healing effects—particularly around trauma, emotional regulation, and communication.

The responses revealed a profound alignment between **Lessac's principles** and the embodied tools needed for healing, resilience, and authentic expression.

Before Training: Disconnection and Diverse Needs

Participants came from diverse backgrounds: some were seasoned performers, others were educators or individuals simply seeking more comfort and power in their voice and body. Despite their differences, many noted a common thread: they entered the Lessac work with **some level of disconnection**—from breath, from presence, from expression.

Some lacked vocal training, others felt physically tense or emotionally "shut down." A few carried deep-seated anxieties about performing or public speaking. For many, this disconnect echoed the same symptoms often associated with trauma: **shallow breathing, body numbness, performance anxiety, or expressive inhibition**.

After Training: Voice, Sensation, and Self-Regulation

Across the board, participants reported noticeable shifts:

- A **deeper awareness** of their bodies and breathing.
- Increased **vocal clarity** and resonance.
- An ability to **self-regulate emotional states** using tone, sensation, and breath.
- Enhanced **confidence and spontaneity**—not only in performance, but in daily life.

The emphasis on sensory engagement—"feeling the voice," "sensing movement," "vibrating with tone"—was repeatedly cited as transformative. Some described the experience as **reclaiming parts of themselves** they hadn't realized were silent or tense.

As one participant wrote: "Lessac didn't just improve my voice—it gave me back parts of my self I didn't know I'd lost."

Energy and Emotional Presence

A particularly striking theme was how **energy** was understood before and after Lessac's work. Prior to training, many associated energy with effort, exertion, or stage presence. Afterward, they described energy as something **lived and sensed**—as something that flowed through breath, vibration, and human connection.

Several described their energy as lighter, more centered, or more expansive. They felt **emotionally clearer**, less likely to "over-perform," and more able to **stay grounded during intense material**.

This aligns beautifully with the DEE Cycle and with the trauma-informed lens we've explored:

- Dynamis: They felt a **renewed potential** for creative and emotional expression.
- Energeia: They engaged with breath, tone, and body to **activate presence**.
- Entelecheia: They completed actions with **authentic communication** and impact.

Therapeutic Insights

Though not all participants explicitly used the word "trauma," many described the Lessac work in therapeutic terms:

- A space for healing and self-care.
- A method to regulate stress and anxiety.
- A tool for **reconnecting with the body and emotions** after periods of suppression or disconnection.

Several suggested that the Lessac approach could support people recovering from trauma, especially when integrated with other forms of therapy or embodied practice.

"The Lessac work was like physical therapy for my inner life."

"I began to understand how my voice was directly linked to my emotional truth."

Who Can Benefit?
Finally, respondents emphasized that this work isn't only for actors. Teachers, public speakers, caregivers, therapists, and anyone struggling with confidence or embodiment could benefit.

Many said the Lessac principles should be part of broader wellness and education programs, noting how **breath, tone, and body awareness** are essential tools for resilience in everyday life.

Synthesis and Closing: Human Theatre as a Practice of Integration

Throughout this chapter, we've explored the profound intersections between **trauma, somatic awareness, and performance**—and how the theatre can serve as a **transformative space** for healing, expression, and reconnection.

We began with the **mask** as a gateway—offering paradoxical freedom by concealing the face and awakening the body. We followed the path of trauma in the performer's body, recognizing the signs: blocked breath, dissociation, hypervigilance, chronic tension. We traced how **Lessac's Kinesensic Training**, informed by the **DEE Cycle**, supported regulation, presence, and creative expression—not just for art, but for survival and emotional restoration.

We discovered parallels between **EMDR therapy** and Human Theatre: both grounded in the body, both dependent on awareness, both aimed at liberating blocked energy and restoring agency.

We unpacked concepts like **interoception**, **proprioception**, and **koshi**—recognizing that when performers are centered in their energetic core and rooted through their pelvis, breath deepens, alignment improves, and presence radiates. Koshi is not simply anatomical; it is a metaphor for grounded power. When the body's base is alive and responsive, the performer finds stillness, strength, and flow.

We reclaimed the **DEE Cycle** not only as a performance principle but as a **pathway for transformation**:

- **Dynamis** as the spark of awareness.
- **Energeia** as the courageous movement forward.
- **Entelecheia** as the embodied completion and reconnection.

We saw how performance techniques can regulate the nervous system, how creative tools can help process trauma without retraumatization, and how being seen

FIGURE 5.27: Human Theatre: A Space of Transformation: The core journey of Human Theatre—where the performer moves from fragmentation to integration, from trauma to transformation. Through breath, voice, koshi alignment, and presence, performers reconnect with their body, channel authentic energy, and reclaim storytelling as a healing act. A reminder that true performance begins with inner awareness and culminates in shared humanity. AI-generated image created with OpenAI's DALL·E (via ChatGPT).

onstage can mirror being seen in the world—for the first time, perhaps, with compassion.

And through it all, we recognized something vital: **Every performer's process is unique.**

There is no singular path to presence. No universal map to healing. What Human Theatre offers is a compass—a way to navigate our histories, sensations, and stories with honesty and care. It's a framework that honors the personal while opening space for shared resonance.

Ultimately, Human Theatre is not about method—it's about integration.

It is about:

- Feeling the **energetic truth** of the body and honoring it.
- Using breath and tone not to "perform" emotion, but to **transform** it.
- Allowing personal history not to limit expression, but to **infuse it with meaning**.
- Making theatre not just a stage for characters, but a **sacred ground for reclaiming self**.

In this approach, theatre becomes **more than storytelling**—it becomes **soul-telling**.

We do not heal by ignoring the body. We heal by **inhabiting it**.

We do not communicate by perfecting our gestures. We communicate by **aligning intention with energy**.

We do not transform by escaping our past. We transform by **holding it**, moving with it, and shaping it into presence.

That is the purpose—and the promise—of Human Theatre (see **Figure 5.27**).

NOTES

1. *Perezhivanie* is a Russian term meaning "living through." It refers to the actor's deep emotional and psychological experience of a role, where they do not simply represent emotions but fully re-experience them onstage, allowing genuine presence to emerge from within the performance.
2. Channels of communication encompass diverse physical and emotional pathways for expressing and perceiving feelings, thoughts, and sensations. Lowen highlighted their significance in fostering authentic connections and self-awareness. He emphasized the body as a crucial medium for communication, asserting that emotional blockages manifest physically and hinder genuine expression. To overcome these obstacles, Lowen encouraged practicing body awareness, breathwork, and movement exercises to open these channels. This holistic approach reflects his belief that emotional health is intrinsically linked to physical well-being, enabling enhanced emotional expression and stronger interpersonal relationships.
3. Dysregulation, particularly emotional dysregulation, refers to the difficulty or inability to manage and respond to emotions in a typical manner. This can manifest as experiencing intense, disproportionate, or prolonged emotional responses that are challenging to control. These responses may manifest as mood swings, anxiety, impulsivity, and other behavioral issues.
4. Antonio Núñez Partido, a renowned Spanish director, teacher, and researcher, significantly contributes to theatre and performance studies. His innovative approaches to actor

training, particularly in physical theatre and movement techniques, emphasize the body's vital role in emotional and artistic expression. Núñez Partido promotes the integration of body awareness and dynamic expression in acting, encouraging dialogue and collaboration between artists and educators. Beyond his directorial projects, he contributes to scholarly discussions on theatrical pedagogy and the role of performance in cultural contexts, making him a key figure in exploring creative expression in theatre.

5. Scott P. Phillips, a scholar and author, is known for his interdisciplinary research on theatre, ritual, and martial arts, especially in Chinese culture. His seminal work, "Theatre, Ritual, and Exorcism in Chinese Martial Arts," explores the historical and cultural connections between theatrical performance, ritual practices, and martial arts traditions in China. Phillips meticulously examines how these elements are intertwined, illuminating their roles in community storytelling, cultural expression, and spiritual concepts. By examining martial arts' performative aspects, he reveals the ritualistic and theatrical dimensions that inform these practices, providing insights into their significance beyond combat. His work contributes to understanding how cultural practices are interconnected and reflect societal values and beliefs.
6. Catharsis refers to the process of releasing and purifying intense emotions, especially through art.
7. Bessel van der Kolk, a renowned psychiatrist and trauma expert, authored *Il Corpo Accusa il Colpo* (*The Body Keeps the Score*). In this influential book, Van der Kolk delves into the profound impact of trauma on individuals' physical and psychological well-being. He seamlessly integrates neuroscience, psychology, and body-based therapies to demonstrate the profound connection between trauma and bodily sensations. Van der Kolk underscores the significance of recognizing and addressing trauma through diverse healing modalities, advocating for a holistic approach that incorporates the body in the healing process. His groundbreaking work has significantly advanced our comprehension of trauma and its enduring effects, making it an indispensable resource for professionals and individuals seeking to comprehend their experiences.
8. Maria Puliatti, an Italian psychotherapist and trauma therapy expert, has made substantial contributions to understanding and treating traumatic experiences. Her book, titled Il *Trattamento dei Traumi* ("The Treatment of Trauma"), presents a comprehensive approach to trauma therapy, detailing methods and techniques for healing and recovery. Drawing from her clinical experience and research, Puliatti emphasizes the significance of addressing the psychological, emotional, and physical aspects of trauma. The book offers valuable insights for practitioners and individuals affected by trauma, providing practical tools for resilience and well-being. Puliatti's work is crucial for comprehending trauma and its pathways to healing.
9. Jíbara music, a traditional folk genre from Puerto Rico's mountainous regions, reflects the cultural heritage of rural Puerto Ricans. It features string instruments like the cuatro and maracas, accompanied by heartfelt vocals. Lyrics often convey themes of love, nature, and

daily life, showcasing the jíbaro people's connection to their environment. Jíbara music's improvisational style and storytelling elements preserve and transmit Puerto Rican rural communities' history and experiences, making it a vital aspect of Puerto Rican identity.

10. Mannerism, derived from the Italian *maniera*, originally referred to the refined and artificially elegant style of art that aimed to embellish reality. Emerging during the late renaissance (1520–1600), mannerism was characterized by complex compositions and stylistic tension, prioritizing form over natural expressiveness. Over time, mannerism became associated with works that distorted the essence of their portrayal due to excessive aesthetic enhancement.

SECTION 3

SYNTHESIS AND APPLICATION OF HUMAN THEATRE

Chapter 6

Human Theatre: Embodying the Performer's Heart

6

Human Theatre: Embodying the Performer's Heart

Part 1—Reframing Dramaturgy: From Ancient Theory to Energetic Expression

The Human Theatre: A New Proposal for a Living Dramaturgy

Dramaturgy has long served as the backbone of theatrical creation—a framework of composition, structure, and interpretation. From Aristotle's *Poetics* to contemporary experimental forms, it has reflected how societies perceive narrative, conflict, and resolution. Traditionally, it emphasized written text, character development, and linear storytelling. But what happens when we shift the center of gravity from script to sensation? From plot to **presence**?

This is where **Human Theatre** takes root.

Human Theatre is not a new aesthetic style—it's a proposal for a new way of experiencing and creating theatre. It centers the performer not as an interpreter of lines, but as a conduit of **energy**. At its core is a belief that **intention**, when amplified by breath, gesture, and awareness, becomes a powerful tool of communication. This energetic exchange is the heart of theatrical meaning.

Rather than rejecting dramaturgical traditions, Human Theatre **reframes** them through the body. Its primary focus is not on verbal expression, but on **energetic presence**. It draws from history but evolves toward immediacy—prioritizing lived truth over narrative structure, and connection over coherence.

FIGURE 6.0: Heart of Resonance. Expression deepens when the heart is awakened. Through this center, feeling becomes movement, radiating through the entire body. AI-generated image created with OpenAI's DALL·E (via ChatGPT).

The dramatic language of Human Theatre is composed of:

- Breath that carries meaning;
- Stillness that resonates;
- Movement that reveals intention;
- Voice used not only to speak, but to vibrate and awaken;
- and above all, energy—transmitted from performer to audience.

This vision is guided by the **DEE Cycle**:

- **Dynamis**—the seed of potential within the performer;
- **Energeia**—the activation of that potential through action;
- **Entelecheia**—the moment it reaches its fullest realization and impacts the audience.

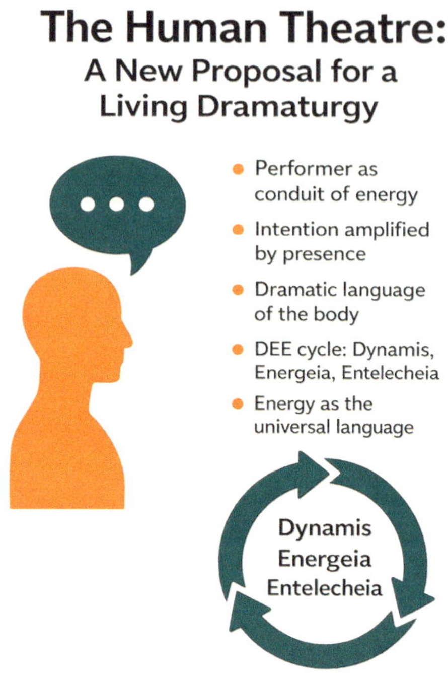

FIGURE 6.1: The Human Theatre Proposal: Energy as Dramaturgy. This diagram visualizes the evolution from traditional dramaturgy—built on character, conflict, and plot—toward Human Theatre, where energy, intention, and presence form the new structural core. The DEE Cycle (Dynamis–Energeia–Entelecheia) becomes not metaphor, but pulse: the living rhythm of a dramatic language rooted in embodiment, not imitation. AI-generated image created with OpenAI's DALL·E (via ChatGPT).

Each cycle renews itself, creating a performance that is not fixed, but **alive**—responsive to the moment, to the space, and to the spectators who witness it.

In Human Theatre, **energy is the message** (see **Figure 6.1**). The performer's body becomes the text. The stage becomes a vessel of transformation.

This dramaturgy is not built on rigid rules, but on sensitivity, empathy, and creative intuition. It is theatre that listens—to impulse, to silence, to the breath of the room.

By placing energy at the center, Human Theatre offers a **universal language**—one that transcends culture and speech, and invites all who witness it to feel, remember, and connect.

From Aristotle to Now: A Journey Through Dramaturgical Models

Dramaturgy has never been a static discipline—it evolves alongside culture, philosophy, and the human need to make sense of experience through performance.

From Aristotle's *Poetics* to the hybrid creations of the twenty-first century, dramaturgical models reflect how we perceive action, character, and meaning onstage. This journey through time allows us to understand how Human Theatre stands on the shoulders of previous thought while offering something radically embodied and new.

Classical Dramaturgy: The Blueprint of Action

Aristotle's model introduced the basic architecture of dramatic composition: unity of time, place, and action; the centrality of plot (*mythos*); the importance of catharsis; and the movement from exposition to climax to resolution. These principles shaped Western theatre for centuries and still influence narrative expectations today.

This model emphasized logic, clarity, and cause-and-effect storytelling, where the audience observed action unfold in a linear progression. Dramatic conflict and character development were used to bring audiences to a moment of cathartic release—an emotional purification.

Modern Dramaturgy: Realism, Psychology, and the Inner World

With the nineteenth century came an embrace of realism and psychological depth. Playwrights like Ibsen, Chekhov, and Strindberg explored the complexities of human behavior and the unconscious. The "fourth wall" convention invited audiences to peer into domestic scenes, where silence, subtext, and gesture often carried more weight than action.

Modern dramaturgy invited empathy and introspection. Conflict remained important, but now it often took the shape of inner turmoil rather than epic clashes. Characters became fragile, nuanced beings. This shift opened the door for the performer to explore emotional and somatic truth.

Postmodern Dramaturgy: Breaking Form, Inviting the Audience

By the late twentieth century, artists began to deconstruct traditional narratives. Postmodern dramaturgy embraced fragmentation, simultaneity, pastiche, and metatheatre. Structures broke open. Logic was replaced by ambiguity. Identity was questioned. The audience was no longer passive.

Playwrights like Heiner Müller[1] or creators like Robert Wilson[2] invited spectators to make their own connections. Meaning became subjective, emerging from association rather than clarity. Performance became a field of possibilities, not prescriptions.

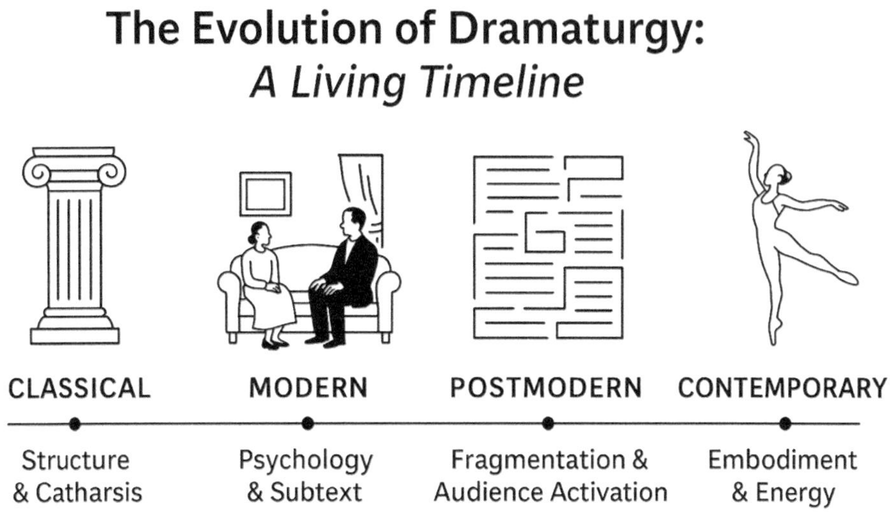

FIGURE 6.2: The Evolution of Dramaturgy: From Aristotle to Human Theatre. This diagram maps the shifting paradigms of dramaturgy across four major eras—Classical, Modern, Postmodern, and Contemporary—each redefining how structure, story, and performer-audience dynamics are understood. The trajectory culminates in Human Theatre, where dramaturgy becomes not just narrative, but energetic architecture—lived, embodied, and aligned with presence. AI-generated image created with OpenAI's DALL·E (via ChatGPT).

Contemporary Dramaturgy: Inclusion, Hybridity, and the Embodied Turn

Today's dramaturgy includes previously marginalized voices and challenges dominant aesthetics. It embraces interdisciplinary methods and global influences. Devised theatre, documentary performance, site-specific work, and immersive experiences all reshape our understanding of what a performance can be.

Most significantly for Human Theatre, contemporary dramaturgy increasingly values the **body**—not just as a vessel for text, but as a source of knowledge and meaning (see **Figure 6.2**). Physical theatre, movement-based forms, and somatic performance methodologies (like those of Pina Bausch or the Lessac approach) center the performer's energy, presence, and lived experience.

It is within this rich, multifaceted evolution that Human Theatre finds its roots. Drawing from the clarity of classical structure, the emotional depth of modernism, the openness of postmodernism, and the embodied intelligence of contemporary practice, Human Theatre proposes not a break, but a synthesis: a re-centering of presence, energy, and intention as the dramaturgical core.

The Body Speaks: Towards a New Dramatic Language

For centuries, dramatic language was defined through dialogue, monologue, and text—tools crafted for clarity, structure, and literary beauty. But as theatre has evolved, so too has the understanding of what constitutes a language onstage. In Human Theatre, we extend the notion of dramatic language beyond the spoken word to encompass the full expressive capacity of the body—gesture, breath, rhythm, and, above all, **energy**.

This new dramatic language is not about rejecting words, but about recognizing the **primacy of presence**. It begins in the body, with its intuitive wisdom and capacity to feel, transmit, and transform. When performers breathe with intention, align their koshi, and charge their gesture with inner meaning, the audience receives the message—not as an idea, but as a **felt experience**. It is not what is said that matters, but what is **sensed**.

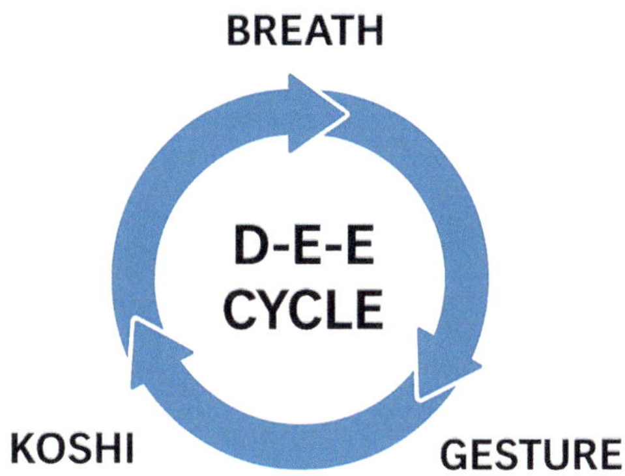

FIGURE 6.3: The DEE Cycle of Human Theatre: From Inner Potential to Embodied Expression. This diagram illustrates the DEE cycle—Dynamis (potential), Energeia (activation), and Entelecheia (realization)—interwoven with the foundational tools of Human Theatre: breath, gesture, koshi, and alignment. These elements form energetic pathways through which the performer transforms internal impulse into embodied expression. The result is not representation, but presence—a form of communication that transcends words and resonates directly with the audience. AI-generated image created with OpenAI's DALL·E (via ChatGPT).

At the heart of this embodied approach is the **DEE cycle**:

- **Dynamis**: The seed of intention, a spark of emotional potential.
- **Energeia**: The energetic manifestation, physicalized in breath, movement, tone.
- **Entelecheia**: The completion, when the energy finds form and meaning in expression.

This cycle is not limited to language or style—it is a **universal energetic structure** that can be applied to tragedy, comedy, ritual, or silence (see **Figure 6.3**). It is the foundation of Human Theatre.

By listening to the body and amplifying its language, performers enter a space of **truthful communication**. This is not mimetic representation—it is energetic transmission. And in this transmission, the audience becomes not just a witness, but a participant. They resonate, reflect, and remember something ancient, something human.

As Gilda Navarra teaches, the body is the original text—the silent well from which every gesture, sound, and dramatic impulse arises (inspired by Gilda Navarra's reflections in *Cartilla de un Officio: Abecedario de un actor-mimo* [2007: 1]). The body becomes the performer's first and most powerful language. In Human Theatre, we read it aloud.

Part 2—The Language of Energy: Incubation, Experimentation, and Embodied Identity

Incubating a Language: Performing Without Words

The journey toward Human Theatre began with a desire: to speak onstage without words. To show the world as I see it, not through text, but through the body's energy—its impulses, its breath, its unspoken truth. What began as curiosity evolved into a deep artistic exploration across traditions where silence carries weight and meaning is shaped by presence.

FIGURE 6.4: Performing Without Words: Expressive Language Beyond Text. This image evokes the core of Human Theatre—where gesture, stillness, breath, and energy become the primary means of storytelling. Here, presence replaces dialogue. Meaning is not spoken—it is transmitted through the body's subtle power to speak in silence. AI-generated image created with OpenAI's DALL·E (via ChatGPT).

To find this new expressive language, I immersed myself in forms where the voice was absent or secondary. I studied **Classical and Contemporary Pantomime**, **Flamenco**, and **Classical and Contemporary Dance**—traditions that elevate the body into a primary instrument of communication. In these disciplines, I discovered not only the aesthetics of movement but also the **poetic potential of stillness**, the vibrational pulse of breath, and the ability to transmit entire emotional landscapes without a single word spoken.

Over time, I became a performer whose body could translate the invisible into action—into Energeia. Not mimicking emotion, but embodying it. Not telling a story, but becoming the story through presence. This shift taught me that what I was searching for wasn't just a performance style—it was a **language of energy**, rooted in the natural alchemy of Dynamis (potential), Energeia (activation), and Entelecheia (expression or fulfillment).

The more I trusted the body, the more I understood: *The body is the original text, and energy is the ink with which it writes.*

In this approach, communication becomes translinguistic. It's not confined by vocabulary or translation. It reaches across borders, across ages, even across disciplines. It touches something universal: the human pulse beneath the performance.

What emerged from this incubation process was a performer trained not only in technique but in perception. Performers who listen with their skin, who breathe with intention, who vibrate with meaning. This is not a rejection of language—it's an expansion of it. A dramaturgy that begins in the breath and extends through every gesture, every pause, every silence filled with presence.

In this context, the performer becomes an amplifier and a renewer of energy. They are not a vessel to deliver lines but a **catalyst of transformation**, transmitting emotion and intention in forms the audience might not consciously recognize—but deeply feel.

This was the first step toward Human Theatre: learning to speak with the full body, to say everything with nothing, and to trust that when the body is clear, the message is unmistakable (see **Figure 6.4**).

Voyage: A First Experiment in Embodied Testimony

What happens when performance becomes a mirror for displacement, identity, and memory? *Voyage* was my first attempt to embody these questions onstage. It was more than a performance—it was an investigation, a testimonial space, and a vessel for collective experience.

At first glance, the two performers—myself and a fellow artist—seemed to have little in common. Our accents, appearances, and upbringings were different. Yet as we began to share personal histories, we discovered a deeper thread: the experience of being immigrants not only across borders but also within our own cultures. We were part of a generation of humans who belonged nowhere and everywhere. This became our point of departure.

From Personal Story to Collective Voice

Voyage was born from our own reflections and expanded through over twenty interviews with immigrants from across the globe—Puerto Rico, Belgium, Brazil, India, New Zealand, the United Kingdom, and more. These testimonials revealed

FIGURE 6.5: Embodied Displacement in Motion. Mid-scene from the Italian premiere of *Voyage*. Through gesture, fractured sound, and sculpted light, the performers invite the audience into the emotional landscape of migration, loss, and identity—not as narrative, but as lived sensation.

astonishing similarities. The same words and emotions repeated across languages and backgrounds: uncertainty, loss, resilience, and a longing to be "citizens of the world."

As we analyzed the interviews, five common stages emerged:

1. **Departure**—the reasons and emotions behind leaving.
2. **The Journey**—displacement, transition, and disorientation.
3. **Arrival**—adapting to unfamiliar lands and customs.
4. **Obstacles**—bureaucracies, language barriers, and alienation.
5. **Realization**—the emergence of a new identity beyond borders.

This structure became the dramaturgical spine of *Voyage*. But the goal wasn't to explain or define immigration. It was to make the audience feel its echoes in its own bodies (see **Figures 6.5** and **6.6**).

Energy as Testimony

Instead of telling the stories literally, we layered video interviews with non-verbal performance. Bodies became the primary instruments of narrative. We used water imagery, breath, stillness, and gesture to evoke the ocean crossings, the hunger for connection, and the silence of not understanding. Suitcases became memory containers. Recorded voices floated through space, not as plot devices but as textures—fragments of lived experience made visible through the performers' energy.

This performative choice created a sensory dislocation for the audience, replicating the feeling of not understanding a language, of being foreign. Rather than dramatizing the immigrant, we invited viewers into the emotional and physiological landscape of migration.

While *Voyage* relies heavily on non-verbal communication, it is not a silent performance. In fact, **the use of layered voices in multiple languages becomes a central dramaturgical device**. These recorded soundscapes do not provide clear narrative exposition—instead, they immerse the audience in a sonic environment that mirrors the emotional confusion and estrangement experienced by immigrants. Words become echoes, texture, and atmosphere rather than clear communication. For many audience members, the inability to fully understand the spoken content becomes a visceral metaphor for displacement, creating empathy through shared disorientation.

Staging Universality

Though *Voyage* was deeply personal, it revealed the power of Human Theatre's tools—nonverbal language, energetic presence, and the DEE cycle—to transmit universal truths.

A particularly moving response came in Croatia, where viewers

FIGURE 6.6: *(top)* The Ocean Between Us. Final scene from *Voyage* (Italian premiere), where two performers stand in silence beside a basin of water. A recurring motif, the basin evokes the ocean—not only as a site of crossing, but of grief, rebirth, and ancestral memory. Breath, gaze, and gesture carry what words cannot. *(bottom)* The Weight of Inheritance. A suitcase in hand, a performer anchors his body to the stage while text is projected above: "I am an American citizen, child of colonialism and imperialism." The juxtaposition of posture and word charges the space with personal and political truth.

described feeling like immigrants within their own families—displaced not by geography, but by mixed heritage and generational rupture (see **Figure 6.7**). The performance became a mirror, showing them parts of themselves they hadn't yet named.

FIGURE 6.7: Fragmented Belonging. Captured during the performance of *Voyage* at the International Theatre Festival in Croatia. In a country scarred by war and migration, the performance resonated as a mirror of inner exile—where many in the audience felt like "immigrants in their own families."

This is the heart of Human Theatre. Not entertainment, but energetic communication. Not spectacle, but presence. Not characters, but carriers of human experience. *Voyage* was the first full realization of this approach.

It taught me that the performer does not always need to speak to be understood. They need to be felt.

One audience member, in Italy, later wrote the message in **Figure 6.8**.

22/04/2017 9:32

[redacted]

Dear [redacted] and Riccardo, I want to thank you again for your piece. It touched me very much and tears naturally came leaving me more free then before. I came to Italy when I was three years old, the first week of kindergarden in the small Italian town I grew up in the 80s (no other immigrants at that time) I was convinced my surname was, now thatwe live in Italy, [redacted] Presente, since that was what we all answeared to the teacher when she called our names to check the presence in class. It was great to have the same name as everybody else although it didn't last long. I found out I was wrong, as many other mistakes I did in the attempts to get as Italian as I could be. I still spell my name a hundred times in the comune etc and most of the times its written wrong and first thing people ask me when I introduce myself is asking me if I m russian. Then I explain and strange enough I feel like I have to justify something. Still. Although the moment where different became special and something to be proud of also already happened. Somehow [redacted] Presente still didn't get it. This is allpersonal story but I want to thank you so much for having pictured the intimate aspects of immigrants idententy seaking and in such a poetic way. I thank you so much for telling my story and those of others. Thank you. Grazie! Danke!!! Great work and personally very much appreciated! It still makes me cry but thats ok.

FIGURE 6.8: *(left)* Scan the QR Code: Watch *Voyage*. This QR code provides access to selected scenes from *Voyage*, inviting the reader to move beyond the page and into the breath, movement, and silence of the performance itself. *(right)* Testimony from the Audience. A message received after the show—one of many. A viewer writes of resonance, healing, and recognition. The true power of *Voyage* lies not only in what is performed but in what is stirred, remembered, and shared.

The Mask as Messenger: Developing a Non-Verbal Communication Channel

As I deepened my practice in physical theatre, my exploration led me to the mask—not merely as a theatrical device, but as a vital communication channel. The mask became a messenger. Stripped of facial expression and fixed in form, it paradoxically allowed for greater emotional complexity. It is in this contradiction that I discovered a new mode of non-verbal storytelling, rooted in energy, presence, and gesture.

My introduction to the mask began with academic studies—first through the pedagogical legacy of **Jacques Lecoq**, whose work emphasized the use of neutral masks as a training tool to awaken the actor's physical awareness and presence. Then, through **Commedia dell'Arte**, where the mask functions as a stylized extension of archetypal energy. In both cases, I saw how the performer's body became more articulate when the face was silenced. The mask required more than movement—it demanded intention.

Later, my encounter with a German theatre company in Berlin opened new questions. During rehearsal, a director told me: "Masks don't align well with drama." The comment struck me. I disagreed instinctively, but I didn't yet have the tools or language to explain why. My intuition told me that the drama wasn't missing—it was simply being carried by another channel.

From that point, I began experimenting. Not to fit the mask into existing dramatic formulas, but to **let the mask reshape the way we tell stories**. I imagined a theatre in which the performer became an instrument of energy transmission—using the mask not to cover identity, but to reveal something deeper: the archetypal, the universal, the unspoken.

In Human Theatre, the mask is both a **filter and a transmitter**. It protects the performer from being judged by appearance, accent, or social markers. It levels the field, inviting the audience to project its own emotions and interpretations onto a neutral face. But far from being static, the mask *absorbs* the energy of the performer's koshi, breath, and gesture. In this dynamic interplay, it becomes a **vessel for emotional resonance**.

The mask doesn't act—it **reacts**. It doesn't express emotions through features, but through energetic suggestion. A tilt of the head, a shift in breath, the weight of a step—these are the new grammar of performance. The audience reads them instinctively, because they belong to a language older than speech: the language of presence.

As my understanding evolved, I began creating my own masks—sculpted not for realism, but for potential. I designed them with a suspended expression, as if they were about to speak. This pause—this moment before articulation—invites the audience to listen more attentively, to fill in the emotional gaps with its own inner world.

In this way, the mask becomes an interface between the personal and the collective. It communicates not as a character would, but as an essence. The performer

FIGURE 6.9: Teatro Umano Masks: Raw Faces of Energetic Expression. This first generation of Teatro Umano masks, sculpted in raw form before painting, captures the moment of creative emergence. Their unfinished surfaces reject fixed identity, inviting emotional projection and non-verbal connection. These prototypes reflect the heart of Human Theatre: presence over persona, vibration over expression.

does not hide behind the mask—they **expand** through it, offering themselves not as an identity, but as a channel. What emerges is a form of theatre that is raw, poetic, and emotionally accessible across cultures and languages (see **Figure 6.9**).

The mask, then, is no longer a theatrical object. It is a **portal**—one that connects the performer's internal world to the audience's subconscious through gesture, rhythm, and energy. It transforms performance into presence. And in doing so, it becomes one of the most powerful tools of Human Theatre.

Part 3—Teatro Umano: Building a Practice

Creating Teatro Umano: A Company of Energetic Presence

The creation of Teatro Umano marked a turning point in the evolution of Human Theatre—not as a style, but as a living practice rooted in energetic exchange, physical presence, and the desire to transcend conventional categories of identity and language.

The company's founding was not merely an artistic decision, but a human one. It came from the need to create a space where performers of diverse backgrounds could express their inner world without being filtered through assumptions about accent, nationality, gender, or physical appearance. In this sense, Teatro Umano is not just a theatre company—it is a **philosophy in motion**, a laboratory for embodied communication (see **Figure 6.10**).

FIGURE 6.10: Teatro Umano Logo: A Visual Manifestation of Energetic Presence. This logo embodies the philosophy of Teatro Umano—a company devoted to fluidity, movement, and embodied human expression. The abstract figure, formed by intertwined organic lines, evokes a performer in motion: aligned through koshi, animated by breath, and alive with Energeia. Its upward flow mirrors the DEE cycle's arc of transformation. The calming hues of green and blue reflect the company's commitment to universal resonance and cross-cultural connection.

Mask as Equalizer and Revealer

One of the earliest insights that led to the formation of Teatro Umano was the realization that **the mask does not hide the performer—it reveals them**. While traditional theatre often relies on external signifiers (costume, makeup, diction) to convey character, the mask in Human Theatre functions as a neutral field. It strips away the surface markers audiences often unconsciously read—ethnicity, age, gender—and forces both performer and spectator to engage on a different level: the **energetic, emotional, and poetic**.

Masks became a **shield against prejudice**, allowing performers to express their humanity in its rawest form. This allowed Teatro Umano to reach audiences across linguistic and cultural barriers, as the work was no longer bound by the limits of spoken language. With text removed or minimal, **energy, gesture, breath, and rhythm** became the true grammar of communication.

Inclusion Through Energy

With each new performance, we saw how the mask could **level the playing field** for performers whose voices had been marginalized—whether due to accent, disability, or simply the way they looked. We began working with actors who had experienced rejection in more traditional contexts, and we witnessed how the language of energy made their inner worlds visible, audible, and profoundly impactful.

Teatro Umano quickly became a space for experimentation—not just with style, but with presence. We focused on training the **DEE cycle** (Dynamis – Energeia – Entelecheia) through exercises in **grounding, koshi alignment, breath, and impulse,** encouraging each performer to become a finely tuned instrument of communication. The more a performer understood their internal energy, the more they could **project presence**—even in stillness, even in silence.

A Theatre Without Borders

What emerged was a form of performance that did not require translation. Audiences from different countries responded to the same gestures, the same tonalities of breath and body. Whether they were from Italy, the United Kingdom, Puerto Rico, or the United States, the emotional clarity of the work crossed cultural thresholds.

We saw that by **removing text**, we were not subtracting meaning—we were **making space** for deeper, more universal resonance. The audience no longer came to decode a plot or analyze a script; they came to feel. And in feeling, they found recognition.

Looking Ahead

Teatro Umano continues to develop performances that respond to the social and emotional urgencies of our time. Whether exploring themes of immigration, grief, inequality, or human resilience, the aim is always the same: to cultivate an **authentic presence** that bridges the performer's inner truth with the audience's need for connection.

Our motto could be this: "We do not act characters. We become messengers of energy."

And in doing so, we open a space where anyone—regardless of language, background, or training—can enter the theatre and recognize themselves.

Beyond the Text: Structure and Composition in *Desconocido*

What does it mean to build a performance from breath, gesture, and energy instead of words? *Desconocido* answers this question by embodying the Human Theatre

FIGURE 6.11: The Trio in Tension. A masked trio mid-dialogue in *Desconocido*. Their exaggerated forms and precise gestures transcend language, inviting projection and emotional interpretation. Here, vulnerability and silent resistance pulse beneath the surface—presence amplified by the absence of words.

methodology: a process that replaces conventional text-driven narrative with structure drawn from energetic intention and emotional resonance (see **Figure 6.11**).

Rather than scripting a traditional plot, the creation of *Desconocido* began with **internal composition**—an exploration of human circumstances, themes, and tensions born from lived experience. The seed was a real story: Anna, a seamstress in wartime Italy, receives letters from her partner Giuseppe, a soldier on the front lines. Their love is strained by separation, illness, and social upheaval. Around them unfold stories of fear, sacrifice, and human connection. But the performance does not dramatize these through dialogue. Instead, it evokes them through movement, music, mask, and space (see **Figure 6.12**).

The **internal structure** of the play followed the **DEE cycle**—Dynamis (potential), Energeia (activation), and Entelecheia (manifested action)—not as a theory but as a tool of composition. Each moment arose from an inner impulse (Dynamis), translated into movement (Energeia), and completed in an action with emotional impact (Entelecheia). In this way, dramatic tension did not arise from external conflict but from the energetic interaction of bodies and environments.

This inner dramaturgy supported the **external structure**, divided into thirteen scenes and two framing moments. It began with Giuseppe writing a letter from the front—an intimate, silent scene amplified by light and music—and transitioned into Anna's world. The simplicity of the set (a sewing machine, a counter, a crib) allowed suggestion to fill in what realism could never fully provide. The space transformed scene by scene, guided by the performers' movement, breath, and the flow of energy—not by scenic changes or spoken exposition.

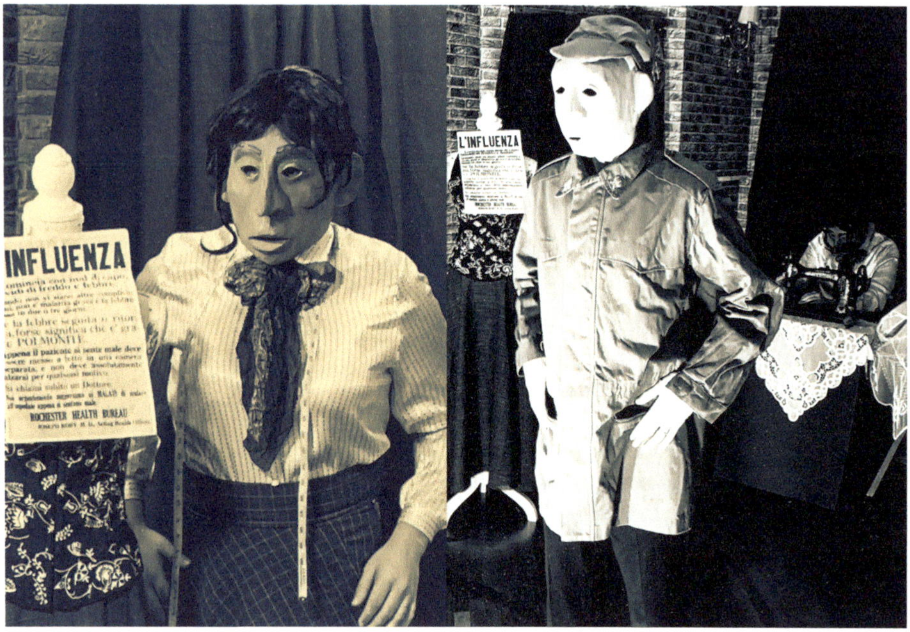

FIGURE 6.12: Anna and Giuseppe: Two Acts of Presence. *(left)* Anna, the seamstress protagonist, wears a humanoid mask in *Desconocido*. Her stillness and posture frame a moment of silent urgency beside a posted influenza notice—an echo of collective vulnerability. *(right)* Giuseppe, isolated in a pool of light, delivers the opening letter from the battlefield. His masked body and grounded voice conjure distance, longing, and the weight of war through stillness and breath.

The **masks** played a crucial role in this structure. As humanoid extensions of the self, they neutralized identity markers like gender or ethnicity, allowing the audience to project its own feelings onto the characters. Audience did not see Anna the Italian seamstress—they saw a caregiver, a survivor, a mirror of its own longing or loss. In this way, the humanoid character served as an **energetic vessel** rather than a fixed personality.

Throughout the development of *Desconocido*, each element—music, costume, mask, object, space—was treated as a **semiotic tool**, selected not for literal realism but for emotional clarity. The storytelling relied on **suggestion, not declaration.** A pot of boiling water evoked anxiety. A single thread across the stage suggested invisible ties between characters and histories. Audiences were invited to **complete the narrative in their own minds**, guided by emotion rather than explanation.

Even the structure of conflict followed this model. Anna's choice to help a stranger—Guglielmo—set off a cascade of actions and consequences, each rooted in human decision rather than external plot devices. Dramatic action emerged not from dialogue, but from choice, breath, and the flow of energy across a shared space (see **Figure 6.13**).

The internal structure of *Desconocido* was mapped visually, showing how narrative transitions, thematic resonances, and energetic pivots interlace to form its dramatic architecture (see **Figure 6.14**). As performers and audiences moved through *Desconocido*, what emerged was not a "story" in the traditional sense, but a **dramatic experience**—visceral, emotional, and open to interpretation. This is the core of Human Theatre's compositional approach: **Structure guided by energy, dramaturgy as embodied presence, and meaning made through mutual resonance.**

FIGURE 6.13: The Arrival of the Stranger. Guglielmo enters Anna's shop in *Desconocido*, a figure of disruption and mystery. His masked stillness fractures routine and kindles connection—an embodiment of the unknown entering the known.

Between Open and Closed: The Dramatic Engine of Desconocido

While *Desconocido* employs an episodic structure reminiscent of open dramaturgy, its emotional build, scenic progression, and character transformations suggest an underlying pulse akin to closed forms. This tension between openness and coherence is part of what gives the piece its dynamic identity.

Scenes unfold like vignettes, often self-contained in rhythm and focus, but linked through energetic arcs, recurring objects (the letter, the mask), and emotional echoes. The dramatic action does not follow a singular goal or hero's journey, but rather an **accumulation of emotional truths.** In this way, *Desconocido* creates a dramaturgy of **presence**, where **conflict is not resolved** but **held, moved through,** and **reflected upon.**

The open nature of the structure also allows for **secondary plotlines**—like those introduced by Rossella—to **emerge without disrupting the emotional thread.** These stories expand the world without deviating from its core energetic intention.

Character as Humanoid: Energy Before Identity

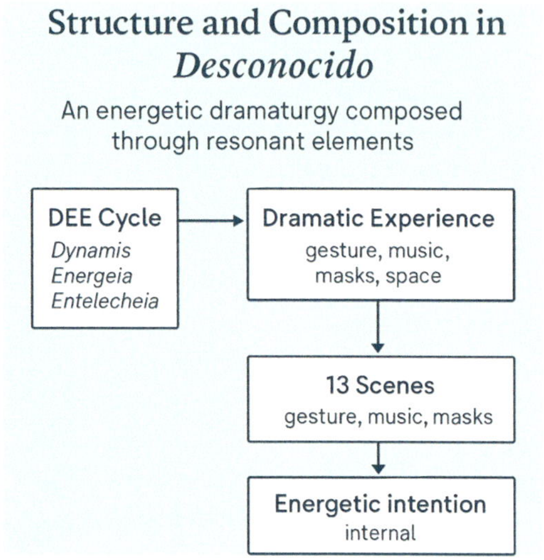

FIGURE 6.14: Structural Map of *Desconocido*. A visual composition of *Desconocido*'s internal dramaturgy and emotional landscape. This flowchart outlines the performance's architecture: narrative transitions, thematic resonances, and energetic pivots that form the backbone of Human Theatre's design. AI-generated image created with OpenAI's DALL·E (via ChatGPT).

What happens when the character onstage is not a "person" as we know it—but an energetic vessel, shaped by movement, gesture, and breath rather than name, gender, or social role? In Human Theatre, this is the essence of the **humanoid**: A figure that transcends surface identity to connect through energetic presence (see **Figure 6.15**).

The humanoid performer is not stripped of humanity but elevated beyond individual biography. They do not "act" in the traditional sense. They do not represent a social type or psychological profile. They project lived emotional states through a channel of **Dynamis–Energeia–Entelecheia (DEE)**—not through words, but through embodied vibration.

The use of masks allows us to reach this state. By concealing the face, we remove the most immediate markers of identity and invite the audience to project meaning based on energy and action. The result is not distance, but intimacy—an uncanny recognition that transcends categories. We no longer ask, *Who is she?* or *Where is he from?* Instead, we feel: *I know that grief, that joy, that struggle.*

These are not anonymous figures—they are **universal mirrors**. And because their identity is not prescribed, their humanity expands. The mask becomes a symbol of the shared soul.

In *Desconocido*, the audience often reacts with surprise when they discover the masked figure they assumed was male is played by a female performer—or vice versa. These reactions are not mere confusion. They reveal how deeply we attach meaning to surface traits. But once the story unfolds, those associations dissolve. The **humanoid character** exists only in the moment of performance, built through breath, presence, and action.

This transformation relies not on abstraction but on **energetic clarity**. When a humanoid receives an action—compassion, rejection, tenderness—the reaction is

FIGURE 6.15: The Humanoid Character: Stillness Before Emergence. In this traditional rendering, the humanoid character stands in a moment of charged stillness—devoid of facial features, yet filled with intent. Here, the body becomes the sole channel of energy, gesture, and presence. This figure embodies Teatro Umano's core philosophy: identity not as appearance, but as energy made visible through form. AI-generated image created with OpenAI's DALL·E (via ChatGPT).

not filtered through personality. It is immediate, elemental. The DEE cycle plays out in real time: potential is activated, shaped, and released into form.

By foregrounding energy before identity, Human Theatre proposes a radical kind of empathy—one that asks us not to categorize, but to connect. This radical empathy comes alive in the physical stillness and alignment of the humanoid performer, where presence is transmitted through gesture, breath, and energetic clarity (see **Figure 6.16**).

Suggesting the World: Space, Time, and the Audience's Mind

In a world saturated with screens, spectacle, and overstimulation, Human Theatre returns to something ancient yet radically vital: suggestion. Rather than relying on elaborate sets, special effects, or literal exposition, this practice proposes that it is the *audience's imagination*—activated by the energy of the performer—that completes the world onstage.

This principle was not theoretical for us. It was tested, lived, and experienced in the performance of *Desconocido* (see **Figure 6.17**). With minimal props and a flexible, intimate set, we trusted that light, music, and the body could evoke an entire world. A sewing machine, a piece of fabric, and the breath of a masked character became more evocative than an entire reconstructed village.

The Space Between Object and Perception

Each element in the performance was chosen not for its realism, but for its *symbolic charge*. The objects became anchors for imagination: a crib suggesting motherhood, a letter channeling love and loss, a suitcase evoking both departure and return. By resisting hyper-realism, we allowed space for projection—for the audience to see its own memories and metaphors reflected in the action. Movement itself expanded space in similar ways (see **Figure 6.18**).

This is the metaphysical theatre Artaud envisioned—not bound by imitation of life, but charged with its essence.

Activating Time Through Presence

Dramatic time in Human Theatre is not clock-bound. It unfolds through rhythm, gesture, and relational tension. The performers' energetic presence bends and shapes time, making a moment stretch or collapse. In *Desconocido*, the moment Anna receives the letter from Giuseppe becomes suspended in emotional time. Everything slows as the performer's breath, posture, and energy shift, inviting the audience into the stillness of grief. This suspended stillness is captured in one of the most powerful images of the piece (see **Figure 6.19**).

The performer doesn't show sadness—they *hold space* for it.

The Audience as Creator

The most remarkable transformation happens in the audience. When offered a suggestion instead of an explanation, they become co-authors

FIGURE 6.16: *Desconocido*: The Humanoid Body in Energetic Expression. This triptych captures three moments from *Desconocido*, illuminating the power of the humanoid performer to communicate emotion without text: *(top)* Guglielmo, energized by internal charge, salutes an unseen presence—embodying tension, duty, and disorientation. *(center)* Don Geraldo's exaggerated theatricality disrupts the moment, while Anna and Rossella respond with micro-gestures and breath, shifting the energetic field. *(bottom)* Anna, in a moment of stillness, cradles her child and clutches a letter—her breath, touch, and gaze transmitting grief, protection, and quiet resilience.

Here, presence is not projected—it's transmitted through gesture, alignment, and stillness.

of the experience. In Sestino, Italy, during an outdoor performance, children played nearby, occasionally shouting. Yet when we asked the audience afterward if they were distracted, they responded: "What children?"

They were inside the world. This is what theatre must aspire to today—not to overpower reality, but to envelop it, and gently transport us somewhere just beyond.

FIGURE 6.17: Minimalism as Portal: Inviting the Audience's Imagination. A scene from *Desconocido*, where fabric walls, symbolic props, and modular set pieces form an open frame for collective storytelling. This space doesn't dictate—it suggests. The emotional atmosphere invites the audience to imagine, fill, and co-create the world from within.

Mask and Metaphor: The Visual Poetics of Suggestion

FIGURE 6.18: Gesture as Geography: Expanding the Stage Through Movement. In this moment from *Desconocido*, a gesture transforms a corner into an unseen interior. The performers expand the performance space not with objects, but with presence. The stage becomes fluid—reshaped by urgency, relationship, and energetic charge.

The mask, too, plays a crucial role in this process. With fixed features and empty eyes, it does not express emotion—it *invites* it. The audience sees what they need to see. A single head tilt, a breath, or a pause becomes a full sentence. The mask becomes a mirror—not of the performer's face, but of the spectator's inner world.

The New Magic of Theatre

Theatre once carried a sacred aura. In Human Theatre, we seek to restore that magic through simplicity, attention, and energetic truth. Suggestion does not mean vagueness. It means *intention so precise* that the smallest gesture carries meaning. It is a trust in the intelligence—and emotional readiness—of the audience.

Through suggestion, we do not escape the world. We reveal it.

Symbolic Characters and Secondary Currents in *Desconocido*

Rossella: The Catalyst of Parallel Worlds

While *Desconocido* centers on Anna, Guglielmo, and Giuseppe, the world they inhabit is shaped and textured by the presence of Rossella—the nurse figure who floats between roles, physical spaces, and emotional atmospheres. Rossella does not just support the action: She **generates parallel stories.** Her appearances signal shifts in rhythm and tone, moving from the comedic to the tragic, from the intimate to the surreal.

Without a single word spoken, Rossella's character navigates secondary plotlines that reflect care, illness, social judgment, and even absurdity. She creates

FIGURE 6.19: The Stillness of Grief: Collective Imagination Through Silence. Anna receives Giuseppe's farewell letter in *Desconocido*. Her masked stillness, underscored by music, offers no fixed emotion—only an open space. The audience completes the moment through projection, memory, and breath. Here, theatrical silence becomes a vessel for shared longing.

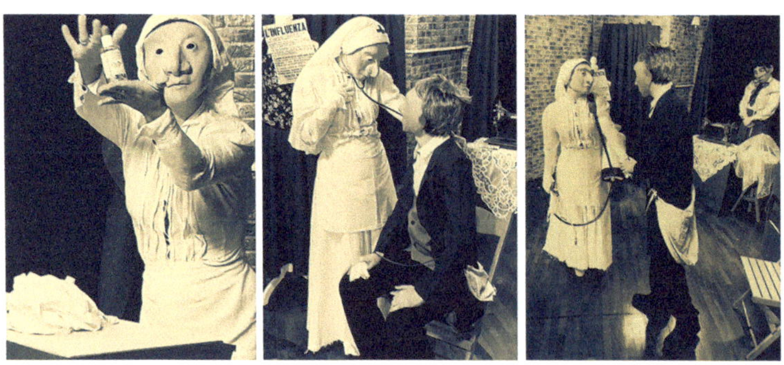

FIGURE 6.20: Ritual, Listening, and Care in the Theatre of *Desconocido*. *(left)* Rossella raises a disinfectant bottle like a sacred relic—elevating the mundane into a symbolic gesture. *(center)* A nurse's stethoscope crosses theatrical distance; Rossella listens not just to breathe, but to the unspoken truth beneath the mask. *(right)* A moment of care—Rossella examines Guglielmo, while Anna witnesses from afar. One act, three emotional currents: compassion, vulnerability, and distance.

bridges between scenes, often arriving before or after a major narrative event to either prepare or cleanse the emotional residue of what occurred. Whether checking Guglielmo's pulse or spraying the room with disinfectant, she acts as both **caretaker and commentator**, grounding the drama while expanding its scope. Rossella's role as ritual-maker and caretaker is especially clear in emblematic moments of the play (see **Figure 6.20**).

Her presence transforms scenic spaces through energetic gesture and stylized repetition, offering the audience a form of **visual continuity and thematic layering**. With Rossella, the narrative becomes three-dimensional—not just a sequence of actions, but a **living system** of parallel energies and emotional tones.

FIGURE 6.21: Geraldine: Poise as Performance, Mask as Metaphor. Geraldine, Anna's wealthiest client, embodies a tension between appearance and suppression. Her rigid posture and stylized mask signal a woman clinging to elegance while struggling to conceal internal disarray—a portrait of fragility beneath status. Geraldine wears the mask of perfection, but within that stillness is a storm of tension. She is not comic, not tragic—she is **poised**, and through this poise, she **invites projection**. Audiences may see in her the part of themselves that has felt unseen or too afraid to speak.

Geraldine: The Mask of Distance

In contrast to the earthy expressiveness of the other characters, Geraldine moves with a restrained elegance, occupying space with a certain height—not just physically, but emotionally and symbolically. She represents **the part of the immigrant self that must remain composed, dignified, and invisible**. Her silence and posture reflect the **fear of revealing what lies beneath the surface**—the foreignness, the fragility, the rage. Geraldine's mask and rigid posture crystallize this fragility beneath poise (see **Figure 6.21**).

As with Rossella, Geraldine allows for a **thematic expansion** beyond the central narrative. She does not propel the action, but she **crystallizes a**

deeper emotional current—the anxiety of assimilation, of judgment, of vulnerability.

Don Geraldo: Opportunism and Folkloric Misinformation

Amid the emotional threads and immigrant journeys of *Desconocido*, Don Geraldo emerges as a figure of comedic contradiction and social commentary. He is the character who speaks the loudest, but says the least of value. Embodying those who profit from fear, he becomes the play's mirror of opportunism—the person who sells hope in a bottle, reassurance in a lie.

Don Geraldo peddles homemade flu remedies, absurd cures, and false wisdom with theatrical conviction. Through him, the piece touches the theme of misinformation, a phenomenon as old as plagues and as recent as the present moment. He's funny—yes—but uncomfortably close to real figures who exploit public vulnerability. Don Geraldo embodies this blend of comic theatricality and exploitation (see **Figure 6.22**).

His exaggerated mask and gestures echo the Commedia dell'Arte tradition of the "charlatan," but re-contextualized in a twentieth-century crisis. In his theatricality, we find both humor and critique—how easily truth is distorted when desperation clouds discernment. Excerpts from Desconocido reveal how this atmosphere plays out onstage (see **Figure 6.23**).

FIGURE 6.22: Don Geraldo: Comedy and Crisis in a Single Gesture. Don Geraldo leans into fear and desperation, hawking remedies with a blend of theatrical charm and exploitation. His performance is both comic and disturbing—revealing how misinformation thrives when vulnerability is met with manipulation.

FIGURE 6.23: Watch *Desconocido*. Scan the QR code to access scenes from *Desconocido*, a masked performance exploring silence, memory, and human resilience.

Part 4—Dramaturgy in Action: Genres, Children, and the Unexpected

Tragedy and Comedy: Complementary Forces in Human Theatre

In Human Theatre, **tragedy and comedy are not opposing genres**; they are complementary forces, two emotional registers vibrating through the same human body. The choice is not between laughter and tears, but in understanding when each vibration is most needed, and how they can coexist within the same theatrical moment.

Take *Desconocido* as an example. At its heart, it is a tragic story—about displacement, war, disease, and identity fragmentation. Yet the performance is filled with laughter. Not as a distraction, but as a counterbalance. The absurdity of Don Geraldo's homemade flu remedies elicits laughter, while at the same time laying bare the desperation of people clinging to false hope. Comedy becomes a mirror—distorted but honest. The tragic silence of Anna's final moment embodies this register (see **Figure 6.24**).

Similarly, the arrival of Guglielmo in Anna's dress shop could be seen as comic—his awkward gestures, the tension of unfamiliar social codes, the miscommunication. But this moment is also deeply human, and in that humanity, tragic echoes are always present. **The shift from laughter to silence is not a rupture—it is a slide.** And that sliding space is where Human Theatre thrives. In *Bar Moments*, the final scene captures this paradox of release and reclamation (see **Figure 6.25**).

In *Bar Moments*—a performance that will be explored in the next chapter—actors devised subtle, silent routines within cafés and transit hubs as public space interventions. What began as comedy—accidental repetitions, strange eye contact, surreal timing—gradually deepened into something else. Audiences leaned in, confused, then enchanted. Some laughed, some cried. But all felt something. That is the goal: a visceral choreography of emotional tones.

FIGURE 6.24: *Desconocido* (Final Scene): Tragic Silence and the Weight of Absence. Anna, consumed by silence, holds her daughter and the letter that seals her fate. The moment radiates stillness, sorrow, and unspoken grief. The audience carries the unresolved energy—a hallmark of Human Theatre's tragic register, where transformation doesn't offer relief, but recognition.

Human Theatre trains performers to **ride emotional waves** rather than impose them. One mask, one gesture, one repeated action can be both comic and tragic depending on rhythm, context, and energy.

FIGURE 6.25: *Bar Moments* (Final Scene): Linear principle. Lila exits, leaving her abusive partner bound and voiceless in the café. The scene resists sentimentality; instead, it pulses with release, survival, and reversed power. Here, comedy is not lightness but reclamation—an energetic aftermath that lifts the weight without denying it.

When done well, these moments invite the audience into a state of paradox—where laughter frees the body, and sorrow opens the heart.

The balance of tragedy and comedy is not just dramaturgical—it is ethical. To laugh with, not at. To witness pain, but not indulge in despair. It is about presence, listening, and trusting that both lightness and weight belong in the same story. Just as they do in life.

While this chapter has focused on *Desconocido*, its deep emotional resonance, and its structure as a tragic arc, in the next chapter we turn our attention to *Bar Moments*—a performance that, while equally grounded in human pain, opens the space for laughter, resistance, and eventual release. These two pieces, when viewed together, offer a full spectrum of Human Theatre's potential.

Theatre for Children: Simplicity, Depth, and Emotional Truth

Theatre for children is often mistaken for a genre requiring less rigor or artistic integrity. Yet within Human Theatre, it demands just as much—if not more—than work created for adults. Children are not passive viewers. They are intuitive, critical, and deeply attuned to emotional authenticity. They don't require elaborate sets or dazzling effects; what they respond to is presence, energy, and truth.

In performances for children, every movement, every pause, every shift in energy is amplified. Performers must be fully alive, listening not just to their partner but to the pulse of the room. There is no hiding. There is no relying on abstract intellectualism. The mask, the gesture, the moment of connection—these become the language of impact.

The creation of children's shows has been a controversial topic. Even today, there are ideas, which I consider outdated, that see children's theatre as a lesser form of theatre. There is an underestimation of children's ability to understand themes and experiences, assuming they do not live through the same situations as adults. It is true that they do not experience them with the same intensity or understanding, but they also face their own challenges.

In Italy, I proposed creating a show about the ephemeral nature of an actor's work and the difficulties of leading a "normal" life, which led us to develop a clown performance. When we presented our ideas to the organizers, they questioned the aesthetic simplicity of the characters, who lacked exaggerated makeup and colorful costumes. For them, children's shows should take place in fantastic worlds where actors transform into animals. But I believe simplicity—when infused with clarity, rhythm, and intention—can reach children with far greater emotional depth.

However, I do not believe that this approach is negative. One of my favorite works is *Mundo Nocturno* by Teresa Valenzuela, a piece that addresses profound themes without traumatizing its young audience. In this play, the main character aspires to be a famous artist and, along the way, interacts with insects that always ask for something in return, ending with a cockroach that traps the bee in its bar. Although the scene implied a loss of freedom, the children were not traumatized; instead, they identified with the mosquito that helped the bee escape.

In my career, I created my own version of *Mundo Nocturno* for a tour in the International Festival of Performing Arts in San Luis, Argentina. We adapted the design to be minimal and portable—it had to travel with us from Puerto Rico to Argentina and adjust to a wide variety of performance spaces, from school classrooms to public piazzas to traditional theatres. The production focused on essential elements: a hat for the scorpion, a striped shirt for the bees, and a piece of fabric for the bar. This simplicity was not a limitation but a strength.

What I discovered was the sheer potency of energetic presence. The children didn't need theatrical illusion—they needed guidance. I began to see how a performer could lead children through the narrative as if taking them by the hand, helping them walk through the story with full emotional participation. This became one of the foundational observations that later helped generate the methodology of Human Theatre.

After performances, we often collected the children's reactions through drawings. Many wrote things like: "The little bee was sad because she wanted to be an artist" or "The little bee didn't want to wake up early to work." Their comments revealed innocence, humor, and surprising insight. Notably, none of them focused on the part where the bee is kidnapped—a moment that might unsettle adults. This contrast made it clear: Children experience theatre with a different lens, one that highlights emotional resonance rather than plot detail.

The transformation begins in the dressing room—where the performer sheds personal identity and steps into the archetypal space of play. Whether through the symbolic color of a red hat or the energetic lift of felt flowers, these performances

FIGURE 6.26: Touring *Mundo Nocturno* (Year Two): Symbolic Simplicity in Design. This image shows the second-year version of *Mundo Nocturno* in Argentina, where a simplified set and costume design—colorful felt flowers, a folding backdrop, and a striped yellow bee shirt—evoked joy, mobility, and symbolic clarity. Every element supported energetic connection through visual immediacy and emotional accessibility.

demonstrate how **less can hold more**: fewer words, simpler designs, but deeper emotional truth (see **Figures 6.26 and 6.27**).

In the tours of *Bar Moments*, which some might consider inappropriate for children, we have always had young people as part of the audience. I remember a girl in Sestino, Italy, who felt fascinated by the masks and decided to attend the presentation with her parents. My character, Lila, was in constant contact with the audience, and I was able to observe this young girl throughout the show. Despite the dark context we were portraying, she was captivated by the masks and their mystery.

Lila, who represents resilience, teaches the child that despite life's difficulties, there are ways to survive those traumas. After the performance, we spoke with the girl and her parents. She shared her thoughts about how the people in the bar treated the owner unfairly and didn't let her daughter play. That sparked a powerful exchange—we talked about gender, control, and imagination, all shaped by her curiosity. That is what children's theatre can and should be: a spark for dialogue, a mirror for feelings, a channel for shared discovery between parents and children.

We do not "play down" to children. We meet them where they are: emotionally vibrant, imaginatively free, and deeply curious. When a masked character cries onstage, we've seen children lean forward, wide-eyed, ready to offer empathy. When a moment of joy erupts, they erupt with it—not because they were told to, but because they were moved to.

FIGURE 6.27: The Puppet and the Red Hat: Traditional Aesthetics for Energetic Engagement. From the earlier year's festival in Argentina, this performance used clown-like makeup and puppet-inspired costuming to evoke classic children's theatre. With just a red hat, gloves, and expressive gesture, the performer created emotional resonance through minimalism, clarity, and embodied play.

One of the most powerful testaments to Human Theatre's effectiveness is the way children linger after performances. They often approach the characters, ask about the masks, or simply sit in quiet reflection. They remind us that theatre is not a product—it's a shared experience.

In performing for children, we are constantly reminded of why we began this journey: to create work that is alive, honest, and transformative. Work that transcends the barrier of language and speaks directly to the soul—no matter the age of the audience.

Part 5—Shifting Paradigms: Postdramatic Influences and Theatrical Hybridity

New Languages, New Codes: From Pantomime to Physical Theatre

Before I understood theatre as a written structure or a series of roles, I understood it through movement. My first impulse as a performer came not from text but from the body—its rhythms, its blocks, its capacity to reveal what words obscure. This embodied beginning led me through an evolving path of pantomime, dance, mask, clown, and ultimately to what I now call *Human Theatre*.

In the early years, I was drawn to pantomime because it stripped the stage of linguistic hierarchy. With no script, no dialogue, the body itself had to generate meaning. The silence of pantomime is not empty—it is vibrating with implication. And in that charged silence, I began to notice the smallest truths: the twitch of a hand, the angle of a neck, the breath before a gesture.

But silence alone wasn't enough. I craved an emotional architecture—a way to link energy and structure, improvisation and intentionality. That's where my journey into **physical theatre** deepened. Influenced by teachers like Todd Farley, Gilda Navarra, Fabio Mangolini, Petra Bravo,[3] and Gradissa Fernández, I discovered how pantomime could be merged with modern dance, ritual gesture, and improvisational timing to create a new language of performance.

This was not merely a stylistic shift. It was a **paradigm change**.

Instead of acting *as if*, I learned to **become**. Instead of mimicking emotion, I learned to **generate energy** through breath, koshi, and sensory imagination. These practices replaced external symbolism with internal transformation. The actor was no longer a translator of text but a transmitter of experience.

Through the *Mythos* workshop at the University of Puerto Rico—*with Gradissa*[4]—my flamenco studies, and my Physical Theatre studies later in Europe, I realized that style is secondary. What matters most is **performers' energy**—their presence, availability, and truthfulness. Even in structured choreographies, the most powerful moments came from surrendering to impulse. The body became the first site of dramaturgy (see **Figure 6.28**).

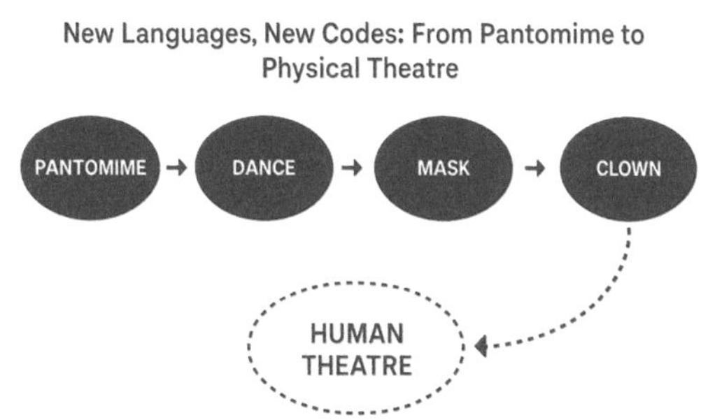

FIGURE 6.28: From Gesture to Presence: The Evolution Toward Physical Theatre. This diagram traces the arc from silent, codified gestures to embodied storytelling, showing how pantomime, clowning, and corporeal mime built the foundation for modern physical theatre. In this lineage, dialogue dissolves, and presence becomes the language—spoken not with words, but with breath, structure, and impulse. AI-generated image created with OpenAI's DALL·E (via ChatGPT).

This experience reshaped how I approached storytelling. My characters stopped speaking and started resonating. I wasn't just representing an idea—I was living it. And I noticed how that energetic authenticity affected audiences. They no longer watched from a distance: They *entered* the world we created.

That was the seed of Human Theatre: A space where codes are not imposed but *emerge* through shared presence. In this process, the performer is no longer merely an actor—they are an **instrument of transmission**, channeling breath, impulse, and memory into immediate poetic form.

As we'll see throughout this chapter, this shift from mimetic acting to **energetic embodiment** is at the heart of the postdramatic movement. But for me, it started in silence—with pantomime—and grew into a polyphonic language of gesture, breath, presence, and play.

Postdramatic Theatre: Breaking Boundaries of Representation

The emergence of postdramatic theatre marked a radical shift in how theatrical works were conceived, performed, and experienced. Coined by Hans-Thies Lehmann,[5] the term refers not merely to a stylistic trend but to a deeper transformation in the role of the text, narrative, and representation within the theatrical event. In postdramatic work, the primacy of the dramatic text gives way to a more open, collaborative, and fragmented mode of creation—one that emphasizes presence, affect, and sensorial experience over linear storytelling.

In the context of Teatro Umano, postdramatic ideas have been instrumental in liberating the dramaturgical process from the confines of literary structure. This liberation doesn't eliminate story or character; instead, it allows them to emerge organically, shaped by the body, rhythm, space, and sound. In this sense, postdramatic theatre aligns with Human Theatre by foregrounding the performer's energy and the moment of encounter with the audience as the core of meaning-making.

Text as One Layer Among Many: In postdramatic theatre, text becomes a material—like light, movement, or sound—rather than the spine of the performance. It may be spoken, fragmented, projected, or even omitted entirely. This opens space for polyphony: multiple perspectives, languages, and textures coexisting onstage. In *Voyage*, the use of projected phrases, overlapping audio in various languages, and non-verbal performance fragments exemplifies this approach. The spectator is not guided by a single narrative line but is instead invited to construct meaning in the gaps between images, sounds, and gestures.

The Crisis of Representation: Postdramatic theatre does not seek to reproduce reality but to expose the theatrical mechanisms through which reality is staged. It breaks the illusion of mimesis and foregrounds the artifice of performance. For Human Theatre, this principle manifests in the visible transitions between characters, the use of masks, and the stylization of emotion through gesture and rhythm.

The audience is not deceived but engaged—aware of the performer's labor and invited into the co-creation of the theatrical world.

Bodies in Space, Presence Over Plot: The postdramatic stage becomes a field of energy rather than a container for dramatic action. What matters is not what happens next in the story, but what happens now between performers and spectators. In *Voyage*, for example, moments of stillness, walking, breathing, or the simple act of holding an object become dramaturgical beats. The narrative arises from the body in space—its weight, resistance, and direction—rather than from scripted dialogue.

Towards a Theatre of Perception: Ultimately, postdramatic theatre encourages a shift from interpretation to perception. The audience is not asked to "understand" the performance in a traditional sense, but to feel it, to dwell in its textures and contradictions. This challenges the passivity of spectatorship and activates a more embodied, intuitive mode of engagement (see **Figure 6.29**).

For Teatro Umano, postdramatic strategies do not serve an aesthetic agenda but a human one. They allow for porous, living dramaturgies that reflect the fragmentation, fluidity, and multiplicity of contemporary life. By moving beyond representation, postdramatic theatre opens the door to a more honest and resonant form of theatrical truth—one that is felt before it is understood.

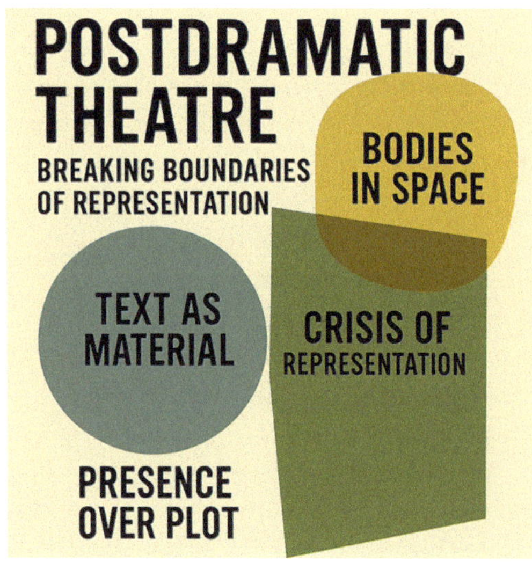

FIGURE 6.29: The Postdramatic Field: Fragmentation, Embodiment, and Co-Creation. This visual distills the essence of postdramatic theatre: fragmentation, simultaneity, physicality, and audience co-authorship. Rather than constructing a linear narrative or stable world, postdramatic performance opens a space of sensory saturation and interpretive ambiguity—where meaning is not delivered but co-created, moment by moment, breath by breath. AI-generated image created with OpenAI's DALL·E (via ChatGPT).

Performance and Embodied Memory: Human Theatre Among Global Influences

Human Theatre emerges not in isolation, but within a global network of theatrical exploration. From the physical intensity of Japanese butoh to the rhythm-based storytelling of African traditions, global performance forms have continuously challenged the idea that language alone is the core of theatre. In these traditions, movement, breath, and energy carry memory—both personal and collective. Human Theatre positions itself in this lineage, exploring how performance can become a space where memory is not only represented but physically evoked and transformed.

While postdramatic theatre has questioned the supremacy of narrative, Human Theatre goes further by questioning the supremacy of character itself. Rather than constructing psychological portraits, performers in this practice inhabit energetic states. These states are shaped by cultural memory, bodily training, and scenographic rhythm. The result is a dramaturgy of vibration—where what resonates is often what cannot be said (see **Figure 6.30**).

FIGURE 6.30: Embodied Memory: A Landscape Beyond Language. This evocative painting symbolizes the convergence of personal memory, cultural lineage, and embodied performance. The figure emerges from a field of abstract textures and gestures—suggesting how Human Theatre draws from the body's deep reservoir of memory to create meaning that transcends narrative or text. AI-generated image created with OpenAI's DALL·E (via ChatGPT).

Embodied memory, in this context, refers to the body's capacity to store and transmit experiences beyond verbal or intellectual knowledge. When an actor trembles, hesitates, or breathes in a certain way, they may be channeling an ancestral gesture, a personal trauma, or a societal rhythm. In Human Theatre, such physical traces are not refined out—they are the material of the work.

This approach has been deeply influenced by training methods encountered in diverse contexts: from the precision and ritual of Balinese dance to the fluid improvisation of contemporary European ensemble work. The performer becomes a channel, not a speaker—one who carries embodied stories through stillness, repetition, and transformation.

In this practice, memory is not something to recall but something to activate. It may appear through the subtle sway of the torso, the contraction of the solar plexus, or the gaze that refuses direct confrontation. These embodied choices are not psychological cues but energetic transmissions. Audiences do not "read" these moments—they feel them.

Ultimately, Human Theatre aims to return the body to its central place—not just as an expressive tool, but as a carrier of cultural, historical, and emotional knowledge. In a world saturated with visual and textual stimuli, it proposes an alternative literacy: one rooted in presence, in vibration, and in the silent memory of the flesh.

Part 6—Poetics of Objects, Masks, and Energetic Transference

Pina Bausch and the Dancer's Soul: Emotional Minimalism in Movement

When we speak of emotional minimalism in performance, it's impossible not to reference the work of Pina Bausch.[6] Her choreography lived in the space between gesture and intention—where movement didn't illustrate emotion, but rather summoned it. Through repetition, silence, and stark, exposed bodies, Bausch allowed her dancers to *become* the emotion, rather than *show* it.

This sensibility profoundly resonates with the principles of **Teatro Umano**, where movement is not ornamental but ontological. In both methodologies, the performer becomes a vessel for memory and presence. The body is stripped of theatricality and returned to raw, grounded truth.

Bausch's work sought moments of rupture—small, precise gestures repeated until they burned themselves into the audience's perception. Similarly, in Human Theatre, the actor's gesture is purified to its energetic core. The movement is not choreographed in the traditional sense, but sourced from breath, weight, and lived emotion. Performers listen to the space, the silence, and their own internal tempo (see **Figure 6.31**).

What distinguishes Teatro Umano's embodied dramaturgy is its integration of objects and masks—not to hide, but to deepen. Where Bausch's dancers revealed vulnerability through exposure, Teatro Umano performers reveal it through **energetic transference**—projecting interior states into external forms. In both approaches, emotion is not dramatized, but distilled into gesture, breath, and presence (see **Figure 6.32**). A gesture toward a mask can hold the same emotional weight as a scream in Wuppertal Tanztheater.

In both practices, narrative dissolves. What remains is transformation—not of story, but of state. The audience becomes a witness not to plot, but to passage. And through that witnessing, a shared emotional truth emerges: ephemeral, intangible, and deeply human.

Object Theatre and the Mask: Symbols of the Unspoken

In Teatro Umano, objects and masks are not accessories; they are vessels of meaning. They carry emotional weight, cultural memory, and symbolic resonance.

FIGURE 6.31: Emotional Minimalism in Motion: Bausch and Teatro Umano in Dialogue. *(left)* A dancer in the spirit of Pina Bausch—grounded, emotionally transparent, minimal in gesture. *(right)* Teatro Umano performer—silent, masked, yet equally expressive. Together, they illustrate a shared language of emotional clarity through restraint—where stillness reveals more than action. AI-generated image created with OpenAI's DALL·E (via ChatGPT).

Where traditional dramaturgy might assign value to words, gestures, or scenic realism, Teatro Umano finds poetry in the inanimate—transforming the mundane into metaphor. This intersection of object and mask creates a dramaturgy of presence, metaphor, and transformation in Human Theatre (see **Figure 6.33**).

A piece of cloth becomes a child. A suitcase becomes a coffin. A sewing machine becomes a ghost of history. These transformations do not rely on elaborate mechanics or technology, but on the performer's capacity to charge objects with energy and significance through presence, repetition, and physical score.

This approach is grounded in **Object Theatre**, a form that recognizes how physical objects can embody narrative. Rooted in traditions from puppetry to visual theatre, Object Theatre strips away the illusion of realism and instead amplifies suggestion. Teatro Umano adopts this form but bends it toward testimony: The objects onstage do not just "stand in" for something else—they carry the essence of the characters' inner worlds. They speak, even when silent. In these transformations, meaning emerges not from realism, but from poetic transference (see **Figure 6.34**).

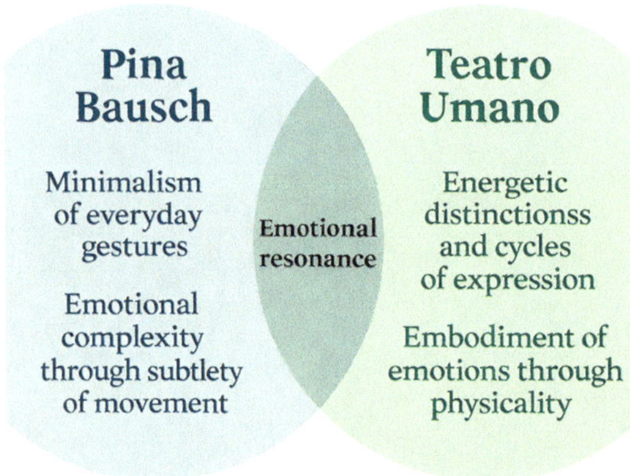

FIGURE 6.32: Overlapping Worlds: The Poetic Intersection of Tanztheater and Teatro Umano. This Venn diagram maps the shared territory between Pina Bausch's Tanztheater and Teatro Umano's embodied dramaturgy. Both forms center gesture, breath, and inner presence as narrative tools—where the spoken word withdraws, and energetic truth emerges. Emotion is not dramatized, but distilled. AI-generated image created with OpenAI's DALL·E (via ChatGPT).

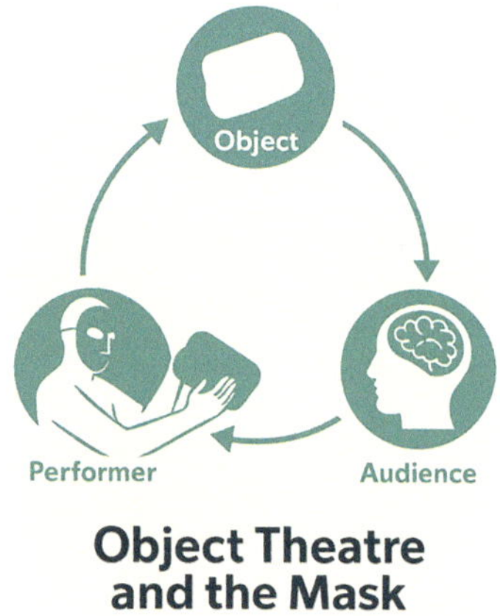

FIGURE 6.33: Diagram illustrating the poetic intersection of Object Theatre and Mask Work within Teatro Umano's methodology. Objects become emotional extensions of the performer, while masks hold and reflect unspoken inner worlds—together creating a dramaturgy of presence, metaphor, and transformation. AI-generated image created with OpenAI's DALL·E (via ChatGPT).

FIGURE 6.34: Object as Character, Absurdity as Mirror. In this solo clown act, everyday items—a shopping cart, a blue cup, a plastic bag—transform into emotional counterparts. The performer invites the audience to see not what these objects are, but what they can become. With minimal setup and maximum imagination, this piece channels the essence of object theatre: where presence animates metaphor, and meaning emerges not from realism, but from poetic transference.

The mask, too, is a central channel in this symbolic system. While masks conceal, they also reveal. In Teatro Umano, masks are **non-verbal voices**—intensifiers of rhythm, emotion, and archetype. Unlike realistic facial expressions, the fixed surface of the mask does not limit interpretation; rather, it expands it. The audience projects meaning into the mask's stillness, and through the actor's breath and gesture, the mask pulses with life.

This dual use of **object and mask** forms the basis of Teatro Umano's symbolic language. When an object is manipulated with authentic energy—lifted, cradled, resisted—it becomes alive. When a mask is worn with full-body engagement, it transforms the actor into a conduit for collective meaning. Here, everyday objects shift into emotional counterparts—mundane items becoming symbolic companions in performance (see **Figure 6.35**).

FIGURE 6.35: Scan to view *Una passeggiata di merda*, a short clown performance by the author. This piece exemplifies object theatre's absurd, metaphorical logic—where mundane items become emotional and symbolic companions.

Together, they offer a space **beyond speech**, where grief, memory, fear, or love can exist without explanation. The spectator is invited to fill in the gaps. This silent contract between performer, object, and audience is not didactic—it is poetic. It is not about making meaning clear, but about making it felt.

Koshi and Energetic Projection: Toward a Universal Theatrical Language

In the heart of Teatro Umano's training lies a subtle yet transformative principle: the koshi. Borrowed from Japanese physical practices, the koshi refers not simply to the hips or pelvis, but to the energetic center of the body—the place from which intention, weight, and impulse are born. It is from here that presence emanates, and it is here that the performer returns when seeking groundedness and projection.

Unlike conventional theatrical traditions that may focus on facial expressivity or spoken articulation, Teatro Umano privileges energetic clarity: the capacity to communicate through breath, axis, rhythm, and energetic direction. The koshi becomes the physical gateway to this language, translating emotional inner states into visible outer form—into action.

In practical terms, this means that a character's decision, doubt, or desire is not first spoken but *felt* through the koshi. This creates a ripple effect that moves through the spine, radiates through the limbs, and eventually meets the audience without necessarily needing words. This is especially relevant in mask work, where facial expression is fixed, and the body must "speak" the entirety of the character's emotional and psychological state.

In performance, this projection is not simply about "big movement" but about clear, directed energy—what some might call *ki* or *chi*. A gesture initiated from the koshi carries intention and lands with precision. Whether in silence or in speech, this kind of projection invites audiences of any culture or language to connect deeply with the action before them.

This approach has proven essential in international touring and multilingual contexts. When language may not be shared, energetic truth becomes the bridge. The audience doesn't need translation when a performer's koshi is truly activated—because the storytelling bypasses words and lands directly in the body of the observer. Energetic projection, then, is not just a performance tool; it is a universal theatrical language (see **Figure 6.36**).

Part 7—Human Theatre and Dramaturgy: A Meta-Perspective

Beyond the Script: Dramaturgy as Creative Framework

In Human Theatre, dramaturgy is not merely the structure of a play—it is the living architecture of performance. It is an energetic map, not just a literary outline. It does not begin with a script, but with questions: What do we want to awaken in the audience? What sensations? What reflections? What memories?

Traditional dramaturgy often begins with a plot and builds outward: characters, scenes, acts. In Teatro Umano, we often begin from the center—the emotional

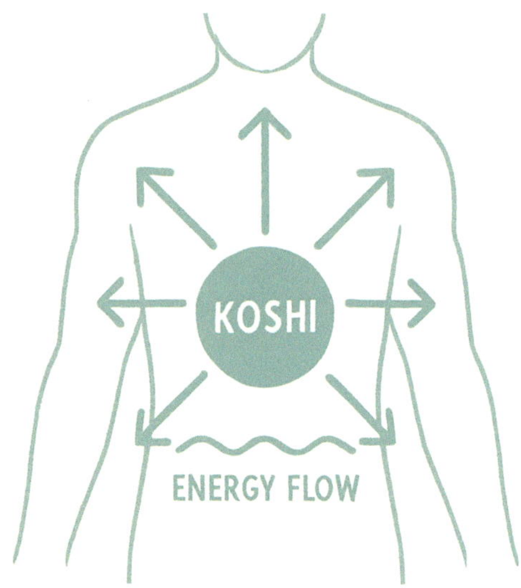

FIGURE 6.36: Koshi as Core: Radiating Presence through Energetic Projection. This diagram visualizes the koshi as the energetic heart of the performer—a source from which presence radiates in every direction. In Teatro Umano, koshi is not merely anatomical—it is the axis of projection, the root of force, breath, and expressive power. From this center, the body becomes a conduit—not of tension, but of intentional release. AI-generated image created with OpenAI's DALL·E (via ChatGPT).

engine, the bodily rhythm, the gesture that holds more meaning than dialogue. Here, dramaturgy becomes a framework for **experience**, a guide not for what will be said, but for how the audience will feel, and how the performer will embody that feeling.

This approach demands an expansion of the dramaturg's role. In Human Theatre, the dramaturg is not only the text analyst or structural consultant, but also a **sensorial architect**, a **movement translator**, and an **empathic observer**. They trace the energetic spine of the performance, ensuring that each beat—whether verbal, visual, or vibrational—contributes to the whole.

Rather than limiting dramaturgy to dramatic conflict and linearity, Human Theatre embraces **interruption, stillness, repetition, silence**. A gesture repeated three times may say more than pages of text. A pause held in breath can hold the weight of a scream. The framework that emerges is not fixed, but flexible—responsive to the present, to the performers, to the space, and most importantly, to the audience. In this way, every element—a gesture, a silence, a structure—carries dramaturgical weight in Human Theatre (see **Figure 6.37**).

The script, if it exists, is one of many tools—not the ultimate blueprint. It may be created in parallel with rehearsal, or even retroactively documented after performance. In some cases, what holds the dramaturgy together is a single gesture, a mask, an object, or a spatial rhythm. The score is kinetic and energetic before it becomes linguistic.

This meta-perspective invites us to see dramaturgy not as a plan to follow but as a living process of meaning-making. Like breath or heartbeat, it is always there—even when invisible. It asks us to trust the intelligence of the body, the clarity of presence, and the audience's ability to co-compose the moment.

Ultimately, dramaturgy in Human Theatre becomes a practice of **attunement**: to sensation, to silence, to surprise. And in this

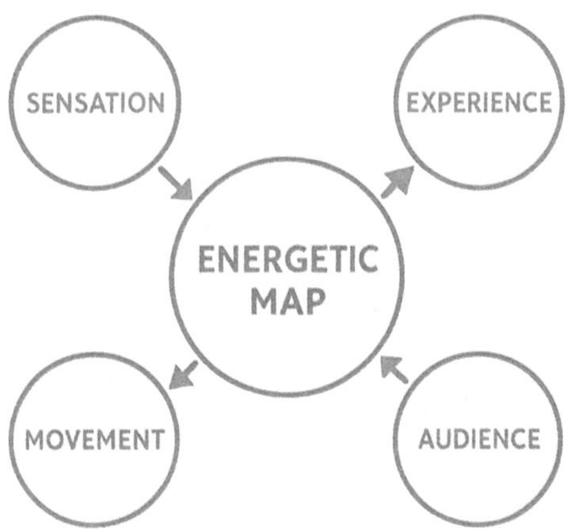

FIGURE 6.37: Dramaturgy as Creative Framework: A Living Cycle. This diagram represents dramaturgy not as fixed text, but as a living, fluid system. Here, the creative process cycles through impulse, structure, embodiment, and reflection—inviting the dramaturg to act as a collaborator of rhythm, space, and meaning, not just a literary interpreter. Every choice is energetic. Every element—a gesture, a silence, a structure—holds dramaturgical weight. AI-generated image created with OpenAI's DALL·E (via ChatGPT).

attunement, a new kind of authorship emerges—one that is collective, embodied, and alive.

Empty Spaces, Open Interpretations: Universality Through Suggestion

In Human Theatre, the absence of elaborate scenery is not a limitation—it is a poetic strategy. The empty space is not a void, but a canvas. It asks the audience to become co-creators, to complete what is merely suggested with its imagination and emotional memory. This openness forms the basis of theatrical universality: when less is shown, more can be felt.

Rather than dictating every detail of time, place, or mood, Human Theatre offers fragments—fabrics that wave like trees, chairs that become doorways, masks that hint at rather than define character. This ambiguity allows the viewer's own cultural, emotional, and experiential references to fill the gaps. It is an invitation, not a prescription.

In *Desconocido*, for instance, a simple curtain becomes a domestic space, a war zone, a dream. A glance or a shift in posture can signify a boundary crossed or a memory returned. In this way, the visual and performative language moves toward a shared emotional code—one not tied to a specific context but resonant across them. This aesthetic of suggestion demonstrates that the less you show, the more you awaken the audience's imagination (see **Figure 6.38**).

This practice draws influence from traditions like Nō Theatre, where minimalism becomes sacred, and from postdramatic theatre, where suggestion often replaces exposition. But in Human Theatre, this minimalism is never abstract for its own sake; it's grounded in energetic and narrative clarity. A performer's intention becomes the strongest scenic element.

By working with restraint—less light, fewer props, limited sound—the stage breathes. It opens room for silence, for stillness, for unexpected connections to arise between gesture, space, and audience. This also echoes a fundamental belief in Human Theatre: that universality is not achieved by generalizing, but by stripping down to the essence of human experience.

The empty space does not speak loudly, but it resonates deeply. And in its quiet invitation, each audience member is allowed to see its own story reflected, reshaped, and made visible through suggestion.

Characters, Cycles, and Structure: Dramaturgy as Internal Compass

In Human Theatre, dramaturgy is not just a blueprint or literary skeleton—it's an inner compass. Rather than following external rules of conflict, resolution, or

FIGURE 6.38: Universality Through Suggestion: The Power of Minimalism. A simple stage—a chair, a table, a sketched window—becomes a canvas for resonance. In this aesthetic of restraint, Human Theatre invites the audience into co-creation. Meaning doesn't arrive—it emerges through silence, presence, and suggestion. The less you show, the more you awaken. AI-generated image created with OpenAI's DALL·E (via ChatGPT).

plot-point timing, the structure of a piece unfolds organically from within: from the breath of a character, the energetic rhythm of a group, or the silence between two gestures. This kind of dramaturgy is embodied.

Characters are not puppets of a narrative line: They are cycles of energy, shaped by repetition, transformation, resistance, and release. A character's journey may not always be psychological or developmental in the traditional sense. Instead, it can be a somatic cycle—a return to a gesture, a breath, or a posture that gains meaning over time. The dramaturgical arc, then, is internal: it moves according to energetic shifts, memory echoes, and emotional resonances that the audience feels more than understands.

Take for example *Desconocido*. The structure does not obey classical acts or scenes. It breathes through the rhythms of the characters. Giuseppe's silent loop with the letter, Anna's unfolding grief, and Rossella's recurring interventions form a circular dramaturgy—a spiral rather than a line. The return of certain objects, sounds, or patterns (like the stethoscope, the sewing machine, or the dance) acts as dramaturgical anchors. These are not arbitrary symbols but energetic cues that signal movement between emotional states. In cyclical dramaturgy, meaning doesn't move forward—it returns deeper, resonating with memory and repetition (see **Figure 6.39**).

This dramaturgy often resembles natural cycles: inhalation and exhalation, blooming and withering, leaving and returning. It resists climax as the only structural goal. Sometimes, the most powerful moments are the pauses, the unresolved endings, the repetitions that deepen instead of "progress."

The role of the creator—be it actor, director, or dramaturg—is to feel these cycles, not force them. Like a choreographer shaping movement or a poet revising a verse, the work is about sensing where energy flows or blocks. In this sense, structure becomes alive, fluid, and responsive. It is not a map, but a pulse.

Thus, in Human Theatre, dramaturgy is not imposed—it is discovered. Not intellectualized—it is lived. It doesn't serve to explain the performance but to hold its energetic truth.

FIGURE 6.39: Cyclical Dramaturgy: A Model of Emotional Return and Energetic Flow. This visual model illustrates how characters, themes, and energies in Human Theatre unfold through recurring loops, not straight lines. Instead of progression, we see repetition with variation—a structure shaped by memory, presence, and transformation. Meaning doesn't move forward; it returns deeper. AI-generated image created with OpenAI's DALL·E (via ChatGPT).

Part 8—Conclusion: Human Theatre as a Living Dramatic Language

The journey of Human Theatre is not one that seeks to impose a final truth or a singular path. Instead, it proposes a living, breathing form of dramaturgy—one that pulses through the body, responds to the world, and invites audiences to become co-creators of meaning. It challenges traditional notions of authorship, identity, and representation, offering instead an approach rooted in presence, intuition, and energetic connection.

Throughout this work, we have traversed different terrains: from ancient dramaturgical models to the postdramatic, from embodied testimony to the power of suggestion, from objects and masks to the breath and the koshi. We have explored the roles of voice, silence, space, gesture, and transformation. In every chapter, what emerges is a theatre that is not defined by plot alone, nor by its text or genre, but by the quality of encounter it facilitates—between performer and performer, between performer and audience, and between the audience and themselves.

Human Theatre does not prescribe a style. It offers a methodology: a system of tuning, of listening, of responding. It reminds us that the dramatic exists not only in what is said or shown, but in what is withheld, in what vibrates silently in the space between. It teaches us that form can emerge from flow, that structure can be born from sensation, and that meaning can arise without needing to be explained.

At its core, Human Theatre trusts the intelligence of the audience. It does not underestimate its capacity to feel, to reflect, to make connections. It invites them into a co-poetic space—one where ambiguity is not a failure, but a tool for liberation; where incompleteness is not a flaw, but an opening.

As we continue creating, devising, and discovering, Human Theatre stands as both an offering and an invitation. An offering to those who seek more than spectacle. An invitation to those who believe that theatre, at its best, can awaken the senses, touch the soul, and remind us of our shared humanity.

It is not a finished method. It is a seed. A living language. And it grows with every breath we take on stage.

NOTES

1. Heiner Müller was a German playwright, poet, and director widely regarded as one of the most important dramatists of the twentieth century after Bertolt Brecht. Known for his dense, poetic language and radical reworkings of classical texts, Müller explored themes of history, power, and identity in postwar Germany. His influential works, such as *Hamletmachine* and *Quartet*, often resist traditional narrative structure, instead employing fragmentation and irony to reflect political and existential tensions.
2. Robert Wilson is an American experimental theatre director, playwright, and visual artist known for his groundbreaking work in avant-garde theatre. Famed for his use of slow movement, minimalist aesthetics, and striking visual composition, Wilson often merges

disciplines like dance, lighting design, and architecture to create nonlinear, dreamlike performances. His collaborations with artists such as Philip Glass (*Einstein on the Beach*) and lucinda childs have had a lasting impact on contemporary performance practice.

3. Petra Bravo, a Cuban dancer and professor, has greatly influenced modern dance and dance education in Puerto Rico. As a faculty member at the University of Puerto Rico, Río Piedras, she teaches contemporary dance techniques and inspires students and audiences through her performances and choreographic works.
4. Gradissa Fernández, a renowned contemporary performer, flamenco dancer, and director in physical theatre and experimental performance, creates immersive experiences that engage audiences emotionally and intellectually through movement, dance, and drama. She explores human relationships and societal issues, actively teaching and mentoring emerging artists to foster a new generation of theatre creators. Fernández's contributions have been recognized at national and international festivals, solidifying her status as a prominent figure in contemporary theatre and a champion of artistic collaboration.
5. Hans-Thies Lehmann was a German theatre scholar best known for his influential theoretical work *Postdramatic Theatre* (1999), which redefined the landscape of contemporary performance. In this seminal text, Lehmann identifies a shift away from narrative-driven drama toward forms that prioritize image, presence, and spatial-temporal experimentation. His analysis captures the evolving aesthetics of late twentieth-century theatre, including fragmentation, intermediality, and the destabilization of character and plot, making his work a cornerstone in the study of avant-garde and experimental performance.
6. Pina Bausch, a German choreographer and dancer, revolutionized contemporary dance and theatre. As artistic director of the Tanztheater Wuppertal, she blended dance, theatre, and spoken word, exploring love, loss, and human relationships through movement and emotional expression. Her innovative works, like "Café Müller" and "The Rite of Spring," challenged traditional performance by emphasizing physicality and dramatic storytelling. Bausch's distinctive style, characterized by powerful imagery and raw emotion, has profoundly influenced dance theatre, inspiring artists and companies worldwide.

Chapter 7

Unmasking Vulnerability Onstage: A Practical Guide to Emotional Presence

7

Unmasking Vulnerability Onstage: A Practical Guide to Emotional Presence

Part 1—Foundations of Embodied Vulnerability

Opening the Curtain: Vulnerability as Presence

Having explored the structure and philosophy of Human Theatre, we now turn to its emotional core: vulnerability. This chapter investigates how embodiment, masks, and neurological empathy work together to activate true presence onstage.

Vulnerability is often misunderstood in performance. It is not fragility. It is not weakness. It is not rawness for its own sake. In the context of Human Theatre, vulnerability is presence. It is the courage to show up with one's whole self—body, breath, energy, silence, and gaze—without hiding behind technical perfection or performative control.

In conventional performance training, actors are often taught to "protect" themselves—to create a psychological distance between their inner lives and the roles they play. While this technique may safeguard the performer's emotional well-being in some settings, it can also result in performances that feel disconnected, mannered, or overly intellectual. The audience may be impressed, but they are not necessarily moved.

Human Theatre takes the opposite approach. It invites the performer to dismantle their internal walls, not by exposing personal trauma, but by becoming radically honest in the moment. Vulnerability here is not about telling all—it is about *being*

FIGURE 7.0: Carrying the Invisible. Gesture arises from subtle vibration. Through the hand, the performer carries the invisible—transmitting what words cannot hold. AI-generated image created with OpenAI's DALL·E (via ChatGPT).

fully receptive, attuned to the present, responsive to impulse. It means allowing the body to tremble, the breath to stutter, the gesture to emerge unpolished—if that is what the moment demands.

This vulnerability does not begin onstage. It begins in training. In breathwork. In silence. In shared glances during improvisation. It begins in the rehearsal space when a performer risks pausing instead of filling the silence, or follows an impulse without knowing where it will lead. It's cultivated in the choice to *listen fully* before reacting, to let presence precede performance.

This is where masks become powerful tools. Paradoxically, the act of wearing a mask often gives the performer permission to be more vulnerable (see **Figure 7.1**). By covering the face, the performer's habitual expressions are removed, making space for a deeper energetic current to surface. It is no longer about showing emotion—it becomes about *feeling truthfully*, and allowing that truth to ripple through the entire body.

FIGURE 7.1: Vulnerability as Presence. An actor steps into the performance space, stripped of ornamentation, embodying the raw vulnerability at the heart of Human Theatre. This is the threshold moment where presence begins—not through spectacle, but through stillness, breath, and the courage to simply be seen. AI-generated image created with OpenAI's DALL·E (via ChatGPT).

Vulnerability is also relational. Mirror neurons—the neurological mechanism that allows us to "feel with" others—are activated not through grand gestures, but through authenticity. When the audience sees a performer breathing honestly, hesitating truthfully, or moving with reverence instead of force, something is awakened in them. They mirror what they witness. They recognize it.

In Human Theatre, vulnerability is the invisible thread that binds the performer and the audience. It is not declared; it is sensed. It asks nothing more—and nothing less—than presence.

From Observation to Embodiment: The Performer as Witness and Vessel

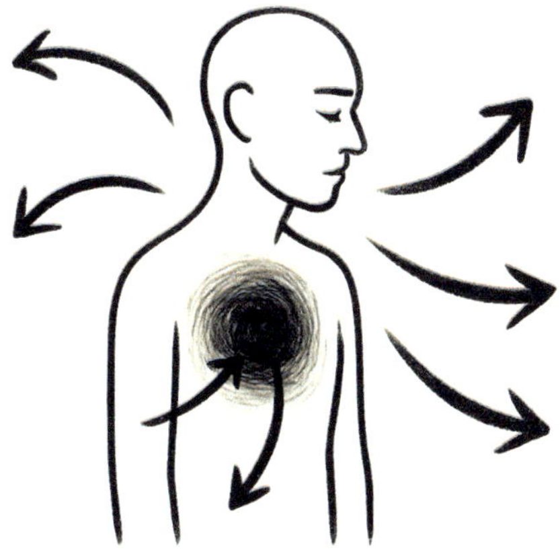

FIGURE 7.2: The Performer as Vessel. Open at the center, the performer absorbs stimuli from the world and radiates energy outward through breath, movement, and presence. This image captures the dual nature of Human Theatre: the performer as both container and conduit of lived and observed emotion. AI-generated image created with OpenAI's DALL·E (via ChatGPT).

In Human Theatre, the performer is more than a storyteller—they are a vessel of experience, a sensitive observer who absorbs and transmits. The process begins not with lines or choreography, but with deep observation: of others, of oneself, and of the world. Every flicker of emotion, every nuanced gesture witnessed in real life becomes raw material—seeds of potential embodiment.

This kind of observation is not passive. It's active, energetic, and empathetic. The performer studies the way a woman wipes her eyes when no one is looking (see **Figure 7.2**), the way children hold their breath before crying, the stiffness of someone trying not to show fear. These human details are not mimicked, but internalized. They enter the body not as gestures, but as resonant energies.

Embodiment, then, is not imitation—it is absorption. It is allowing the body to become a porous membrane through which emotion and action pass. Performers do not "play" a character, but rather let that character emerge as a vibration through their own body, informed by observation and attuned to the present moment.

The mask deepens this process. It removes the face, our habitual channel of expression, and forces performers to speak with their whole body. Subtlety becomes power. Observation becomes precision. The vessel becomes charged. In this way, the performer is not merely interpreting the world—they are translating it into movement, breath, and presence.

To embody is not to control—it is to surrender. Human Theatre teaches performers to become instruments of feeling, not vehicles of demonstration. And in that space of surrender, the invisible becomes visible. The audience does not see the performer "acting." They witness a body in resonance, a soul remembering something unspeakable. And that is where transformation begins.

Activating the Invisible: A Performer's Inner Guide

The most powerful tools of the performer are often the ones the audience cannot see: Impulses, sensations, intuitions, and emotional undercurrents that move silently beneath the surface. In Human Theatre, these invisible forces are not secondary—they are primary. They guide the performer like an inner compass, shaping action from the inside out.

To activate this internal guide, performers must cultivate a deep state of listening—listening not just to their fellow actors or to the external environment, but to the micro-signals of the body. The flutter in the gut. The catch in the breath. The pull behind the eyes. These are not distractions: They are messages. The training, then, is to become fluent in their language.

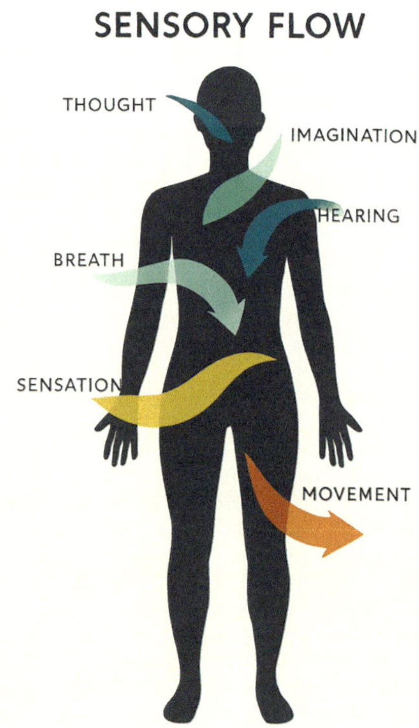

FIGURE 7.3: Intuition in Motion. The performer is enveloped in an energetic field, guided by internal impulses rather than external commands. Here, inner sensing shapes outer expression—a moment where movement is born from silence, and presence from intuition. AI-generated image created with OpenAI's DALL·E (via ChatGPT).

This process does not begin with the character. It begins with the self (see **Figure 7.3**). Before a mask is worn, before a gesture is shaped, performers tune their body and breathe to a state of sensitivity. This may involve somatic warm-ups, grounding exercises, or simply a moment of stillness. The goal is to lower the noise of performance anxiety and amplify the signals of inner clarity.

In this sense, the inner guide functions almost like a tuning fork. It resonates with what is true. It allows the performer to notice when they are faking an emotion, forcing a movement, or hiding behind a technique. And it also knows when something is alive—when the body is speaking without censorship, when the moment becomes charged.

At the heart of this activation is the performer's **inner guide**, an embodied intelligence honed through practice, sensitivity, and trust. The performer becomes a channel—absorbing emotional truth, filtering it through breath and movement, and transmitting it through presence. This is not simply "acting": It is **energetic listening**, and **embodied storytelling**.

A foundational mechanism in this process is the **DEE Cycle**:

- **Dynamis** (Desire/Intention).
- **Energeia** (Activation).
- **Entelecheia** (Outcome/Effect).

But the DEE Cycle is not a formula—it is a **rhythm.** It lives in the timing of a glance, the tension of a still body, the disruption of an unexpected gesture. It unfolds through breath, gesture, and silence. When fully activated, it allows the **mirror neurons** of the audience to resonate with the inner life of the character, **bridging empathy without explanation.**

In Human Theatre, we use this invisible guide to navigate each moment of creation. It tells us when to pause, when to move, and when to connect. And most importantly, it tells us when we are truly present.

Mirror Neurons and Emotional Connection

One of the most compelling scientific bridges between performance and empathy lies in the discovery of **mirror neurons**—a network of cells in the brain that fire both when we perform an action and when we observe someone else performing that same action. In the context of theatre, this discovery affirms something that performers have intuited for centuries: that emotional resonance between actor and audience is not abstract—it is neurological.

When a performer expresses a gesture of tenderness, pain, or joy (see **Figure 7.4**), the spectator doesn't simply witness it—they **feel** it. This is because mirror neurons allow us to internally simulate what we see. Our bodies participate in the emotional

FIGURE 7.4: Energetic Transmission Through Embodied Gesture. As the performer expresses emotion through breath and gesture, the audience's mirror neurons activate—creating a shared, felt experience across space. This is not performance as representation—it is presence as emotional resonance. AI-generated image created with OpenAI's DALL·E (via ChatGPT).

landscape before our minds fully process it. This simulation creates **empathy**, a visceral connection that bypasses language and logic.

Human Theatre is built upon this principle. It places less emphasis on explanation and more on **evocation**. It relies on the actor's ability to embody an emotion with energetic truth, rather than to imitate its external signs. The presence of the performer becomes a stimulus for the audience's inner mirror system—inviting not only comprehension, but **identification**.

This is why stylized movement, breathwork, and mask performance can be so powerful. They bypass cognitive filters and speak directly to the nervous system. A trembling hand, a shift in weight, a breath held too long—these are not just details. They are activators.

In this sense, the audience becomes a **partner** in the performance—not passively consuming, but actively experiencing. Its mirror neurons fire in response to the performer's authenticity. The more embodied the actor's presence, the more the spectator is drawn into emotional attunement.

Ultimately, mirror neurons help explain what Human Theatre aims to cultivate: a stage where stories are not just told, but **felt**, co-created in the shared space between body and gaze, movement and memory, impulse and recognition.

The Mask and the Amplification of Emotion

In Human Theatre, the mask is not a tool for concealment—it is a device for revelation. It strips the face of its familiar micro-expressions and forces the performer to communicate from deeper, more embodied sources. In doing so, the mask becomes a paradox: by hiding the face, it reveals the soul.

Without access to the usual facial cues, the performer must activate the entire body as a channel of meaning. Breath, posture, rhythm, and gesture take center stage. The audience, unable to rely on the face for emotional cues, becomes more attuned to energetic signals, sensing the emotional field rather than reading it. In this heightened relational space, the performer's inner landscape becomes amplified, and small impulses can ripple with unexpected power.

Masks also offer protection—psychologically and energetically. By shifting identity away from the personal, they enable the performer to go further emotionally without collapsing into vulnerability. The performer does not perform "as themselves," but as a vessel, inhabited by impulses, stories, and archetypes. In this way, the mask becomes a mediator between inner truth and external form.

The energetic demands of masked performance align beautifully with the DEE cycle (see **Figure 7.5**): the spark of **Dynamis** (impulse), the activation of **Energeia** (movement, sound, vibration), and the fulfillment of **Entelecheia** (presence, expression). The mask does not speak, but it listens. It does not show, but it reveals. It creates a threshold through which energy passes—amplified, refined, and offered with intensity.

In rehearsal, we often notice that once the mask is worn, something clicks. Movements become clearer, more decisive. The breath deepens. The performer stops "acting" and begins "being." This shift, subtle but profound, lies at the heart of Human Theatre. It is not about pretending to feel. It is about allowing the emotion to inhabit the form—and trusting that the mask will carry it forward.

Wearing a mask is not a performance of falseness—it is a discipline of truth.

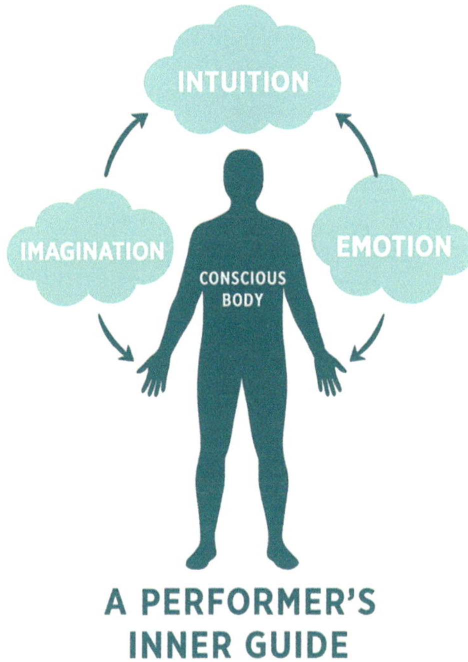

FIGURE 7.5: The Energetic Compass of Human Theatre. A triad of intuition, imagination, and emotion drives the performer's internal world, shaping physical expression and embodied presence. This diagram visualizes the invisible guidance system that leads the performer from sensing to action. AI-generated image created with OpenAI's DALL·E (via ChatGPT).

DEE in Action: Awakening Empathy Through the Mask

In Human Theatre, the DEE cycle—**Dynamis, Energeia, Entelecheia**—is not only a tool for internal alignment or stage composition; it becomes an instrument for activating empathy in the audience. When performed through the mask, this energetic progression intensifies, bypassing cognitive resistance and inviting direct emotional resonance.

The mask, in this context, functions not as concealment but as magnification. It filters out the superficial self, silencing the performer's personal ego and amplifying inner intention. The audience does not project onto a blank slate—they project onto a vessel in motion. The mask, stripped of facial micro-expression, calls for a bolder transmission of Energeia: movement, breath, rhythm, and posture must all speak louder, with more precision and emotional clarity.

When this energy is rooted in Dynamis—an authentic inner impulse—it becomes contagious (see **Figure 7.6**). Through this resonance, audiences feel **with** the performer, not just about them. This is the moment of Entelecheia: When the story materializes not only in performance, but in perception. It lives simultaneously in both performer and viewer.

In neuroscience, mirror neurons fire not only when we move, but when we see someone else move with emotional intention. A masked performer who embodies Dynamis does not offer generic gestures: They offer **emotional signals**. These activate the viewer's own neurological circuits for empathy, which is why the audience often report feeling a deep connection with masked characters—despite their apparent "anonymity."

This is the paradox of the mask in Human Theatre: By removing the personal face, we invite deeper personal projection. By limiting one channel of expression, we amplify others—gesture, breath, koshi, timing. The performer becomes energetically transparent, allowing the DEE cycle to shine through.

This kind of presence doesn't emerge from acting. It emerges from **being**—from the discipline of sensing, trusting, and letting the body's inner compass guide expression outward. The DEE cycle, then, is not theoretical. It is experiential. It is how we feel others feel.

And in that space, between movement and recognition, between impulse and reception, empathy is not just awakened. It is **shared**. This process is captured visually in **Figure 7.7**.

A further visualization of this process in ensemble performance is shown in **Figure 7.8**.

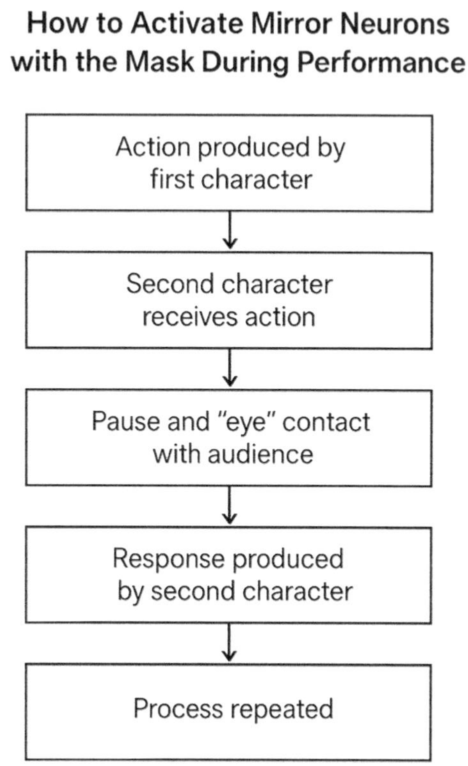

FIGURE 7.6: The Cycle of Emotional Echo. Step-by-step visualization of how mirror neurons are activated in masked performance—through rhythm, pause, and presence. Action, reception, and response form a loop that draws the audience into a shared energetic space. AI-generated image created with OpenAI's DALL·E (via ChatGPT).

Part 2—Human Theatre in Practice: Case Study and Reflection

Bar Moments: "Italy Yesterday as Today" (Case Study)

In continuing our exploration of embodied vulnerability onstage, *Bar Moments* offers a case study in how theatrical silence, physicality, and energetic storytelling can awaken both personal and collective memory.

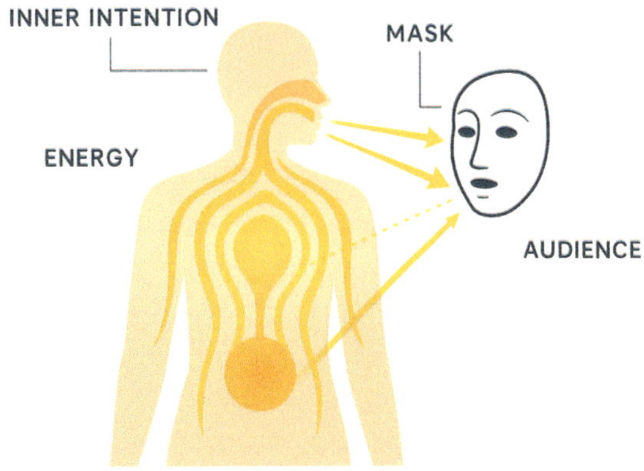

FIGURE 7.7: The Performer as Resonant Filter. This model illustrates how the performer absorbs, processes, and transmits emotional energy. Through awareness and inner flow, emotion becomes embodiment and embodiment becomes shared feeling. AI-generated image created with OpenAI's DALL·E (via ChatGPT).

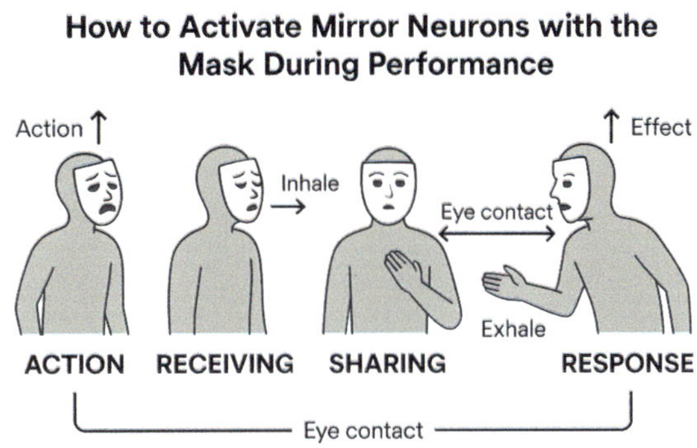

FIGURE 7.8: The DEE Cycle Embodied in Ensemble Work. Masked performers demonstrate the DEE cycle of Demonstration → Empathy → Echo, pausing to include the audience as emotional witnesses. Energy flows from one body to another—creating not just empathy, but transformation. AI-generated image created with OpenAI's DALL·E (via ChatGPT).

Bar Moments was born from a desire to explore a painful moment in Italy's history—the Fascist era—not as a static narrative, but as a recurring cycle of behavior, silence, and resistance. The goal was not to recreate historical events but to reflect on how the ghosts of the past continue to haunt the present. The subtitle *Italy Yesterday as Today* encapsulates this thematic intention: History repeats, sometimes subtly, sometimes loudly, but always embodied.

Synopsis of Bar Moments*: In a provincial bar, on the brink of 1940, the modest and monotonous life of Lila, the bar owner, her daughter, and the regular customers unfolds. The characters meet, clash, and reveal contradictions, reminding us of how fragile the line between past and present is. It is a masked comedy, sometimes cutting, that gives voice to Italian stereotypes from all times, demonstrating that experience is the true teacher of personal growth.*

Bar Moments explores Italian identity through a blend of character, movement, and emotional authenticity (see **Figure 7.9**). Characters such as **Lila, Gianni, Sister Magdalena, Maia, Lili**, and **Truffini** each embody societal forces (see **Figure 7.10**)—patriarchy, religion, political authority, and the yearning for liberation. Every gesture, every breath, is charged with intention.

The performance is set in a bar—a simple, unremarkable place that becomes a microcosm for society. Within its walls, characters gather: the bar owner Lila, the politician Truffini, the nun Magdalena, and a chorus of townspeople. The action unfolds through movement, gesture, and stylized interaction.

FIGURE 7.9: Publicity and synopsis for *Bar Moments*. The visual and textual material here frames the performance as a meditation on resistance, identity, and inherited silence.

FIGURE 7.10: Embodied Archetypes in *Bar Moments*. *(left)* Lila, the play's emotional core, channels lived trauma through grounded stillness and restrained gesture. Her body becomes a vessel for pain, resilience, and transformation. *(center)* Magdalena, cloaked in spiritual austerity, embodies repression. Her stillness creates discomfort—presence through absence. *(right)* Truffini, the opportunist politician, asserts power through angular, dominating movement—embodying performative control and ideological force.

FIGURE 7.11: Gianni, Lila's husband, personifies fascist-era machismo in *Bar Moments*. His presence reflects a generational suppression of female autonomy through gesture, posture, and spatial control.

There is no spoken dialogue. The masks speak instead—not with words, but with posture, tension, stillness, and impulse. This silence creates space for the audience to lean in, to listen more deeply—not only to the story but to themselves.

Among them, Gianni—Lila's husband—embodies the weight of patriarchal expectation through domineering physicality and machismo (see **Figure 7.11**), contributing to the oppressive rhythm that drives the bar's atmosphere.

Each character's journey follows the DEE cycle:

- **Desire** (a wish, a longing, an intention).
- **Energeia** (the action or struggle taken to pursue that desire).
- **Effect** (the consequence, internal or external, of that action).

Each character's arc follows the DEE cycle:

- **Gianni** reflects fascist machismo, restricting Lila's autonomy.
- **Sister Magdalena** silences joy with religious repression.
- **Lili**, a sex worker, embodies sensual liberation in defiance of church and state.

Each moment is **played physically, deliberately, with emotional precision**, allowing the audience to feel before they understand. This is how the DEE cycle awakens mirror neurons: through presence, rhythm, and authentic embodiment.

Lila, the central character, is a survivor. She is not loud or overtly heroic. Her strength lies in her ability to observe, to endure, and eventually, to act. Her gestures are subtle but deliberate. She wipes down tables, rearranges glasses, tends to the bar—each action layered with unspoken emotional weight. The environment becomes charged as others enter: Truffini, full of pompous self-importance; Magdalena, obsessed with moral purity and control. Their behavior imposes a rhythm that Lila initially follows ... until she doesn't.

FIGURE 7.12: Lila's Final Gesture. In locking the bar behind her, Lila symbolically closes a chapter of submission in *Bar Moments*. Her poised stance reflects the energetic shift from survival to self-possession—a quiet act of liberation.

In the final scene, Lila locks the bar door, symbolically containing the forces that have manipulated her life (see **Figure 7.12**). She doesn't shout, she doesn't fight. She acts. The stillness in her final gesture is louder than words.

Audiences often describe the piece as cathartic—not because it explains, but because it reveals. They see reflections of their own societies in the interactions, their own silences mirrored in Lila's, their own need for liberation echoed in her gesture. The DEE cycle is fully present here: Lila's *Dynamis* is her quiet resilience; her *Energeia* emerges in physical resistance; and her *Entelecheia* is the reclaiming of agency, through one final, wordless act.

The piece does not offer clear answers—it offers sensation, recognition, and, above all, presence. By blending historical themes, embodied memory, and the poetic potential of silence, *Bar Moments* activates both individual and collective empathy. It becomes a mirror where the audience sees not only Lila, but themselves.

Breath and Timing

Breath becomes the lifeline: the inhale to draw in the world and the exhale to respond to it. The manipulation of time—stretching moments just long enough—ensures the DEE cycle unfolds with the right rhythm to resonate on a visceral level.

This is the alchemy of theatre: by mastering these elements, the performer transforms the stage into a space where empathy thrives, stories unfold naturally, and audiences do not merely observe—they feel.

The goal is not just to tell a story, but to create a shared experience that transcends language and culture. The audience leaves the theatre not just having watched a play, but having lived it.

To be human is to feel—pain, joy, fear, and pleasure. But to understand these emotions, especially when they are not our own, is an act of conscious effort and courage. In performance, this understanding is not intellectual—it is embodied. For the performer, empathy must be lived through the body. And for the audience to feel this truth, the performer must activate the DEE cycle: **Desire/Intention/Dynamis**, **Energeia**, and **Effect/Entelecheia**.

The creation of *Bar Moments* came from this exact practice: placing myself in others' shoes and confronting the layered moral, religious, and social constructs surrounding them. My time observing in the bar revealed, in subtle and repeated gestures, a culture that imposed boundaries and obligations on women—rarely rights. What struck me most were the micro-aggressions veiled as everyday behavior.

One vivid moment stayed with me: An older man walked up to the bar, ordered a drink, then turned to me with a smirk, saying: "Giovane, in cerca della topa, ah." I didn't understand it at first. But the owner's discomfort was clear. Later, I learned the phrase's meaning—crude, sexist, and dismissive. That moment of ignorance and realization became a source of transformation, pushing me to write Gianni.

Gianni, Lila's husband, embodies the fascist-era machismo that diminished women's autonomy. He operates within a framework where women are idealized as "mothers, wives, and tireless angels of the home." These were not compliments—they were constraints. His character is a mirror to the society that bred him.

Enter **Sister Magdalena**, a symbolic extension of the Catholic Church's complicity (see **Figure 7.13**). In a key scene, Lila dances freely to the sound of Trio Lescano. The nun silences the radio. A moment of eye contact follows. No words, just breath, stillness, and unspoken tension. (Lila's **Desire**: joy and release. Her **Energeia**: the dance. The **Effect**: silence, shame, and repression. The mirror neurons of the audience absorb her disappointment.)

Through **Maia**, Lila's child, the audience witnesses generational cycles of social conditioning (see **Figure 7.14**). Early on, Lila tries to pass down her routines. But by the end, she chooses to return Maia's toy bear—choosing her child's joy over tradition. (Lila's **Desire** shifts from preserving norms to protecting innocence. The **Energeia** is the internal struggle. The **Effect**: liberation for both.)

Lili, on the other hand, brings explosive contrast (see **Figure 7.15**). As a sex worker, she challenges both fascist and religious control over the female body. Her sensual presence creates a metaphysical moment—*Artaud's dream realized*. When she seduces Gianni, causing him to collapse at her feet, it's not simply about power—it's about reclaiming agency. (Her **Desire**: freedom. Her **Energeia**: presence. The **Effect**: disruption and chaos.)

FIGURE 7.13: Sister Magdalena silences joy in *Bar Moments*. Religious repression becomes embodied—her restraint carries the weight of institutional denial and spiritual censorship.

Maia's interruption cuts through this scene, returning us to the world of moral judgment. When Lila finds Maia playing with Lili's belongings, something unspoken shifts. This subtle moment of perceived corruption and fear echoes in every breath of the performer.

FIGURE 7.14: Maia, Lila's child, stands as a living thread between generations in *Bar Moments*. In her gestures, the audience witnesses how social conditioning echoes, repeats, and begins again.

The emotional peak arrives when Lila attempts reconciliation. Gianni performs a romantic game, blindfolding her in a moment that hovers between seduction and manipulation. As Lila stands vulnerable, Gianni steals alcohol and exits. When the blindfold comes off, her realization is immediate—and devastating. She finds a single flower on the ground, a visual metaphor for betrayal. (Desire: reconnection. Energeia: surrender. Effect: abandonment. The breath here is broken, the time suspended. The audience feels the betrayal before they process it.) This emotionally charged sequence is illustrated in **Figure 7.16**.

Truffini, the fascist politician, adds yet another layer—this time of political and institutional power. He and Sister Magdalena lock horns through passive-aggressive gestures: a campaign poster, a portrait of the Pope. Their battle unfolds over coffee orders and space occupation. But Lila, once again, intervenes—offering cake, peace, and temporary calm. Their symbolic power struggle and Lila's interruption are depicted in **Figure 7.17**.

FIGURE 7.15: Lili's entrance. Her first encounter with the nun becomes a threshold moment—charged with both innocence and the foreboding weight of authority.

FIGURE 7.16: *(left)* Gianni steals alcohol, a gesture of secret consumption and careless dominance. *(right)* Lila's betrayal realized. Her stillness becomes charged with the shattering recognition of broken trust.

When a radio announcement reveals a new property tax, Lila's perspective shifts. She ejects both church and state from her space. (**Desire:** peace. **New Desire:** autonomy. **Energeia:** action. **Effect:** self-empowerment.) The emotional impact of Lila's reckoning is visually represented in **Figure 7.18**.

In the final moments, Lila doesn't just resist—she transcends. She becomes a symbol of change, embodying a rupture with roles that have long confined her. Her final breath onstage isn't just a sigh of relief—it's an invocation of hope.

Through *Bar Moments*, we see how simple actions—pauses, shared breaths, and indirect cues—open emotional pathways in the audience. These pathways are personal. They allow the viewer to connect, remember, and reflect. And in doing so, they do not just witness history—they *feel* it continuing in the present. This act of symbolic release is captured in **Figure 7.19**.

FIGURE 7.17: *(top)* Magdalena initiates a symbolic confrontation—the Church versus Government. *(bottom)* Lila interrupts the staged conflict and shares the symbolic "cake"—an embodied challenge to the false dichotomy of power.

FIGURE 7.18: Lila's moment of reckoning. Her body folds into a visceral collapse—the weight of betrayal by once-revered institutions becomes physically inescapable.

Embodied Empathy as the Ultimate Goal

The true gift of this work is not catharsis—it is **shared recognition.** The DEE cycle makes visible what is invisible. The body becomes the score. The mask, the amplifier. Breath, the pulse of the story. Mirror neurons bridge the space between self and other, allowing the audience to become more than observers—they become **participants in empathy**.

To be human is to feel. But to embody another's feeling with integrity requires discipline, honesty, and surrender. It is in this sacred space that Human Theatre finds its power—not in spectacle, but in **resonance**. A QR code linking to video excerpts of this work can be found in **Figure 7.20**.

Bar Moments: *A Case Study in Energetic Flow and Disruption*

This case study invites us to observe performance not through character or plot, but through energy—how it builds, resists, releases, and transforms. In *Bar Moments*, we witness a live anatomy of presence: where alignment falters, breath hesitates, or gesture fails to find completion.

Viewed through the lens of the DEE Cycle—Dynamis, Energeia, Entelecheia—we can trace how intention begins, how it either flows or is blocked, and what ultimately manifests. When tension is unconscious, the cycle stalls. When tension

FIGURE 7.19: Symbolic liberation. In one sweeping gesture, Lila releases the weight of institutional control. This is not rebellion—it is energetic emancipation.

is acknowledged and worked with—as proposed in the TDTETE model—a new rhythm emerges: One that restores coherence and resonance.

These moments are not theatrical mistakes. They are thresholds. Each one holds the potential for transformation—if the performer learns to listen.

Embodied Resistance: Performing Empathy Through the DEE Cycle

In the world of Human Theatre, performance is not merely an act of representation—it is an act of resistance. Resistance against numbness, disconnection, and superficial storytelling. And the root of that resistance is empathy—an embodied, felt, and vibratory empathy that activates the DEE cycle not as a technique, but as a lived, transformative process.

FIGURE 7.20: Scan to watch scenes from *Bar Moments*. The QR code grants access to excerpts where breath, gesture, and silence speak louder than dialogue.

To feel deeply and to respond honestly onstage requires more than talent. It requires a body that has been trained to listen, to hold, and to release. It requires an actor who is not performing emotion, but moving through it in real time—without collapsing into it. This is the delicate power of the DEE cycle: **Dynamis** (the potential), **Energeia** (the activation), and **Entelecheia** (the fulfillment), all flowing through breath, gesture, and impulse.

Empathy, in this context, is not about imitation. It is not about imagining how someone else feels—it is about allowing the body's sensory intelligence to mirror, absorb, and respond to another's energetic state. It's a willingness to be affected, to tremble with the tremble of another, to become a porous vessel without losing your center.

Human Theatre trains this capacity through exercises that ask the performer to:

- Ground in koshi while holding presence through the breath.
- Engage with the audience not through facial expression, but through tone, posture, and spatial relation.
- Release control and allow emotion to arise from sensation, rather than from intellectual direction.

This embodied resistance breaks the mold of theatrical "productivity." It replaces planned emotion with organic emergence. It shifts the goal of theatre from performance to connection, from spectacle to communion. One such moment of grounded resistance is shown in **Figure 7.21**.

In this way, each performance becomes a ritual of shared humanity. It challenges the performer to move beyond aesthetic polish and toward emotional truth. It challenges the audience to let go of judgment and meet the moment with its nervous system—not just its intellect.

To perform empathy is to insist that presence matters. To activate the DEE cycle is to reanimate the body's wisdom. To engage Human Theatre is to return to theatre not just as art, but as offering.

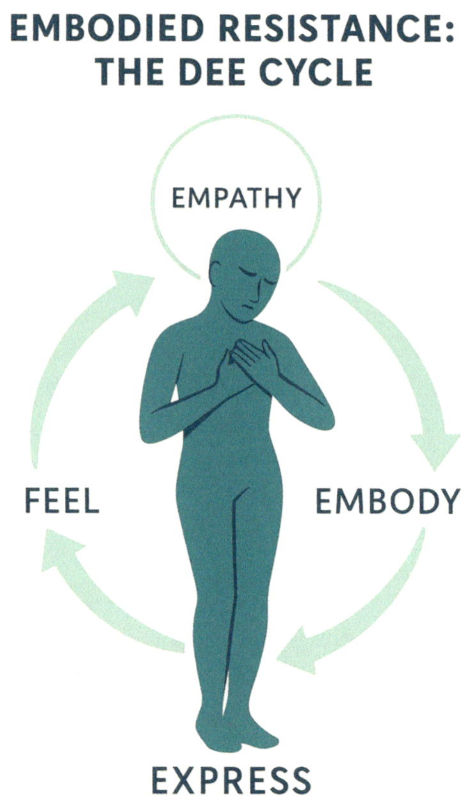

FIGURE 7.21: Embodied Resistance: The DEE Cycle in Action. A moment of grounded defiance. The performer draws power from koshi, channels breath and feeling, and moves through Dynamis → Energeia → Entelecheia. Here, resistance becomes not a reaction, but a form of empathetic presence—a physical response rooted in clarity and care. AI-generated image created with OpenAI's DALL·E (via ChatGPT).

Weaving the Threads: Vulnerability, Energy, and Empathy

Throughout this chapter, we have explored how Human Theatre engages the body not merely as a tool of expression, but as a vessel of transmission—a space where emotion, memory, and presence converge. Vulnerability, in this context, is not weakness. It is the gateway to authenticity. It is the condition that allows energy to circulate freely, to touch the self and the other without defenses, without masks—unless, of course, we use the mask as a paradoxical tool for liberation. This integration of energy, empathy, and vulnerability is diagrammed in **Figure 7.22**.

From the activation of mirror neurons to the energetic DEE cycle, from the breath that roots us to the koshi that grounds us, we've seen how performance in Human Theatre is an act of shared becoming. The performer is not simply interpreting a role, nor merely reenacting emotion—they are channeling it, becoming porous enough to allow the audience to feel what is not spoken, to understand what is not explained.

Empathy, in this framework, is not abstract. It is physical. The audience responds because they see a body that is present, unguarded, and alive. They mirror the performer's openness not through analysis, but through breath, tone, posture, and gaze. This is the heart of the theatrical encounter. And it is the beating core of Human Theatre.

In weaving these threads—vulnerability, energy, empathy—we return to the essence of performance not as spectacle, but as communion. Not as fiction, but as the energetic echo of what it means to be alive.

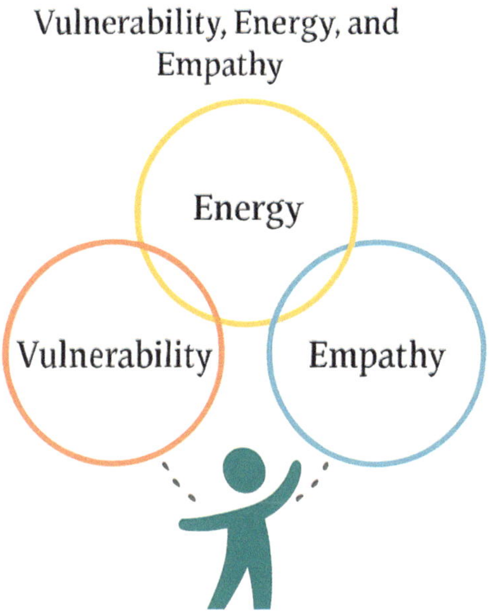

FIGURE 7.22: Vulnerability, Empathy, and Energy: The Performer's Inner Compass. This visual embodies the quiet force of Human Theatre: where vulnerability is not weakness, but access, empathy is not emotion, but attention, and energy is not force, but flow. These three threads, when woven together, form the deep resonance that makes truth visible onstage. AI-generated image created with OpenAI's DALL·E (via ChatGPT).

Weaving the Threads of Human Theatre

Having journeyed through the foundations, experiments, and expressions that shape Human Theatre, we now arrive at a moment of synthesis. This chapter is not a closing—it is a weaving together of threads into a tapestry still in progress.

We began by exploring the essential shift from text to embodiment. Dramaturgy, we discovered, is not merely a literary or structural device—it is a framework of perception, a way of listening to the world, the body, and each other. From Aristotle's *Poetics* to postdramatic expressions, from mask work to object theatre, each chapter peeled back a layer of theatrical tradition to reveal a more intuitive, inclusive, and energetic model of performance.

The DEE Cycle—Dynamis, Energeia, Entelecheia—emerged as a central axis. It is not a formula, but a pattern of transformation: from internal potential to energetic activation to expressive manifestation. Whether through breathwork, rhythm, gesture, or silence, the performer channels this cycle not to illustrate meaning, but to **become** it.

We explored the performer as a codified instrument—trained, sensitive, and energetically alive. We examined how embodiment, when combined with somatic regulation and creative exploration, leads to a more grounded, resilient actor—one who not only performs, but also heals. Human Theatre does not avoid trauma; it holds space for it, listens to it, and transmutes it into presence.

The introduction of masks—humanoid yet poetic—challenged traditional identity markers, allowing emotion to rise beyond speech and physicality. With them, and through them, performers activate mirror neurons in the audience, sparking empathic resonance. In this act, we transcend representation and enter communion.

And throughout, one principle remained constant: **vulnerability**. Vulnerability is not weakness. It is the quiet bravery of showing up with nothing but breath and intention, of offering your energy in service of collective meaning. It is the soul of Human Theatre.

An Invitation Forward

Human Theatre is not a finished method. It is a living language—a practice of presence that adapts to the times and to the humans who inhabit it. Its tools are simple: body, breath, intention, and space. But in the hands of an attuned performer, these tools become portals.

As theatre artists, educators, healers, and witnesses, we are invited to keep evolving this language. To let it be shaped by our histories, our wounds, our joys. To offer performances not as answers, but as questions. Not as spectacles, but as gestures of connection.

Final Words

Human Theatre reminds us that theatre is not merely an art form—it is a mirror, a gesture, a breath shared in time. In its vulnerability lies its greatest strength: the

FIGURE 7.23: Human Theatre as an Evolving Energetic Language. This spiral represents the unfolding of Human Theatre as more than a method—it is a living language of breath, presence, and transformation. Each turn echoes a cycle of tension and release, memory and motion, intention and expression. The performer does not master the form—they become it. In this evolving field, the body speaks not from tradition alone, but from awareness, attunement, and the energy that flows between. AI-generated image created with OpenAI's DALL·E (via ChatGPT).

power to awaken, connect, and heal. It does not need to be technically perfect; it must be true. Authenticity is its compass. Presence is its language. The evolving spiral of Human Theatre as a living language is visualized in **Figure 7.23**.

Part 3—It's Your Turn: Training for Human Theatre

The Performer's Preparation: Sensing Before Acting

Before stepping into character, before entering the scene, before uttering a single word—there is the body. This is the first space of performance, and in Human Theatre, it is treated not as a tool to be manipulated but as a landscape to be attuned.

This section invites the performer to engage in deep sensory preparation—not to "warm up" in the conventional sense, but to return to a state of heightened presence, receptive to inner movement and outer connection.

In Human Theatre, sensing comes before doing. This reverses the dominant paradigm of action-first training and reminds us that every gesture, tone, and breath onstage carries energetic residue. To act with authenticity, the performer must know what they are carrying—and where it is held in the body.

This awareness becomes the performer's compass. It is through sensation that we locate our emotional terrain. The breath becomes our barometer. The skin becomes our instrument of resonance. And the koshi—our energetic core—becomes the anchor from which all presence arises.

The preparation, then, is not ornamental. It is essential. To sense is to listen. To listen is to receive. And in receiving, we begin to activate the invisible.

Practical Exercises: Sensing Before Acting

These practices are designed to be done before rehearsal or performance, either solo or in groups. The goal is to **awaken inner awareness**, ground the body, and align with the energetic field of the present moment.

1. ***Five-Minute Body Scan (Eyes Closed)***
    - **What to do:** Stand or sit in stillness. Slowly bring awareness to each part of the body, starting from the feet and moving upward: soles, ankles, knees, thighs, hips, spine, chest, arms, hands, neck, face, and crown.
    - **Why:** This cultivates interoception and reclaims awareness of body parts often numb or neglected due to tension or trauma.
2. ***Breath-Skin Listening***
    - **What to do:** Place one hand on the chest, one on the abdomen. Breathe deeply through the nose. As you inhale, feel not just the expansion inside but the skin's subtle response. Then exhale slowly and silently.
    - **Why:** This invites sensory receptivity and enhances breath awareness—two foundational principles in Human Theatre.
3. ***Weight and Contact Awareness***
    - **What to do:** Stand in stillness and bring attention to the soles of your feet. Shift your weight slightly side to side, forward and back, then center. Feel the contact with the floor. Ask: Where does the ground meet me?
    - **Why:** Reorients proprioception and deepens grounding—critical for accessing koshi-centered energy later.
4. ***Energetic Temperature Check***
    - **What to do:** Ask internally: What is the energetic weather in my body right now? (Calm? Stormy? Fragmented? Tight?) Without judging, describe it to yourself silently or with movement.
    - **Why:** Builds a habit of self-check-in that leads to emotionally intelligent performance.

5. ***Sensation Mapping (with Partner or Mirror)***
   - **What to do:** Perform a simple gesture (lifting an arm, turning the head). Do it slowly, then pause. Ask: What sensation just arose? Where did it begin? Where did it end?
   - **Why:** Develops precision and somatic curiosity—inviting the performer to sense the impulse before acting on it.

These exercises are not about mastery, but about awakening. They offer a pathway into the deeper landscape of the performer's body—where impulse, energy, and emotion coalesce into presence. The more we sense, the more we see. The more we see, the more we can offer.

Tuning the Instrument: Breath, Koshi, and Resonance

If Human Theatre begins with presence, then breath is its first language. The performer's body is not simply a tool—it is an instrument. And like any fine instrument, it requires tuning. Tuning the performer means aligning physical, energetic, and emotional channels. In this section, we explore how breath, the koshi, and resonance shape a performer's readiness to connect and communicate onstage.

The Breath: Entry Point to Presence

The breath is the primary gateway to awareness. It registers emotion before words do, and reveals the state of the nervous system. Shallow breath often accompanies anxiety, while expansive, diaphragmatic breath signals regulation, openness, and readiness.

In Human Theatre, we treat breath not only as a physiological necessity but as an energetic field. We sense where breath moves freely, where it gets blocked, and how it carries emotional tone.

> To breathe with awareness is to feel the boundary between the self and the world dissolve.

Breath becomes visible in the quality of movement and the tone of voice. In this way, it is both internal and external—felt and perceived. Performers learn to sense breath not just in themselves but in the ensemble, building rhythmic attunement that lays the foundation for collective storytelling.

Koshi: Center of Energy and Grounding

Rooted in Japanese somatic philosophy, the **koshi** refers to the lower back and pelvic basin—the body's energetic and physical center. It is not merely anatomical; it is the hinge point of movement, balance, and intention.

In Human Theatre, we emphasize the koshi as the axis around which energetic presence flows. An activated koshi allows for grounded stillness, explosive movement, and dynamic transitions. When it is collapsed or disengaged, movement becomes disconnected; when awakened, the performer radiates power from the center.

The koshi unites verticality and earthiness. It is where "being" meets "doing."

Resonance: Voice as Vibration

Resonance refers to the quality of sound that emerges when the breath meets open, aligned space in the body. Lessac's principles of tonal and structural sensation guide performers toward discovering resonance as a **felt** phenomenon.

Rather than focusing on volume or projection, Human Theatre develops **vocal presence** through the inner experience of vibration. This includes:

- Tonal play through humming.
- Placement of tone in bones and cavities (skull, chest, pelvis).
- Imagining sound as light or color to support emotional texture.

The performer's voice, in this framework, becomes an extension of breath, koshi, and intention. It is not something to push—it is something to uncover.

Practical Exercises: Awakening Breath, Koshi, and Resonance

Here are a few foundational practices used in Human Theatre to support this tuning process:

1. ***Breath Sensing and Grounding***
    - Lie on your back with knees bent.
    - Place one hand on your belly, one on your chest.
    - Inhale slowly through the nose, allowing the belly to rise.
    - Exhale through a relaxed mouth and feel the weight of your body sink into the floor.
    - Repeat for 5 minutes, listening to the breath like a wave.

Purpose: Establish breath awareness, calm the nervous system, increase body sensitivity.

2. ***Koshi Activation: Spiral Walk***
    - Stand in a relaxed, upright posture with slightly bent knees.
    - Begin walking slowly in a circular path.

- Place attention on your lower back and hips.
- Let your steps spiral from the koshi, sensing it as a weight that guides your movement.
- Allow the upper body to follow without tension.

Purpose: Connect koshi to locomotion, develop grounded movement.

3. *Tone Mapping*
   - Begin with gentle humming.
   - Let the hum travel through different parts of the body: chest, jaw, nose, and crown of the head.
   - Place your hands on those areas and notice where you feel vibration.
   - Now, walk slowly and hum while moving. Try changing direction or posture and notice how the vibration shifts.

Purpose: Develop awareness of resonance and explore the voice-body relationship.

Final Reflection

In traditional training, breath, posture, and voice are often separated. In Human Theatre, they are unified through the koshi. The koshi becomes the bridge between impulse and action, breath and tone, body and meaning. The performer who cultivates this integration finds not only more expressive power—but more stability, more empathy, and more presence.

They become not just an actor of words, but a resonant body of feeling—attuned, alive, and tuned to the world.

Mask Work: Awakening Energetic Awareness

In the realm of Human Theatre, the mask is not a disguise—it is a magnifier. It silences the face in order to amplify everything else: the breath, the alignment, the movement, and above all, the energy. Working with the mask requires a radical shift in awareness. The performer can no longer rely on facial expressions to communicate emotion. Instead, presence must arise from within, through clarity of intention and energetic direction.

This is where energetic awareness becomes indispensable. The performer learns to "fill" the mask—not with mimed emotion, but with breath and attention that emanate from the whole body. The mask invites stillness as much as motion; it teaches us to listen before acting, to settle before expressing. It confronts us with the essential question: what am I communicating when I do nothing?

A key tool in this process is the **neutral mask**—a foundational practice in physical theatre traditions, particularly in the lineage of Jacques Lecoq. The neutral mask offers a blank canvas, erasing the habitual patterns of expression and gesture we accumulate through life. Its blankness levels the playing field, allowing the performer to encounter space, impulse, and rhythm with fresh attention.

Working with the neutral mask is a rigorous training in presence. It reveals every tension, every unconscious movement, every moment of indecision. Because the face cannot assist, the entire body must become articulate. Movement becomes thought. Stillness becomes a statement. The performer becomes aware not only of the actions they take, but of the energy that precedes them—the micro-moments of transition between intention and action.

Core Exercises in Energetic Mask Work

- **Stillness and Breath Expansion**: With the neutral mask on, the performer stands in space and focuses on the breath. They observe how energy radiates outward through the limbs, spine, and gaze—even in stillness. The mask becomes animated by the internal movement of the breath alone.
- **Impulse and Direction**: The performer explores initiating movement from different body centers—pelvis, heart, forehead—while maintaining clarity and economy. Each movement must be intentional and radiate beyond the self.
- **Listening to the Space**: A group of performers wear masks and enter the stage one by one, not to act, but to "read" the energy of the space. They adjust their posture, pace, and gaze according to what they sense—not what they assume. This heightens group awareness and spatial intelligence.
- **Weight and Gravity**: Through floor work and slow transitions, the performer becomes attuned to how the mask responds to shifts in weight. They learn to modulate energy by sensing gravity, resistance, and flow.

In my own practice, I have witnessed how this kind of work dissolves performance habits and awakens something deeper—an intuitive presence that listens with the skin and responds from the center. The mask gives permission to step beyond persona and into archetype, beyond character and into essence.

It is here, in the silence of the mask, that Human Theatre comes alive—not through what we try to show, but through what we allow ourselves to become.

The DEE Cycle in Practice: Micro and Macro Exercises

The DEE Cycle—**Dynamis, Energeia, Entelecheia**—is more than a theoretical framework; it is a dynamic guide for embodied presence. When integrated into the performer's process, it offers a powerful map to access truth in expression while remaining grounded in the body. But how do we move from concept to experience?

This section proposes a series of **practical exercises** to help performers activate and embody the DEE Cycle, both in small, everyday moments (micro) and in fuller, performative explorations (macro). These tools can be used in rehearsal, performance, or personal somatic training.

Micro Exercises: Awakening Awareness

These are short, focused practices to develop sensitivity and presence in the body.

1. ***Koshi Pulse Check***
   - *Dynamis*: Sit or stand in stillness, place your awareness at the koshi (pelvic center).
   - *Energeia*: Begin gently rocking the pelvis or shifting your weight side to side. Feel the koshi as a source of rhythm.
   - *Entelecheia*: Allow this internal movement to subtly affect your upper body, arms, or breath. Let the motion travel and "speak."
2. ***Breath as Bridge***
   - *Dynamis*: Inhale fully and hold the breath for a moment. Sense the potential.
   - *Energeia*: Exhale slowly on a vowel sound or humming tone, letting the breath animate the voice.
   - *Entelecheia*: Let the breath carry intention—whether calm, longing, or joy—and observe how it changes your face, posture, and presence.
3. ***Gesture Seed***
   - *Dynamis*: Place your hand on your chest or belly. Ask yourself, "What wants to move?"
   - *Energeia*: Let a gesture slowly emerge, even if it's tiny. Stay with it.
   - *Entelecheia*: Complete the gesture and let it inform a facial expression, a stance, or a single word.

Macro Exercises: Deepening Expression

These longer, integrative exercises explore the full cycle in a performative or improvisational setting.

4. ***The Energetic Monologue***
   Choose a memory or imagined situation (grief, joy, reunion).

- *Dynamis*: Stand in silence and feel the emotional charge inside—before any action.
- *Energeia*: Begin moving slowly, letting that inner charge initiate movement. Use the whole body, voice optional.
- *Entelecheia*: Speak a single sentence or phrase that arises. Repeat the cycle with new energy. Repeat the sequence, observing how each layer changes what and how you express.

5. ***DEE Character Walk***
   Choose a character or archetype.
   - *Dynamis*: Explore their internal engine—what drives them? What is unresolved?
   - *Energeia*: Let that charge animate the walk, posture, and breath.
   - *Entelecheia*: Arrive at a moment of stillness, where characters "become" through their action, tone, or gaze. Use this cycle to build a character from the inside out—not by imitation, but through energetic logic.
6. ***The Partner Mirror Cycle***
   Work with a partner. One person begins by holding a silent energy (Dynamis).
   - The second mirrors the energy with movement (Energeia).
   - Both transition to a shared expression (Entelecheia): a shared gesture, breath, or vocal tone. This builds attunement, empathy, and responsiveness.

Final Note: Practicing with Sensitivity

While these exercises offer structure, they are not prescriptions. The key is to approach them with **curiosity and non-judgment**, allowing the body to lead. Let the DEE Cycle reveal itself in your own rhythm, and revisit it often.

In time, performers find that **DEE becomes second nature**—not something they do, but something they live through the body, moment by moment. This is the heart of Human Theatre: a return to authenticity through energy, breath, and truth in motion.

Mirror Neurons in Training: Observation, Repetition, Transmission

Within the performer's journey, one of the most subtle yet powerful mechanisms of connection lies in the function of **mirror neurons**. These neurons, discovered in the 1990s by neuroscientists studying monkeys, fire both when an individual performs an action and when they observe the same action performed by someone else. In short, the brain "mirrors" what it sees—even without physical participation.

In theatre, this process becomes a **core training principle**. The actor observes, repeats, and eventually internalizes movements, gestures, and emotional textures. But beyond technical imitation, the mirror neuron system allows us to **feel what we see**. It's what makes an audience flinch when someone falls, or cry when a character grieves—because on a neurobiological level, **we are experiencing with them**.

This neurological reality affirms a foundational belief of Human Theatre: the body is not only capable of empathy—it is wired for it.

Training Implications

For performers, the mirror neuron system opens new approaches to embodiment:

- **Sensory attention** sharpens as we attune to how others move, breathe, and shift.
- **Repetition with presence** allows observed gestures to become lived experience.
- **Subtle imitation** becomes a doorway to emotional alignment and transformation.

In my own training, I have experienced moments where watching a gesture over and over created a resonance inside me—a moment when the gesture was no longer "copied," but somehow **mine**. This is when the mirror neuron system shifts from mechanical to poetic—from neuroscience to empathy in action.

The Mask as Mirror

The mask deepens this process. When an audience sees a masked figure express vulnerability or joy, its mirror neurons do not interpret a face—they interpret movement, rhythm, posture, and breath. This abstraction reduces distraction and increases **embodied resonance**. They don't see *someone* crying—they feel *the act* of sorrow.

This is why mask performance is not impersonal—it is **intensely human**. And for the actor, performing in mask becomes a profound training in **non-verbal empathy**: in transmitting emotion not through facial expression, but through full-body communication.

Beyond Performance: Mirror Neurons and Empathy

In Human Theatre, we train not only to portray emotion but to **transmit** it. This is not about manipulation—it is about authenticity. When the performer's action is rooted in genuine internal activation, the audience does not watch—they *feel*.

This understanding reframes the role of rehearsal: not as a space to perfect, but as a space to **attune**. Through mirroring, repetition, and somatic recall, performers build a language of movement that resonates across the boundary between stage and seat.

In essence, mirror neurons remind us that presence is not performed alone—it is a shared physiological event. It is the invisible thread between the witness and the witnessed. In Human Theatre, this thread becomes the stage itself.

From Vulnerability to Visibility: Journaling, Improvisation, Reflection

In Human Theatre, the inner life of the performer is not secondary—it is the material. Before any script is memorized, before any blocking is marked, the performer must first engage in a process of discovery: uncovering the layers of emotional residue, hidden impulses, and unconscious resistance that shape how they move, speak, and listen onstage.

Three essential practices serve this excavation: **journaling, improvisation, and reflection**. These are not add-ons, but core components of an actor's preparation. They allow vulnerability to move from the hidden margins of the psyche into the visible center of the work.

Journaling: Excavating the Inner Terrain

Journaling is the performer's private mirror. It allows them to track sensations, record emotional triggers, reflect on rehearsals, and capture fleeting thoughts that may later become embodied gestures or choices in performance. It is not only analytical but poetic—a space where the performer can write freely about dreams, sensations, memories, or even recurring physical reactions during training.

Suggested Practice—Sensory Journaling After rehearsal or training, write for 10 minutes without stopping using these prompts:

- What did my body experience today?
- What surprised me about my breath, movement, or voice?
- What sensations returned? What disappeared?
- *Where did I feel disconnected, and why might that be?* This practice sharpens interoception and deepens the performer's awareness of recurring themes or energetic blocks.

Improvisation: Rehearsing Vulnerability

Improvisation in Human Theatre is not about cleverness or inventiveness—it's about presence. The aim is not to entertain, but to reveal. We use improvisation to test the emotional truth of a gesture, to follow a breath into an impulse, to experiment with the unknown. This is where performers learn to trust not only their technique but their intuition.

Suggested Practice—Breath-to-Motion Improvisation

Begin seated. Inhale and notice where your breath wants to go. Let the first movement emerge from that place. Follow it. Let each breath begin a new motion. Continue for 5–7 minutes. End by standing and letting stillness arrive. This develops a dynamic connection between inner impulse and outer action—a fundamental skill for vulnerability onstage.

Reflection: Giving Language to the Intangible

The third component—reflection—invites the performer to articulate what they've discovered. Sometimes this happens in conversation with a director or peer; other times, it takes place in silence, on the walk home. What matters is not "getting it right," but beginning to notice the links between sensation, memory, behavior, and performance.

Reflection closes the loop between embodied experience and cognitive understanding. It brings coherence to the work and gives performers tools to regulate, repeat, or revise their approach. It also supports integration—so that what happens onstage can influence personal healing, and vice versa.

Together, these three tools allow vulnerability to become a resource—not something to hide, but something to shape. Not a weakness, but a deepening of expressive capacity. As performers move through journaling, improvisation, and reflection, they learn to become not only more honest—but more **visible**.

In Human Theatre, we don't just perform emotion. We track it. We tend it. We give it form.

Final Invitation: Building Your Own Scene of Presence

As we draw this chapter to a close, it becomes clear that Human Theatre is not a fixed script or a codified technique—it is a call. A call to listen more deeply, to move more honestly, and to allow our bodies to become the instrument through which unseen energies take shape. Vulnerability is not a liability in this space—it is the compass. It is what directs the actor inward toward authenticity and outward toward connection.

To activate this space of presence in your own work, begin with a simple but profound prompt: Create a Scene Without Words.

Let the scene unfold from the following questions:

- What does your body want to say today?
- What gesture keeps returning, even when you're still?

- If you could breathe color, what color is your breath right now?
- Where is the tension—and what story is it holding?

Find a small space. Strip it down. Choose one object. Allow your body to enter the space not with the intention to perform, but with the invitation to reveal. Let each movement arise from breath. Let each stillness speak. If you feel discomfort, lean into it. That is the edge where performance begins. Use the mask, if you have one. Or simply imagine your face as a neutral field, your presence as a mirror for the audience. Trust that your vulnerability is legible. That the small tremors matter. That what you withhold can be just as powerful as what you show. This scene does not need to be shared to be real. But if it is, let it be incomplete. Let the audience fill in the rest. *Let Human Theatre live—not just on a stage, but in your breath, in your listening, and in your becoming.*

> The true essence of a captivating performance lies beyond impeccable technique; it requires the harmonious blend of mind, body, and heart. Without this synthesis, art loses its soul, transforming into mere exhibition. It is this alchemical fusion that breathes life into a performance, transforming it from mere execution to true artistry. Remember it doesn't have to be perfect but authentic.

About the Author

Richard Martínez is a theatre artist, an educator, and an interdisciplinary creator devoted to the transformative power of embodied performance. He is the founder of Teatro Umano and the originator of Human Theatre, a methodology rooted in energy, presence, and somatic intelligence.

Born in Puerto Rico, Richard's creative spark was ignited through the influence of Gilda Navarra. Though they never worked together directly, her fearless fusion of flamenco, mime, dance, and theatre deeply inspired his own artistic journey. Her ability to merge forms into a personal, expressive language helped catalyze his own.

Richard holds a **Bachelor's degree in Theatre/Drama**, an **MBA in Business Administration**, an **MFA in Physical Theatre** (earned in the United States with intensive training across Europe —**Germany, Italy, and the Czech Republic**), and a **Ph.D. in Performing Arts** developed through academic and artistic research in **Madrid, Spain.** His MFA thesis, "Towards a Human Theatre: An Analysis of the Use of Energy in the Practice of Todd Farley, Gilda Navarra, Fabio Mangolini, Scott Putman, Arthur Lessac, and Eugenio Barba," laid the foundation for his unique approach to performance.

His Ph.D. dissertation, "Human Theatre: Dramatic Language Based on the Analysis of Energy Use in the Practice of Todd Farley, Gilda Navarra, Fabio Mangolini, Scott Putman, Arthur Lessac, Antonin Artaud, and Eugenio Barba, and Its Benefits on the Physical and Mental Health of the Performer," further developed this vision—positioning performance as a transformative practice for both artistic and personal integration.

Richard's training spans a wide range of disciplines—including physical theatre, flamenco, clowning, Commedia dell'Arte, mime, and various somatic and vocal traditions. He is also a certified Lessac Kinesensic practitioner and EBAS method trainer. Notably, he co-created the first Spanish-language workbook for Lessac training in collaboration with Dr. Elga Sepúlveda, under the mentorship of Deborah Kinghorn—extending the accessibility of Lessac's work to Spanish-speaking communities.

In parallel to his artistic work, Richard is an experienced computer programmer. His digital platforms—created to support cultural institutions and manage artistic archives—reflect his commitment to uniting creativity, technology, and social purpose.

He currently lives and works in **Italy**, where he teaches, performs, and collaborates with cultural associations while continuing to develop and share Human Theatre through workshops, mentorship, and performance. His work speaks to artists, educators, therapists, and those seeking to reconnect with their bodies as expressive, healing instruments.

Richard's contributions to performance and education have been recognized internationally, with awards in **Italy**, and honors from governmental and cultural institutions in **Puerto Rico**, the **Dominican Republic**, **Argentina**, the **Senate of the United States**, and the **Senate of Puerto Rico**.

Earlier in his career, he founded and produced *Fiesta en las Américas: teatro, baile y algo más ...*, an international festival held in Puerto Rico that celebrated the vibrancy and diversity of Latin American performance traditions. Though the festival was held only once, it marked a foundational moment in his dedication to intercultural dialogue through the arts.

At the heart of Richard's work is a deep belief: that theatre is not only craft or spectacle, but a ritual of return. Human Theatre is both a personal evolution and a shared invitation—a way back to breath, body, and presence.

Theatre gave me back my breath—and through it, my voice and my body.

info@teatroumano.com
www.teatroumano.com
www.richardmartinez.it

Richard Martinez

Bibliography

Arcangeli, Massimo. "Cosa Vuol Dire 'Catarsi'?" *Il Post*, June 16, 2017. https://www.ilpost.it/2017/06/16/cosa-vuol-dire-catarsi/#. Accessed July 22, 2024.

Artaud, Antonin. *El Teatro y su doble*. Translated by Enrique Alonso and Francisco Abelanda, Pocket edhasa Edición, 2011.

ArtSocial. "La comunicación empática." *ArtSocial*, n.d. https://www.artsocial.cat/articulo/la-comunicacion-empatica/. Accessed July 22, 2024.

Arunima. "Yakshagana: The Art of Telling Stories Through Music, Dance and Dialogue." *Tell-A-Tale*, September 13, 2016. https://www.tell-a-tale.com/yakshagana-the-art-of-telling-stories-through-music-dance-and-dialogue/. Accessed March 11, 2017.

Barba, Eugenio. *The Paper Canoe: A Guide to Theatre Anthropology*. Translated by Richard Fowler. Routledge, 2005.

Barba, Eugenio, and Nicola Savarese. *L'arte segreta dell'attore: Un dizionario di antropologia teatrale*. Edizioni di Pagina, 2011.

Caldwell, Rachel. "VCU Professor Scott Putman's Structural Reeducation Practice." *Dance Teacher*, DanceMedia LLC, May 11, 2017. https://www.dance-teacher.com/2016/05/higher-ed-vcu-professor-scott-putmans-structural-reeducation-practice/. Accessed July 22, 2017.

Castañeda Pavón, Alberto. *El actor y el arte de actuar*. Palibrio | Author Solutions, 2013. iBook.

Cazorla, Gemma. "Reiki – Origen y definición de Reiki." *Medicina Natural y Alternativa—Salud Terapia*, March 7, 2017. https://www.saludterapia.com/glosario/d/95-reiki.html. Accessed May 11, 2017.

Destro-Bisol, Giovanni. "Genetica, il Dna Degli Italiani È il Più Variegato d'Europa." *Il Giornale*, January 9, 2014. https://www.ilgiornale.it/news/cultura/genetica-dna-degli-italiani-pi-variegato-deuropa-981257.html. Accessed July 22, 2025.

Doménech, Fernando. *Manual de Dramaturgia*. Ediciones Universidad de Salamanca, Real Escuela Superior de Arte Dramático de Madrid y Los Autores, 2016.

Dougherty, Elizabeth. "What Are Thoughts Made Of?" MIT School of Engineering, n.d. https://www.engineering.mit.edu/engage/ask-an-engineer/what-are-thoughts-made-of/. Accessed May 23, 2017.

"Edward W. Said Biography." *Encyclopedia of World Biography*, Advameg, Inc., n.d. https://www.notablebiographies.com/supp/Supplement-Mi-So/Said-Edward-W.html. Accessed July 22, 2017.

Ehrenreich, Steve. "Yi Chuan Kung Fu—Interview with Master Cheuk Fung." *Yi Chuan Kung Fu*, Master Cheuk Fung, 2009. https://www.yichuankungfu.com/. Accessed July 22, 2017.

EMDR España. "¿Qué es EMDR?" *EMDR España*, n.d. https://www.emdr-es.org/Sobre-EMDR/Que-es-EMDR. Accessed July 22, 2024.

"Emerge Pediatric Therapy. "¿Qué es la propiocepción?" *Emerge Pediatric Therapy*, n.d. https://www.emergepediatrictherapy.com/que-es-la-propiocepcion/. Accessed July 22, 2017.

"Energy | Definition of Energy in English by Oxford Dictionaries." *Oxford Dictionaries*, 2018. https://www.en.oxforddictionaries.com/definition/energy. Accessed July 22, 2017.

FallenTowers. "Moses with Todd Farley." YouTube, July 8, 2012. https://www.youtube.com/watch?v=mt0bvJ0XyD4. Accessed June 29, 2017.

Farley, Todd. "Re: Interview I." Email interview with Richard Martinez, June 17, 2017.

Fernández, Montse. "Neuronas Espejo y la Teoría de la Empatía." *Awen Psicología*, January 15, 2024. https://www.awenpsicologia.com/las-neuronas-espejo/. Accessed July 22, 2024.

Flavio~. "Modern Flamenco: Carmel Natan Sheli." Flickr, Yahoo!, June 30, 2011. https://www.flickr.com/photos/37873897@N06/5886901514. Accessed July 22, 2017.

FranticGrass. "Ancient Chinese Kunqu-Opera—'The Dream in Visiting the Garden'." YouTube, January 11, 2012. https://www.youtube.com/watch?v=N3Z9F8eC31A. Accessed February 26, 2017.

"Google Ngram Viewer." Google Books, Google, n.d., https://books.google.com/ngrams/graph?year_start=1800&year_end=2008&corpus=15&smoothing=7&case_insensitive=on&content=energy&direct_url=t4%3B%2Cenergy%3B%2Cc0%3B%2Cs0%3B%3Benergy%3B%2Cc0%3B%3BEnergy%3B%2Cc0. Accessed March 14, 2017.

Gustavothomasteatro. "Mei Lanfang Hands Gestures (edited)." YouTube, February 10, 2010. https://www.youtube.com/watch?v=sFUC5ROtN8M. Accessed February 20, 2017.

Hart, Hilary. "Do You See What I See? The Impact of Delsarte on Silent Film Acting." *Mime Journal*, vol. 23, 1 (2005): 184–99. https://doi.org/10.5642/mimejournal.20052301.11.

Hay, Maciamo. "Genetic Origins of the Italian People." *Eupedia*, July, 2013. https://www.eupedia.com/genetics/italian_dna.shtml. Accessed July 22, 2024.

Indiavideodotorg. "Describing a Heroine in Kutiyattam, Koodiyattam, Performing Arts, India, Kerala Videos." *India Video*, March, 2017. https://www.indiavideo.org/kerala/arts/performing-art-forms/kutiyattam/description-of-a-heroine-in-kutiyattam-403.php. Accessed March 6, 2017.

Indiavideodotorg. "Kutiyattam Part 1, Kailasodharanam, Invis Multimedia, DVD." YouTube, June 11, 2010. https://www.youtube.com/watch?v=N3Z9F8eC31A. Accessed March 6, 2017.

Institute, Lessac. "Arthur Lessac." Lessac Institute, n.d. https://lessacinstitute.org/about/arthur-lessac/. Accessed May 16, 2017.

Institute, Lessac. "What is Kinesensic Training?" Lessac Institute, n.d., https://www.lessacinstitute.org/about/. Accessed May 16, 2017.

Izutsu, Toshihiko, and Toyo Izutsu. *The Theory of Beauty in the Classical Aesthetics of Japan*. Martinus Nijhoff, 1981.

Jie, Yang. "Distinguishing Features of Kunqu Opera." *CCTV News—CNTV English*, *Global Times*, March 9, 2010. http://english.cntv.cn/20100309/101385.shtml. Accessed February 26, 2017.

"Kunqu." *Encyclopædia Britannica*, Encyclopædia Britannica, Inc., November 8, 2010. https://www.britannica.com/art/kunqu. Accessed February 20, 2017.

Larousse, Éditions. "Définitions: énergie – Dictionnaire de français Larousse." *Dictionnaires Larousse*, n.d. https://www.larousse.fr/dictionnaires/francais/%C3%A9nergie/29421. Accessed March 14, 2017.

Lecoq, Jacques, et al. *El cuerpo poético: una pedagogía de la creación teatral*. Alba, 2014.

Lessac, Arthur. *Body Wisdom: The Use and Training of the Human Body*. 2nd ed., Lessac Institute, 1990.

Lessac, Arthur. *The Use and Training of the Human Voice: A Bio-Dynamic Approach to Vocal Life*. McGraw-Hill, 1997.

López-Ligero, Mar. *La Obra de Teatro: Manual Técnico de las Artes Escénicas*. Editorial UOC, 2017.

Lowen, Alexander. *La Bioenergética*. Editorial Sirio, 2012.

Mangolini, Fabio. "Commedia dell'Arte e Kyōgen: Due teatri agli estremi della Via della Seta." Purdue University, 1994.

Mangolini, Fabio. "Attraversando il ponte." PhD dissertation, Facoltà di Lettere e Filosofia, Università di Bologna, 2006. Unpublished.

Mangolini, Fabio. "About Me." Fabio Mangolini website, 2017. https://www.fabiomangolini.com/About_Me.html. Accessed August 27, 2017.

Mangolini, Fabio. "Re: Pregunta." Email interview with Richard Martinez, February 27, 2017.

Marsella, Stacy C. et al. "An Exploration of Delsarte's Structural Acting System." *Intelligent Virtual Agents Lecture Notes in Computer Science*, (2006): 80–92. https://doi.org/10.1007/11821830_7.

Mime Corporel Dramatique. "Etienne Decroux and Corporeal Mime." Ecole Internationale de Mime Corporel Dramatique — Paris, August 19, 2017. https://www.mimecorporel.com/etienne-decroux-and-corporeal-mime/. Accessed July 22, 2017.

Muni, Bharata. *Natyashastra (with English Translations)*. Translated by Manomohan Ghosh, Asiatic Society of Bengal, Calcutta, Internet Archive. https://archive.org/details/NatyaShastra/natya_shastra_translation_volume_1_-_bharat_muni/. iBook. Accessed July 22, 2017.

Navarra, Gilda. "Trayectoria del actor-mimo." *SMJEG-UPRRP* (1983): 31–49. http://smjegupr.net/wp-content/uploads/2012/05/Trayectoria-del-actor-mimo-Gilda-navarra.pdf. Accessed March 11, 2017.

Navarra, Gilda. *Cartilla de un oficio: Abecedario de un actor-mimo*. Vol. 1. Fragmento Imán Ed., 2007.

Navarra, Gilda, and Jorge Rigau. "Detrás del silencio: una vida, un oficio, un camino: autobiografía pictórica." Revés, 2006.

Nearman, Mark J. "*Kyakurayka*: Zeami's Final Legacy for the Master Actor." *Monumenta Nipponica* XXXV, 2, (1980): 153–87.

Nearman, Mark J. "*Kaky*: Zeami's Fundamental Principles of Acting." *Monumenta Nipponica* XXXVII, 3, (1982–83): 333–74, 459–96.

Nearman, Mark J. "Feeling in Relation to Acting: An Outline of Zeami's Views." *Asian Theatre Journal* 1, 1, (1984): 40–51.

Núñez-Partido, Antonio. "Integración Cuerpo, Emoción Y Mente: El Enfoque Bioenergético de A. Lowen." Asociación De Psicoterapeutas Laureano Cuesta, September 17, 2009. https://www.psicologoslaureanocuesta.org/articulos/bioenergetica.pdf. Accessed July 22, 2017.

Obregón, Osvaldo. "Acercamiento al teatro puertorriqueño contemporáneo (crónica)." *Arrabal*, vol. 0, 7 (2010): 47–62. http://www.raco.cat/index.php/Arrabal/article/view/229322. Accessed August 27, 2017.

"Organic | Definition of Organic in English by Oxford Dictionaries." *Oxford Dictionaries*, 2017. https://www.en.oxforddictionaries.com/definition/organic. Accessed July 22, 2025.

Pellecchia, Diego. "Aesthetics and Ethics in the Reception of Nō Theatre in the West." Royal Holloway, University of London, 2011, 149–75.

Phillips, Scott P. "Theater, Ritual and Exorcism in Chinese Martial Arts." *Daoist Studies*, DaoistStudies.org, 2010. https://www.daoiststudies.org/node/11835. Accessed July 22, 2017.

Piacenza-Cabrera, Giorgio. "Glosario De Términos Griegos En Filosofía." *Glosario De Filosofía Griego*, July 22, 2012. https://www.terminosgriegosdefilosofia.blogspot.it/2012/07/glosario-de-terminos-griegos-en-filosofia.html. Accessed May 11, 2017.

Prado, Bernat Castany. "Edward W. Said. Orientalismo." *Cartaphilus. Revista de Investigación y Crítica Estética*, 2009. https://www.revistas.um.es/cartaphilus/article/view/91321/88001. Accessed July 22, 2017.

"Propiocepción." *Barnaclinic*, January 25, 2019. https.//www.barnaclinic.com/blog/traumatologia-deportiva/2019/01/25/propiocepcion/. Accessed July 22, 2025.

Puliatti, Maria. *Il trattamento dei traumi: Un protocollo integrato EMDR-Somatic Oriented*. First edition, Giunti Psicologia, 2023.

Putman, Scott. "Aligning the Pathways Within." Teachers Manual Level I, 2017.

Ottaviani, Gioia. *Introduzione allo studio del teatro giapponese*. La Casa Usher, 1994.

Randi, Elena. "From the Gestural and Phonetic Sign of Everyday Life to the Actor's Sign: Aspects of François Delsarte's System." *KODIKAS/CODE. Ars Semeiotica*, (2017): 1–10. https://www.periodicals.narr.de/index.php/kodikas_code/article/view/1067/1046. Accessed July 22, 2017.

Rimer, J. Thomas, and Masakazu Yamazaki. *On the Art of the N. Drama: The major Treatises of Zeami*. Princeton University Press, 1984.

Russo, Alessandra. "Sette Caratteristiche dell'estetica Zen." *Sesshū Tōyō (1420–1506)*, 2017. https.//www.sesshutoyo.com/il-rotolo-lungo-delle-quattro-stagioni/estetica-zen/sette-caratteristiche-dell-estetica-zen/. Accessed December 7, 2017.

Said, Edward W. et al. *Orientalismo*. Debolsillo, 2013.

Santana Mojica, Carmelo. "Gilda Navarra: Maestra de Maestras." *Revista del Instituto de Cultura Puertorriqueña*, July 8, (2003): 93–104.

Sarti, Marco. "Negli ultimi 15 anni sono morti nel Mediterraneo oltre 30 mila migranti. La maggior parte resta ancora senza un nome." *Linkiesta*, March 17, 2017. https://www.linkiesta.it/it/article/2017/03/17/negli-ultimi-15-anni-sono-morti-nel-mediterraneo-oltre-30mila-migranti/33575/. Accessed July 22, 2017.

Scott. "Elemental Body Alignment System." *Elemental Body Alignment System*, n.d. https://www.doebas.com/. Accessed July 22, 2017.

Shanghai, Xinhong. "Mei Lanfang." *Mei Lanfang*, Cultural, 2007. http://en.chinaculture.org/gb/en_artqa/2003-09/24/content_27424.htm. Accessed February 26, 2017.

Shukla Chatterjee (Mandal), Smt. "Balancing Tradition and Modernity: A Reading of Tendulkar's Ghasiram Kotwal." *Performance Studies: Rupkatha Journal on Interdisciplinary Studies in Humanities*, vol. 5, 2 (2013): 230–35.

Sini, Maria Alessi. "Rapporti tra teatralità e ritualità con particolare riferimento a Bartabas." Corso di laurea magistrale in antropologia culturale ed etnologia, Tesi di Laurea, Facoltà di Lettere e Filosofia, Università degli Studi di Sassari, 2011. https://www.alessiasini.eu/it/teatro-rito-mito.html. Accessed July 22, 2017.

Smithsonian Institution. "Puerto Rican Bomba and Plena: Shared Traditions—Distinct Rhythms." *Smithsonian Folkways Recordings*, Smithsonian Institution, https://www.folkways.si.edu/puerto-rican-bomba-plena-shared-traditions-distinct-rhythms/latin-world/music/album/smithsonian. Accessed July 22, 2017.

Stebbins, Genevieve. "Delsarte System of Dramatic Expression." *Internet Archive*, 2007. https://www.archive.org/details/delsartesystemof00stebuoft. Accessed July 22, 2017.

Teruel, Tomàs Motos, Antoni Navarro Amorós, and Xema Palanca Santamaria, eds. *Artes Escénicas y Danza*. Algar Editorial, 2016.

Tristesse1. "Amazing Flamenco." YouTube, November 27, 2011. https://www.youtube.com/watch?v=sFUC5ROtN8M. Accessed July 22, 2017.

UNESCO. "Intangible Cultural Heritage." UNESCO, January 1, 2004. https://www.unesco.org/culture/ich/en/state/india-IN?info=projects. Accessed March 10, 2017.

van der Kolk, Bessel. *Il corpo accusa il colpo: Mente, corpo e cervello nell'elaborazione delle memorie traumatiche*. Edited by Maria Silvana e Alessandro Vassalli, Raffaello Cortina Editore, 2015.

Vázquez, Dan. "Bomba Puertorriqueña." YouTube, September 14, 2013. https://www.youtube.com/watch?v=ZummXOaoXuo. Accessed July 22, 2017.

Weill, E. B. "Maximilien Decroux, Pour une modernité du geste." Maximilien Decroux website, n.d. https://www.maximilien.decroux.free.fr/index.php?rub=1, 2016. Accessed July 22, 2017.

"Yakshagana." *Encyclopædia Britannica*, Encyclopædia Britannica, Inc., July 15, 2014. https://www.britannica.com/art/yakshagana. Accessed March 6, 2017.

"Yakshagana—Ramayana—1—Shoorpanakha." YouTube, December 22, 2014. https://www.youtube.com/watch?v=O-EA4v4kDFg. Accessed March 6, 2017.

Yepes Stork, Ricardo. "El Origen de la Enérgeia en Aristóteles." *Anuario Filosófico*, vol. 22, no. 1 (1989): 93.

Yepes Stork, Ricardo. "Origen y Significado de la Entelecheia en Aristóteles." *Thémata*, vol. 9, (1992): 361–74.

Index

This index is a cartography of your inner and outer landscapes as a performer. It gathers the pathways of the body, the mind, and the energetic field, offering a structured map of the concepts, practices, and models that shape Human Theatre and Energetic Alchemy. The methodology itself unfolds in a progression—from the somatic to the emotional to the energetic—and each entry reflects this movement. Likewise, the pedagogical arc that guides the work—activation, opening, encounter, revelation, and integration—quietly underpins the organization of ideas contained here.

Within these pages, tensions become teachers, spirals awaken movement, and revelations open the emotional body. Each entry gestures toward a wider constellation of ideas; each subentry becomes a doorway into your body's intelligence and the method's evolving vocabulary. Figures, noted in italics, illuminate the visual architecture that supports this work. You are invited to navigate the index not only intellectually but somatically—moving through it as you would through a practice: with curiosity, attention, breath, and an openness to transformation.

How to Use This Index

This index is designed not only as a reference tool, but as a companion to your embodied journey through *Human Theatre and Energetic Alchemy*.

1. Follow conceptual clusters rather than isolated terms.
   Entries are grouped to reflect the natural progression of the methodology: from somatic foundations → emotional processes → energetic dramaturgy.
2. Allow the subentries to guide you through transformation arcs.
   Many concepts evolve across multiple chapters. Subentries reveal how an idea unfolds in the body, mind, and energetic field.
3. Use cross-references ("see also") as somatic pathways.
   These connections reflect the fluidity of the work. Follow them the way you follow breath or impulse: to discover deeper relationships.

4. Notice which concepts include figures (in italics).
   These visual anchors complement the textual explanation and help you embody the method's architecture.
5. Navigate the index somatically.
   With curiosity, breath, and attention—much like the practice itself. Let the index support you as both a map and a living companion.

A

activation, *see also* flow; impulse; somatic activation
  activation and tremble response 53–59
  activation patterns 41–45
  emotional activation, (somatic/emotional) 42–49 somatic activation, (somatic) 39–44
  energetic activation 11–14, 168–73
affect 42–49
  affect–body relationship 43–45
alignment, *see also* axis; C-curve; grounding; koshi; somatic architecture
  alignment and koshi 82–90
  axis alignment 69–83
  general principles 20–23, 69–80
  misalignment patterns 74–77
  pelvic alignment 74–79
  spinal alignment 70–76
  weight and grounding relations 72–79
aliveness 4–7
allowing 17–19, 33–37
ancestry, performer ancestry 196–99
archetypal gesture 130–32; *see also* gesture; expression
audience–performer field 176–82; *see also* energetic dramaturgy; perceptual gates; presence
  collective presence 180–82
  energetic feedback (energetic) 177–80
  field awareness (perceptual) 188–93
  resonance loops 179–81

B

balance (somatic) 71–79
Bar Moments (case study) 227–31
Barba, Eugenio 198–200; *see also* theatre anthropology; presence
behavioral patterns 110–18
bioenergetics 112–20, 131–36; *see also* Reich, Wilhelm; Lowen, Alexander; grounding; tension
  bioenergetic charge and discharge 11–14, 118–19
  Lowen's contributions 113–14
  Reichian lineage 110–16
blockages *see also* somatic armor; tension; residue (emotional); compression
  emotional blockages 51–53
  energetic blockages 110–16
  somatic blockages 50–53
bodymind relationship 3–5, 112–16
breath *see also* diaphragm; emotion; grounding; zones of energy (diagram)
  activation (somatic/energetic) 17–23
  breath as emotional gateway 22–25
  breath–emotion link 22–26
  diaphragmatic gating (somatic/emotional) 18–23
Brecht, Bertolt 109
bridge (energetic/emotional) 43–45, 171–76; *see also* flow; revelation; DEE Cycle
  bridge and DEE transitions 168–72
  bridge to revelation 171–76

Bomba (Afro-Caribbean tradition) 196–99
embodied ancestry 196–99

C

Casaca, André 68–69
Castañeda Pavón, Alberto 109
C-curve (Lessac) 68–69; *see also* alignment; grounding; Lessac, Arthur; koshi
postural influence 70–76
relation to grounding 72–79
character, *see also* ego tension; mask work; presence; TDTETE Model
character habits 124–28
character tension (somatic/emotional) 118–26
character vs. presence 118–22
emotional posture 125–28
mask influence 128–31
somatic character architecture 123–30
charge (energetic) 11–14, 118–19; *see also* release; activation; tension
bioenergetic charge 113–14
closure (dramaturgy) 169–70; *see also* recomposition; integration
reintegration and closure 203–08
collapse (somatic/emotional) 114–18, 216–21; *see also* vulnerability; contraction; opening
collapse as emotional contraction 114–18
collapse–opening cycle (somatic/emotional) 213–17
collective presence 180–82; *see also* presence; audience–performer field
compression (somatic/emotional) 45–47, 118–24; *see also* contraction; tension; blockages
compression and tension patterns 118–31
connection (internal/external) 15–20
connection and flow 42–49
connection to breath 17–23
consciousness, somatic 4–6
containment (somatic/emotional) 16–17, 116–17; *see also* safety; dissociation; training principles
containment and safety 131–36
inner container 16–17
contraction (somatic/emotional) 45–47, 114–18; *see also* compression; emotional flow; tremble response
contraction–release cycle 47–52
cycles, *see also* DEE Cycle; flow; dramaturgy
DEE Cycle 11–22, 168–77
dramaturgical cycles 168–77
somatic cycle (closure–reintegration) 203–08

D

development (dramaturgy) 166–67; *see also* narrative arc; dramaturgy
developmental arc 165–70
DEE Cycle 11–22, 168–77; *see also* flow; energy; revelation; energetic dramaturgy; pedagogical arc
Energeia 14–18, 170–73
Entelecheia 18–22, 173–77
embodied understanding 43–49
DEE Cycle (diagram) *8*
Dynamis 11–14, 168–70
transitions 12–21, 168–76
diaphragm (somatic/emotional), *see also* breath; expression; zones of energy (diagram)
diaphragm and breath 17–23
diaphragmatic gating 18–23
role in emotional regulation 22–26
directionality (energetic) 172–75

discharge (somatic/energetic) 47–49, 118–19; *see also* tremble response; release; flow
- bioenergetic discharge 113–19
- discharge and tremor 53–59

dissociation 131–36; *see also* safety; overwhelm; containment
- dissociation and overwhelm 216–18
- somatic dissociation 132–35

dynamis 11–14, 168–70; *see also* DEE Cycle; impulse; activation
- action-impulse 11–14

E

EBAS (Elemental Body Alignment System) 68–69; *see also* Putnam, Scott; alignment; C-curve

ego tension 119–22; *see also* tension; somatic armor; character tension
- ego–body patterns 119–22
- embodiment in dramaturgy 168–77

embodiment, *see also* presence; gesture; revelation
- emotional embodiment (somatic/emotional) 218–24
- expressive embodiment 127–30
- somatic embodiment (somatic) 3–7, 118–22

emergence (somatic/emotional) 42–52; *see also* unfolding; gesture; flow
- emergence of impulse 11–14
- emotional emergence 42–49
- gesture emergence 46–52

emotion, *see also* vulnerability; revelation; expression; contraction
- emotional arcs (micro-arcs) 45–48, 220–26
- emotional contraction (somatic/emotional) 114–18
- emotional embodiment 218–24
- emotional flow (somatic/emotional) 42–49
- emotional release (somatic/emotional) 47–49, 118–19, 221–26
- emotional residue 112–14

energeia 14–18, 170–73; *see also* DEE Cycle; flow; revelation
- energetic expansion 170–73

energetic dramaturgy 168–77; *see also* dramaturgy; DEE Cycle; presence; revelation
- application to performance 168–77
- audience–performer field 176–82
- definition and framework 168–77
- energetic arcs 171–76
- energetic dramaturgy (diagram) *169*
- flow shifts 172–75

energetic field 4–6, 176–82; *see also* audience–performer field; presence
- field resonance 179–81

energetic flow 17–21, 71–74; *see also* flow; activation; koshi
- flow and spirals 76–82
- flow patterns 17–21

energetic mapping 118–40, 198–203; *see also* TDTETE Model; somatic architecture; tension
- mapping dramaturgical arcs 198–203
- mapping tension 118–36

energetic structure 66–74, 198–203; *see also* somatic architecture; koshi

entelecheia 18–22, 173–77; *see also* DEE Cycle; revelation
- end-state revelation (emotional/energetic) 173–77

engagement frameworks 12–22, 39–44, 168–77; *see also* perception; presence; practice (conceptual)
- emotional engagement 42–49
- energetic engagement 168–77

perceptual engagement 182–90
somatic engagement 39–44
exploration, principles of 25–37; *see also* practice (conceptual); training principles; vulnerability
emotional exploration 42–49
energetic exploration 168–77
somatic exploration 25–33

F

Farley, Todd 68–69
mimestry lineage 68–69
somatic expressivity 46–52
fear response (somatic/emotional) 216–18; *see also* safety; dissociation; vulnerability
fear and overwhelm 216–18
feedback (energetic) 177–80; *see also* resonance; audience–performer field
feedback loops 179–81
field awareness (perceptual) 188–93; *see also* perceptual gates; presence
awareness of energetic field 176–82
flow, *see also* spirals; emergence; release; DEE Cycle
emotional flow 42–49
energetic flow 17–21, 71–74
flow shifts in dramaturgy 172–75
flow–gesture relationship 46–52
focus, *see also* awareness; perception
inner focus 15–17
outer focus 176–80
soft focus 15–17
frustration (energetic/emotional) 42–45
frustration in activation patterns

G

gates (perceptual/energetic) 182–88; *see also* thresholds; perceptual gates (diagram); awareness
energetic doorways 184–90
thresholds of perception 183–89
gesture, *see also* alignment; koshi; spirals; expression; emergence
archetypal gesture 130–32
expressive gesture 47–52
gesture emergence (somatic/emotional) 46–52
gesture families 48–52, 126–32
gesture–emotion relationship 45–48
somatic origins of gesture 47–50
grounding 17–22, 72–79, 236–38; *see also* koshi; alignment; zones of energy (diagram); practice (conceptual)
ground–pelvis connection 72–79
grounding and energetic zones 17–25
grounding through exposure 236–38
gravity (somatic) 72–74

H

habits (somatic/emotional), *see also* tension; somatic armor; character; training principles
character habits 124–28
emotional habits 112–18
habitual tension patterns 110–18
movement habits 47–52
head–heart–pelvis alignment 72–76; *see also* alignment; koshi; axis
alignment of vertical centers 69–76
holding patterns (somatic/emotional) 51–53, 112–19; *see also* somatic armor; contraction; residue (emotional)
emotional holding 114–18
energetic holding 113–17
holding and armor 112–19
Human Theatre (methodology) 3–9, 168–208; *see also* DEE Cycle; somatic architecture; TDTETE Model; practice (conceptual)
applications in dramaturgy 168–208
foundation and purpose 3–7

energetic/somatic integration 3–9
methodological pillars 3–9
pedagogical arc 11–22, 213–27

I

identity softening (somatic/emotional) 214–20; *see also* vulnerability; revelation; mask work
identity suspension through mask 128–31
softening and exposure 213–17
immediacy (expressive) 220–24; *see also* revelation; expression
immediacy and presence 220–24
impulse (energetic/emotional) 11–14, 42–44; *see also* activation; flow; gesture
impulse and DEE Cycle 11–14
impulse to gesture 47–48
somatic impulse (somatic) 39–44
inner observer 224–29; *see also* self-observation (diagram); witnessing; presence
inner witness 224–29
meta-awareness loop 225–29
inner space 15–17; *see also* presence; awareness
inner spaciousness and breath 17–23
somatic inner space 15–17
insight zone 19–25; *see also* zones of energy (diagram); expression; revelation
energetic vertical mapping 17–25
integration 58–59, 135–39, 203–08; *see also* recomposition; revelation; pedagogical arc
integration and closure 203–08
post-release integration 135–39
somatic–energetic integration 203–08

K

kinesthetic awareness 40–43, 187–91; *see also* perception; presence; training principles
perceptual refinement 187–91
somatic attention 40–43
koshi, *see also* alignment; axis; grounding; somatic architecture; spirals
definition and function 81–94
dramaturgical koshi 198–203
energetic center 82–90
koshi and somatic architecture (diagram) *84*
pelvis connection 82–90
spine–koshi axis 88–92

L

layers (somatic/emotional) 45–52, 120–31, 238–42; *see also* tension; emergence; revelation
layered release 47–52
layered tension structure 120–31
layers in vulnerability work 213–20
Lessac, Arthur 68–69; *see also* alignment; grounding; EBAS
C-curve method 68–69
listening, *see also* awareness; perceptual gates; presence
inner listening (somatic) 15, 40–41
kinetic listening (somatic/emotional) 187–91
listening as presence 176–82
perceptual listening (energetic) 176–82
line of action, 47–48; *see also* gesture;
flow gesture trajectory 46–52
Lowen, Alexander 113–14; *see also* Reich, Wilhelm; bioenergetics; tension
bioenergetic lineage 113–14
grounding and charge 113–14

M

Mangolini, Fabio 68–69; *see also* EBAS; alignment; koshi
mask work 126–32; *see also* character; identity softening; vulnerability

expressive mask (emotional/somatic) 129–31
identity suspension 128–30
mask and character tension 125–31
mask and somatic impulse 47–48
neutral mask (conceptual) 127–29
mimestry 68–69; *see also* gesture; movement qualities
Farley lineage 68–69
mimestry and somatic expressivity 46–52
mirroring (somatic/emotional) 191–93, 225–28; *see also* resonance; witnessing; self-observation (diagram)
emotional mirroring 224–28
mirroring in self-observation 224–29
somatic mirroring 191–93
mobility–stability interplay 72–79; *see also* alignment; grounding; axis
movement balance 72–76
structural stability and koshi 82–90
movement qualities 46–52, 74–80; *see also* gesture; flow; spirals
qualities arising from gesture 46–52
qualities within somatic architecture 74–80

N

Navarra, Gilda 68–69
narrative arc 165–70, *168*; *see also* dramaturgy; energetic dramaturgy; closure
classical structure 165–69
closure 169–70
crisis 167–68
development 166–67
resolution 168–69
trigger 165–66
neutral
neutral mask, *see also* mask work
neutrality in presence 118–22
nervous system activation (somatic/energetic) 53–59; *see also* tremble response; activation; safety
autonomic shifts 53–59
neurogenic tremor 56–58

O

opening (somatic/emotional) 213–17; *see also* softening; vulnerability; revelation; contraction
opening as pedagogical phase 213–17
opening in vulnerability work 213–17
opening through breath 17–23
overwhelm (somatic/emotional) 216–18; *see also* safety; dissociation; vulnerability
overwhelm and dissociation 216–18
threshold of overwhelm 218–22

P

patterns, *see also* tension; somatic armor; habits
character patterns 124–30
emotional patterns 112–18
movement patterns 46–52
somatic patterns 110–18
tension patterns (somatic/emotional) 118–31
pelvis, *see also* alignment; koshi; grounding
ground–pelvis relationship 72–79
pelvic alignment 74–79
pelvis and koshi 82–90
power zone 18–22
pedagogical arc 11–22, 213–27; *see also* DEE Cycle; practice (conceptual); training principles
activation phase 11–14
encounter/emergence 42–52
integration/recomposition 203–08
opening phase 213–17
revelation phase (emotional/energetic) 218–25

perception, *see also* awareness; perceptual gates; field awareness
energetic perception 176–82
inner perception (somatic) 15–17
perception in dramaturgy 176–82
somatic perception 182–90
perceptual thresholds 183–89; *see also* perceptual gates; vulnerability
perceptual gating 182–88
threshold of exposure 218–22
practice (conceptual) 11–22, 39–49, 213–27; *see also* exploration, principles of; training principles; vulnerability
practice and presence 176–82
practice as container 16–17
practice phases (activation → revelation → integration) 11–22, 213–27
states of practice 39–44
presence, *see also* witnessing; energetic dramaturgy; revelation; listening
collective presence 180–82
performance presence 176–82
presence and immediacy 220–24
presence vs. character 118–22
somatic presence 3–7
pressure (somatic/emotional) 114–18; *see also* contraction; blockages; tension
internal pressure and contraction 114–18
pressure release cycles 47–52
Putnam, Scott 68–69; *see also* EBAS; alignment; grounding
EBAS method 68–69
somatic alignment work 68–79

R

Reich, Wilhelm 110–16, 120–21; *see also* Lowen, Alexander; bioenergetics; somatic armor
character armor theory 112–19
influence on bioenergetics 113–14
Reichian lineage 110–16
release (somatic/emotional/energetic), *see also* contraction; tremble response; revelation; DEE Cycle
emotional release 47–49, 118–19, 221–26
energetic release/discharge 113–19
release in emotional arcs 220–26
release–revelation sequence 218–25
somatic release 52–54, 72–76
rebound (somatic) 56–58; *see also* tremble response; activation
rebound effect in tremor response 56–58
recombination/recomposition 203–06; *see also* integration; closure; pedagogical arc
closure and recomposition 169–70
post-process reintegration (somatic/emotional) 203–08
residue (emotional) 112–14; *see also* somatic armor; release; contraction
repressed emotional charge 112–14
residue and armor formation 112–19
resistance (emotional/somatic) 113–17; *see also* somatic armor; tension; vulnerability
resistance as armor 113–17
resistance in energetic work 168–73
resonance 44–46, 179–81, 129–31; *see also* mirroring; presence; audience–performer field
emotional resonance 42–49
resonance loops (audience–performer) 179–81
somatic resonance (gesture/emotion) 129–31
revelation (emotional/energetic) 218–25; *see also* vulnerability; expression; DEE Cycle; pedagogical arc

release–revelation cycle 221–26
revelation and DEE Cycle (Entelecheia) 173–77
revelation during emotional emergence 218–24
somatic cracking-open 218–23
ritual performance 194–99; *see also* ancestry; presence
ancestral activation 196–99
Bomba tradition 196–99
embodied ritual presence 194–97

S

safety (somatic/emotional) 131–36; *see also* dissociation; overwhelm; containment; training principles
emotional safety during release 135–39
safety in pedagogical progression 213–17
somatic safety principles 131–35
scaffolding (somatic/energetic) 70–74; *see also* somatic architecture; koshi; alignment
energetic scaffolding in koshi 82–90
structural scaffolding for alignment 70–74
self-observation 224–29; *see also* witnessing; mirroring; presence
meta-awareness loop 225–29
self-observation (diagram) *225*
somatic observation (somatic/emotional) 224–29
sensation 40–43
sensation and emergence 42–49
somatic sensing 40–43
sequencing (somatic/emotional) 33–37, 49–53; *see also* emergence; training principles; flow
sequencing in pedagogical arc 11–22
somatic sequencing in gesture emergence 46–52
shaking/tremor response (somatic/energetic) 53–59; *see also* release; activation; discharge
bioenergetic tremor release 56–59
neurogenic trembling 53–56
rebound effect 56–58
softening (somatic/emotional) 213–17; *see also* opening; vulnerability; revelation
softening and opening 213–17
softening before revelation 218–24
somatic, *see also* alignment; gesture; tension; koshi
somatic activation 39–44
somatic architecture (diagram) *84*
somatic architecture 66–74
somatic armor 112–23
somatic dissociation 132–35
somatic emergence 45–52
somatic mirroring 191–93
somatic perception 182–90
somatic transparency (somatic/emotional) 213–16
somatic truth 219–24
space (internal/external) 15–20, 176–82; *see also* presence; field awareness; perception
external space (energetic) 176–82
internal space (somatic) 15–17
relational field 176–82
spirals (somatic/energetic) 76–82; *see also* flow; koshi; somatic architecture
energetic spirals in koshi 80–82
spiral pathways in movement 76–80
stability 72–80; *see also* alignment; grounding; koshi
relationship to grounding 72–79
stability–mobility dynamics 72–79
Stanislavski, Konstantin 109
Strasberg, Lee 109

structure (dramatic) 165–70; *see also* narrative arc; energetic dramaturgy
dramatic progressions 165–69
suspension (somatic/energetic) 73–76; *see also* alignment; koshi; scaffolding
suspension in somatic architecture 73–76
suspension vs. collapse 114–18

T

tension (somatic/emotional), *see also* compression; contraction; somatic armor; TDTETE Model
character tension 118–26
ego tension 119–22
habitual tension 110–18
release of tension 221–26
suppressed tension 113–17
tension grids 120–36
tension patterns 118–31
mapping tension (TDTETE Model) 118–40
TDTETE Model (Mapping Energy Through Tension) 118–40; *see also* tension; somatic architecture; energetic mapping
application to performance 144–47
definition and framework 118–31
energy mapping 118–40
somatic tension grid 120–36
tension architecture 118–31
thresholds (perceptual/energetic) 183–89; *see also* perceptual gates; vulnerability; revelation
performative thresholds 172–76
threshold of exposure 218–22
tremble response, *see* shaking/tremor response
training principles 11–22, 33–37, 131–39
safety 131–36; *see also* exploration, principles of; practice (conceptual); safety
attentional practices 15–20
containment 16–17, 116–17
sequencing 33–37
threshold navigation 183–89
truth (somatic/emotional) 219–24; *see also* revelation; vulnerability; expression
somatic truth in revelation 219–24
truth and exposure 218–25

U

unfolding (somatic/emotional) 42–52; *see also* emergence; flow; revelation
emotional unfolding 42–49
gesture unfolding 46–52
unfolding within pedagogical arc 213–17
unmasking (somatic/emotional) 126–32; *see also* mask work; vulnerability; presence
identity suspension 128–30
mask removal as opening gesture 127–30
revealing somatic truth 129–32
unresolved emotion 112–16; *see also* somatic armor; release; contraction
blocked emotional charge 113–17
emotional residue (somatic/emotional) 112–14

V

verticality 71–73, 80–82; *see also* alignment; axis; grounding; koshi
vertical alignment and koshi 82–90
vertical axis 69–75
vibration (somatic/energetic) 56–58; *see also* tremble response; discharge; activation
tremor vibration 53–59
vibratory release 118–19

vitality 3–6, 47–50; *see also* flow; activation; presence
vital force in expression 47–50
vital somatic presence 3–7
activation and vitality 11–14
vulnerability 211–26; *see also* revelation; presence; witnessing; opening
emotional exposure (somatic/emotional) 212–24
identity softening 214–20
overwhelm and vulnerability 216–18
rebuilding after exposure 225–27
somatic transparency 213–16
somatic vulnerability 213–17
thresholds of exposure 218–22
vulnerability in training 231–38

W

weight transfer 74–80; *see also* grounding; alignment; koshi; stability
somatic balance 74–76
weight, grounding, and koshi 72–79
witnessing 224–29; *see also* self-observation; mirroring; presence; vulnerability
emotional witnessing 224–28
inner witnessing (somatic/emotional) 224–25
somatic witnessing 225–29
witnessing (diagram) *225*
will (energetic impulse) 11–14; *see also* impulse; DEE Cycle; activation
will and action-impulse 168–70
will as dynamis 11–14

Z

zones of energy (diagram) *20*; *see also* grounding; breath; expression; insight
breath/diaphragm zone 18–23
emotional expression zone (chest) 19–24
grounding zone (legs) 17–22
insight zone (head) 19–25
power zone (pelvis) 18–22
vertical mapping of zones (somatic/emotional/energetic) 17–25